The Secret Garland

AAR
AMERICAN ACADEMY OF RELIGION

AAR RELIGION IN TRANSATION

SERIES EDITOR
Mark Csikszentmihalyi, University of Wisconsin–Madison

A Publication Series of

The American Academy of Religion
and
Oxford University Press

THE DAOIST MONASTIC MANUAL
A Translation of the *Fengdao Kejie*
Livia Kohn

SACRED AND PROFANE BEAUTY
The Holy in Art
Garardus van der Leeuw
Preface by Mircea Eliade
Translated by David E. Green
With a new introduction and bibliography by
Diane Apostolos–Cappadona

THE HISTORY OF THE BUDDHA'S RELIC SHRINE
A Translation of the Sinhala Thūpavamsa

Stephen C. Berkwitz
DAMASCIUS' *PROBLEMS AND SOLUTIONS CONCERNING FIRST PRINCIPLES*
Translated by Sara Ahbel–Rappe
Introduction and Notes by Sara Ahbel–Rappe

THE SECRET GARLAND
Āṇṭāḷ's *Tiruppāvai* and *Nācciyār Tirumoḻi*
Translated with Introduction and Commentary by Archana Venkatesan

The Secret Garland

Āṇṭāḷ's *Tiruppāvai* and *Nācciyār Tirumoḻi*

Translated with Introduction and Commentary

BY ARCHANA VENKATESAN

OXFORD
UNIVERSITY PRESS
2010

OXFORD
UNIVERSITY PRESS

Oxford University Press, Inc., publishes works that further
Oxford University's objective of excellence
in research, scholarship, and education.

Oxford New York
Auckland Cape Town Dar es Salaam Hong Kong Karachi
Kuala Lumpur Madrid Melbourne Mexico City Nairobi
New Delhi Shanghai Taipei Toronto

With offices in
Argentina Austria Brazil Chile Czech Republic France Greece
Guatemala Hungary Italy Japan Poland Portugal Singapore
South Korea Switzerland Thailand Turkey Ukraine Vietnam

Published by Oxford University Press, Inc.
198 Madison Avenue, New York, New York 10016

www.oup.com

Library of Congress Cataloging-in-Publication Data

Venkatesan, Archana.
The secret garland : Āṇṭāḷ's Tiruppāvai and Nācciyār tirumoḻi / translated with introduction and commentary by Archana Venkatesan.
p. cm.
Includes bibliographical references and index.
ISBN 978-0-19-539174-9; 978-0-19-539175-6 (pbk.)
1. Āṇṭāḷ. Tiruppāvai. 2. Āṇṭāḷ. Nācciyār tirumoḻi. I. Āṇṭāḷ.
Tiruppāvai. English. II. Āṇṭāḷ. Nācciyār tirumoḻi. English. III. Title.

PL4758.9.A58T5339 2010
894.8'1111-dc22 2009046234

9 8 7 6 5 4 3 2 1

Printed in the United States of America
on acid-free paper

For Amma and Appa

Acknowledgments

I first encountered Āṇṭāḷ and her poems in the winter before I began graduate school. Through all these many years, friends, family, colleagues, and mentors have helped me make sense of my fascination with Āṇṭāḷ, and have gently guided my great love for her poetry to productive ends. I take great pleasure in acknowledging their wisdom and compassion that have seen this book to its completion.

Professor Maraimalai, Visiting Professor at U.C. Berkeley (1997–98) patiently read the *Tiruppāvai* and *Nācciyār Tirumoḻi* with me, along with innumerable commentaries. George Hart, an exemplary translator and wonderful mentor, encouraged my first tentativeattempts at translation, showing me how to improve my work without making me feel foolish or discouraged. Kausalya Hart was always generous with her encyclopedic knowledge of Tamiḻ language and literature, as well as with her time. Professor Steven Hopkins, a precious friend, gave me the gift of his sensitive translations of Vedānta Deśika, and inspired me to do better by Āṇṭāḷ. Professors Indira Peterson and Vasudha Narayanan have supported this work since its nascent stages and their comments on Āṇṭāḷ in general and these two poems in particular have enriched my understanding of the *Tiruppāvai* and *Nācciyār Tirumoḻi* immeasurably. I am grateful to Davesh Soneji for his friendship and for his enthusiasm and support for this project. Frank Clooney helped me take the initial steps toward publication by suggesting the American Academy of Religion's Texts and Translation Series as a possible home for this book. Anne Monius, the editor for the series, shepherded me through the entire process with patience and kindness. I am immensely thankful to both of them for having faith in the value of a new translation of Āṇṭāḷ's *Tiruppavai* and *Nācciyār Tirumoḻi* . The incisive and thorough comments from the anonymous reviewers for Oxford University Press have shaped this into a much better book. I thank them for the care and the attention they gave my work.

Katherine Ulrich and Gwen Colvin, with their keen editorial eye have done a magnificent job in preparing this manuscript for publication. My heartfelt thanks to Molly Balikov and Anastasia Aizman, the designer not only for designing a beautiful cover, but for also so patiently listening to all my many concerns, and for accommodating them. Gayatri Devi Menon, graduate student at UC Davis, copy-edited the manuscript and prepared the Index. Without her help, it would have taken me twice as long to complete this book.

The people of Śrīvilliputtūr added enormously to my understanding of Āṇṭāḷ. Extemporaneous discussions of a particular verse, or its use to make a subtle point in a story about her, never failed to deepen my appreciation of the intricacies of her poetry. In particular, I would like to thank Raghurama Bhattar, Govindaraja Bhattar, the late Vedappiran Bhattar, Tiruvenkatammal and Srinivasa Araiyar for sharing their knowledge and their time so freely. Mr. M. Kannan of the French Institute of Pondicherry was an invaluable resource during my year of dissertation research. I would also like to thank Narendran and Ramanujam, librarians at the French Institute of Pondicherry for their able assistance in procuring me a wealth of books and photocopies. Sri Varadadesikar of the École Française d'Extrême-Orient patiently clarified my many questions on Śrīvaiṣṇava theology, and steered me through innumerable Sanskrit and Maṇipravāḷa tellings of the Āṇṭāḷ story. It is through his deeply felt expositions of *āḻvār* poetry that I came to appreciate the subtle and delightful craft of the Śrīvaiṣṇava commentator.

My sister Aarathi dragged me out of my dimmest writing moments with her usual good humor and zest for life. Her twenty questions, asked and pondered during our many long walks, forced me to reexamine some of my most basic presumptions about Āṇṭāḷ. My uncle S.Raghunath has been an unshakeable and quiet source of strength through all the many years of graduate school.

My husband Layne, fellow scholar and translator, read through these translations too many times to count. His suggestions were always insightful and his gentle criticisms were unerringly accurate. His unwavering support and belief in this project has been instrumental in bringing it to fruition.

There are two extraordinary artists, whose mastery of their crafts emboldened me in a task that often appeared insurmountable. The first is the great

English poet John Keats, whose letters and poems impressed me even as a young girl. Little did I know that I would have the great fortune to discover another poet who captured my imagination with the same intensity that he had. This translation owes as much to the lyricism of Keats' great works as it does to Āṇṭāḷ's. Like Keats' nightingale, the beautiful, crisp music of the late, great Karṇāṭak musician K.V. Narayanaswamy kept me company in the lonely night hours. His renderings of the *Tiruppāvai* brought Āṇṭāḷ alive for me every day, and with this gift imbued every moment of the laborious task of translation with beauty.

Āṇṭāḷ ends the *Tiruppāvai* and almost every decad of the *Nācciyār Tirumoḻi* with a reference to Viṣṇucittaṉ, the person she identifies as her spiritual guide, and the one she regards as instrumental in the fulfillment of her greatest desire. He is her teacher, her initiator, and her mentor. My parents Krishna and Jayashree Venkatesan have played just as pivotal a role in my life. It is their infectious love for music, for reading, and for learning seeped into every corner that set me on this path. But without their unflagging faith and their loving encouragement, I know that I would never have been able to finish it. It is in their honor that this book is dedicated.

Contents

Note on Transliteration, xiii

Introduction, 3

Tiruppāvai (Thirty Verses for the Drum of Māl), 51

Commentary and Notes to the *Tiruppāvai*, 81

Nācciyār Tirumoḻi (Fourteen Songs for the Love of Māl), 147

Commentary and Notes to the *Nācciyār Tirumoḻi*, 189

Appendix 1: *Taṉiyaṉ* to the *Tiruppāvai* and *Nācciyār Tirumoḻi*, 223

Appendix 2: Major Myths, 227

Appendix 3: Index of Myths and Names in the *Tiruppāvai* and *Nācciyār Tirumoḻi*, 235

Glossary, 241

Bibliography, 249

Index, 255

Note on Transliteration

Transliteration posed some difficulty as I was dealing with Tamiḻ, Sanskrit, and Maṇipravāḷa words. I have transliterated Tamiḻ words according to the conventions of the *Tamiḻ Lexicon*. Sanskrit words used in a Tamiḻ context are transliterated as such. So, I use *Nālāyira Diyva Prabandham* instead of *Nālāyira Tivviya Pirapantam, utsavam* in place of *uṟcavam*, Raṅgamaṉṉār and not Raṅkamaṉṉār Sanskrit words have generally been transliterated according to the conventions of the Monier-Williams *Sanskrit-English Dictionary*. All place names have been transliterated throughout the book. I have spelled the names of contemporary authors and informants as they choose to render them in English, and have not used diacritical marks. I have transliterated the names of all historical personalities.

The Secret Garland

Introduction

Kōtai of Viṣṇucittaṉ
lord of Putuvai
city of towering mansions that rise like mountains
sang this garland of sweet Tamiḻ
to plead with Kāmadeva
with his sugarcane bow and five-flower arrows
to unite her with the lord
who broke the tusk of the elephant
as it screamed in agony,
who ripped apart the beak of the bird
that one dark and lustrous as a gem.

Those who sing this soft song of plea
will remain forever at the feet
of the supreme king of the gods.

Nācciyār Tirumoḻi 1.10

If one goes by Kōtai's lavish descriptions in her *Tiruppāvai* and *Nācciyār Tirumoḻi*, the town of Putuvai was a wealthy metropolitan hub, overflowing with abundance, populated by perfect priests and incomparable mansions. It was a blessed land, mythical in its scope, for it was here that Kṛṣṇa sported and played. Today, Putuvai is identified with Śrīvilliputtūr, a dusty town about seventy-five kilometers south of the bustling Tamiḻ cultural capital, Maturai. Surrounded by lovely hills, their crests tipped with dark clouds, the Śrīvilliputtūr landscape is dominated by an imposing temple tower that rises colorful and majestic, audaciously confronting the neighboring hills. The temple is this otherwise ordinary town's claim to fame, for it marks the birthplace of the celebrated ninth-century Tamil̲ Vaiṣṇava poet, Kōtai, who a few centuries later was apotheosized into the goddess Āṇṭāḷ. It is her remarkable legend, her beautiful love poems, and the temple she shares with her immortal husband, Viṣṇu (locally known as Raṅgamaṉṉār) that command the landscape and contour the experiences of local devotees and visiting pilgrims alike. It is her *caritam*—her story—that forms the backdrop against which medieval commentators and contemporary devotees alike express their enjoyments (*anubhava*) of her two poems. So we begin here, with the story of her miraculous and improbable love for Viṣṇu.

Speak Not of Mortal Men: Āṇṭāḷ's Story

One day Viṣṇucittaṉ, a humble, Brahmin garland maker at the Vaṭapatraśāyi temple of the reclining Viṣṇu at Putuvai, found a lovely baby girl under a sacred *tulasī* plant. A voice from the heavens instructed him to take the little girl home and raise her as his own. Viṣṇucittaṉ named the child Kōtai and lovingly brought her up, inculcating in his adopted daughter a deep love for Viṣṇu. As she grew older, Kōtai resolved to marry Viṣṇu and no one else. Every morning, she enacted her fantasy as Viṣṇu's divine bride by ignoring the rules of ritual purity and donning the sacred garland meant for him. One morning, Viṣṇucittaṉ inadvertently caught her in the act, chastised her for the ritual transgression, and refrained from offering the polluted garland to the deity in the local temple. But to his astonishment, Viṣṇu appeared in a dream that same night to reveal his attachment to the special garland that Kōtai had first worn, earning her the epithet, *cūṭikkoṭuttavaḷ*—she who gave what she had worn. Still Viṣṇucittaṉ remained oblivious to Kōtai's adamant desire to become Viṣṇu's bride, even as she grew more pale and feverish. When her father mentioned marriage, she rejected the very notion saying, "if there is even talk of mortal men . . . I will not live."[1] It was in the throes of her overwhelming passion and the subsequent crushing disappointment that she composed two poems, the *Tiruppāvai* (The Sacred Vow) and *Nācciyār Tirumoḻi* (The Woman's Sacred Words). Viṣṇucittaṉ finally comprehended the full scope of her longing and anxiously inquired: "Which of the many forms of Viṣṇu do you wish to wed?"

Kōtai replied, "Sing their praises to me."

And so Viṣṇucittaṉ began describing all of them in loving detail, but when he described the lord of Śrīraṅgam, he noticed the faraway look in Kōtai's eyes and the sheen of unrequited desire.

He despaired: "How can I fulfill my daughter's mad desire?"

Once again Raṅganātha, the lord of Śrīraṅgam appeared in his devotee's dream and directed him to bring Kōtai dressed in full bridal regalia to his temple. Viṣṇucittaṉ promptly did as directed and arrived with his daughter in Śrīraṅgam. And there, witnessed by devotees, kings, Viṣṇu's attendants, and her father, Kōtai boldly strode into the *garbha gṛha*, climbed atop the beautiful image of the reclining Viṣṇu, and simply disappeared. From that point on Kōtai was known as Āṇṭāḷ—she who ruled—for she had won her lord's heart like no other before her.[2]

The Historical Āṇṭāḷ and Her Place Among the Āḻvār

The remarkable legend of Āṇṭāḷ recorded in oral and written hagiographies since the eleventh century reveals very little that is historically verifiable about her.[3] The sparse biographical information contained in the *phala śruti* verses (benedictory verses) that close the *Tiruppāvai* and each of the fourteen sections of the *Nācciyār Tirumoḻi* offer nothing more than a silhouette of the poet who called herself Kōtai.[4] She probably lived in a town called Putuvai (lit. New Town) that she also referred to as Villi's Putuvai[5] and which she praised for its beauty and prosperity. She was related in some way to the *āḻvār* poet Viṣṇucittaṉ (commonly referred to as Periyāḻvār), who is identified in the hagiographic traditions as her father. Based on a verse like this,

> Viṣṇucittaṉ has heard
> these words of truth spoken
> by the mighty and righteous king
> of Tiruvaraṅkam:
>   "Those who love me
>   I will love in return."
> If even his words are proved false
> what is there left to believe?
>
> *Nācciyār Tirumoḻi* 11.10

the Śrīvaiṣṇava commentarial literatures on the *Tiruppāvai* and *Nācciyār Tirumoḻi* also assert that Viṣṇucittaṉ was Āṇṭāḷ's teacher (*ācārya*).[6] Viṣṇucittaṉ does not mention Āṇṭāḷ by name in his composition, the *Periyāḻvār Tirumoḻi*, while Āṇṭāḷ herself only obliquely alludes to their relationship in the *Tiruppāvai* and *Nācciyār Tirumoḻi* by using a generic possessive such as "Viṣṇucittaṉ's lovely Kōtai" (*Viṣṇucittaṉiṉ viyaṉ Kōtai*). However uncertain the exact nature of the relationship between these two, the internal evidence of Viṣṇucittaṉ's

Periyāḻvār Tirumoḻi (Sacred Words of Periyāḻvār) reliably places him in the ninth century, making Āṇṭāḷ his contemporary and part of the devotional milieu of the Tamiḻ *bhakti* poets.[7]

Āṇṭāḷ is the only woman of the twelve *āḻvār* poets (600–900 C.E.), whose devotional poems comprise the *Nālāyira Divya Prabandham* (The Divine Collection of Four Thousand), the Tamiḻ canon of the Śrīvaiṣṇavas. But Āṇṭāḷ's position as one of the *āḻvār* is tenuous, and she is sometimes excluded from this list. By the eleventh century, and dovetailing with the systematic development of Śrīvaiṣṇava theology under the direction of Rāmānuja (traditional dates, 1017–1137 C.E.), the *Nālāyira Divya Prabandham* became a revealed text, with a place of primacy reserved for Nammāḻvār's *Tiruvāymoḻi* (ca. 9th century), which is revered as the Tamiḻ Veda. The apotheosis of the Tamiḻ canon activated a reciprocal apotheosis of its composers, who by the thirteenth century are transmogrified into various divine emanations (*aṁśa*) of Viṣṇu. Within the parameters of this new scheme, Kōtai the poet was recast into the role of the secondary consort Bhū Devī, placing her in a position of intimacy with Viṣṇu that for the Śrīvaiṣṇava theologians and commentators was far superior to that of the other male *āḻvār*.

By the time of the important Śrīvaiṣṇava philosopher, poet, and theologian, Vedānta Deśika (1268–369 C.E.), lists of the *āḻvār* begin to omit Āṇṭāḷ, indicating her already-contested place as a poet, saint, and goddess, although her two poems (especially the *Tiruppāvai*) continued to occupy a central place in the religious and ritual imagination of the community. By the mid-sixteenth century, the ninth-century poet Kōtai is distinctive enough to merit an important temple site dedicated to her, counted as one of the 108 sacred sites (*divya deśa*) of the Śrīvaiṣṇavas.[8] Once a part of the devotional milieu, by the late medieval period in South India she herself has become the recipient of *bhakti* songs -are composed for her, temples are built in her honor, and endowments are made in her name.

The ambiguity of Āṇṭāḷ's position as an *āḻvār*-goddess and the well-integrated position of her texts into the Tamiḻ canon are most clearly in evidence at Śrīraṅgam's annual *Adhyayanotsavam* (Festival of Recitation) celebrated in the auspicious month of Mārkaḻi (December–January). During this festival, the sacred space known as the "Hall of Thousand Pillars" is imagined to recreate a divine court where Viṣṇu, accompanied by his consorts Śrī and Bhū, enjoys a liturgical recitation and on occasion dramatic enactments of the entire *Nālāyira Divya Prabandham*. Bronze images of the *āḻvār*—except Āṇṭāḷ—and the *ācāryas* are hierarchically placed in the sacred arena for the duration of the Festival of Recitation. Āṇṭāḷ's marked absence among the *āḻvār* is explained away because of her eternal presence beside Viṣṇu as his secondary consort Bhū. As the

Tiruppāvai and *Nācciyār Tirumoḻi* are ritually recited during the first ten days of the *Adhyayanotsavam*, while Āṇṭāḷ's image is excluded from Viṣṇu's devoted retinue of poet-saints, this festival enunciates her dual identity as both an *āḻvār* and a goddess.[9]

Āṇṭāḷ and Other Women Poet-Saints of India

Women's literary compositions in India, particularly in the pre-colonial period, have largely been in the realm of devotional or religious literature. The sixth-century B.C.E. Buddhist *Therīgāthā* is the earliest compilation of women's writing in India. In these early poems, the domestic drudgery of a woman's duties becomes an effective metaphor for life as suffering. The Buddhist nun Muttā makes the point eloquently in the poem below:

> So free am I, so gloriously free,
> Free from three petty things—
> From mortar, from pestle, and from my twisted lord,
> Freed from rebirth and death I am,
> And all that has held me down
> Is hurled away.
> (Trans. Uma Chakravarti and Kumkum Roy)[10]

In the Tamiḻ context, the earliest female poets are contributors to the secular Caṅkam anthologies (first–third century C.E.). Of the 2,381 Caṅkam compositions, at least 154 in both the love (*akam*) and war (*puṟam*) genres bear female signatures. Because, like their male counterparts, these women poets composed poems that were strictly governed by the conventions of Caṅkam poetics, it is difficult, perhaps even impossible, to discern a distinctively female voice in this early corpus of secular Tamiḻ poetry.

By the beginning of the late fifth century, secular literature and the massive literary accomplishments of Tamiḻ Buddhists and Jains gave way to the newly emergent *bhakti* ethos. One of the earliest participants in this new poetic and religious world was the female *bhakti* poet and devotee of Śiva, Kāraikkālammaiyār (ca. 6th century). Although she was neither a contemporary of Āṇṭāḷ, nor a poet with a similar poetic temperament, as the only woman among the sixty-three canonized Śaiva saints (*nāyaṉmār*), Kāraikkālammaiyār is often regarded as Āṇṭāḷ's Śaiva counterpart. According to her hagiography, her husband, awed by her mystical powers, released Kāraikkālammaiyār from her obligations to him, thereby enabling her to devote herself completely to Śiva. Her move away from the normative social order is marked by a radical transformation that remakes her beautiful body into that of a skeletal ghoul. The climactic moment of the hagiography occurs when she climbs sacred Mount Kailāśa on her hands, so as to refrain from defiling its hallowed ground with her feet. Upon seeing such dedication, Śiva, lauded as one who has neither beginning nor end, is said to have welcomed Kāraikkālammaiyār to his celestial abode by addressing as her as "Mother!" As Norman Cutler points out, "Kāraikkālammaiyār's story . . . expresses an underlying tension between the saint's intuitive calling to serve Śiva and her responsibilities in the social realm."[11] But this tension between social responsibility and service to Śiva does not dominate the tone or content of Kāraikkālammaiyār's *Aṟputatiruvantāti, Tiruiraṭṭaimaṇimālai*, and the two *Tiruvālaṅkāṭṭu Mūtta Tiruppatikams*. Instead, like the poems of the earliest *āḻvār* poets, Kāraikkālammaiyār's compositions are uncomplicated in form and even content, but are nonetheless profoundly speculative. A wonderful example is from *Aṟputatiruvantāti* 61:

> I became your slave
> even though I couldn't see you,
> and now your image still eludes my eyes—
>   when people ask me
>   "how does your lord appear?"
>   what can I say?
>
>   which among all these forms is yours?[12]
>
> (Trans. Norman Cutler)

In contrast, Āṇṭāḷ's *Nācciyār Tirumoḻi* is replete with vociferous rejections of marriage to a mortal, an attitude that eventually becomes the centerpiece of her hagiographic narrative. As Āṇṭāḷ's story develops, her bold assertions are subsumed into a theological position that implies that only a divine being—Āṇṭāḷ as Bhū Devī—can achieve something as extraordinary as marriage to Viṣṇu.[13]

In an article on women saints in India, A. K. Ramanujan suggests that unlike men, women often have to reject normative family life to pursue their spiritual goals.[14] In some instances, like that of Kāraikkālammaiyār, the husband or family sanctions such a rejection. In the case of the twelfth-century Kannada poet Mahādevīyakka, the transgression of social norms is extreme—she walked naked—and is sanctioned by no one. Āṇṭāḷ falls somewhere in between these two figures—her poetry, especially the *Nācciyār Tirumoḻi*, is radical for its frank eroticism and disturbing images of violence. But her mythic life, enshrined in the hagiographies, presents a more comfortable picture, where the father aids in securing his daughter's impossible goal of marriage to Viṣṇu.

It is no surprise that the story of Āṇṭāḷ's love for Viṣṇu and her eventual marriage to him has invited parallels to Mīrā, the sixteenth century North Indian poet-saint. Hagiography tells us that Mīrā rejected her royal husband and her duties as a daughter-in-law for Kṛṣṇa, the divine lover with whom she eventually merged. Such superficial similarities aside, there are significant differences between these two female poets that nonetheless speak to the difficulty that Āṇṭāḷ and Mīrā present to their respective religious communities. Whereas we are reasonably certain that the poet Kōtai composed the *Tiruppāvai* and *Nācciyār Tirumoḻi,* the same cannot be said of Mīrā. John Stratton Hawley suggests that "it is much harder in Mira's case than in that of her male rivals to have any confidence that she actually composed a substantial portion of the poetic corpus attributed to her."[15] There is a Mīrā tradition in which poems are composed in her name and are used to embellish the legend of the Mewar princess. The closed and canonical nature of the *Nālāyira Divya Prabandham* disallowed the kind of organic production of poetry for Āṇṭāḷ, or any of the *āḻvār* poets, that is the hallmark of the Mīrā traditions. There is no evidence of poets appropriating Āṇṭāḷ's name (or indeed that of any of the other *āḻvār*) to add to her fairly slim contribution of just 173 verses. But there are plenty of verses in praise of Āṇṭāḷ, beginning with the laudatory verses, known as *taṉiyaṉs* that are appended to the *Tiruppāvai* and *Nācciyār Tirumoḻi.*[16] Undoubtedly, this important distinction between the Āṇṭāḷ and Mīrā traditions has much to do with two very different systems of producing and transmitting knowledge. Nevertheless, it also says something important about the ways in which widely divergent religious communities deal with problematic female poets. In point of fact, it might be said that Āṇṭāḷ and Mīrā are mirror images. The legend of Mīrā is shocking in its dramatic rejection of wifely and royal duties, while those poems attributed to her are not, even when they allude to the abuses she withstood. Her poems tend to be meditative and enigmatic, and her persona in these poems is as much lover as ascetic.[17] Here is a good example of a poem from the Mīrā tradition:

My dark one has gone to an alien land.
He's left me behind,
  he's never returned,
    he's never sent me a single word,
So I've stripped off my ornaments,
  jewels and adornments,
    cut the hair from my head,
And put on holy garments,
  all on his account,

seeking him in all four directions.
Mīrā: unless she meets the Dark One, her Lord,
she doesn't even want to live.[18]
(Trans. John S. Hawley)

On the other hand, Āṇṭāḷ's poetry, especially the *Nācciyār Tirumoḻi,* is transgressive, sensual, and bold. Below is an example from one of the later sections of the *Nācciyār Tirumoḻi*:

My breasts seek the gaze of the one
whose beautiful hand lifts the discus.
Bound tightly in a red cloth, their eyes
shy away from the gaze of mere mortals
desiring none other than Govinda.
I cannot live here a moment longer
Please take me to the shores of the Yamunā.
Nācciyār Tirumoḻi 12.4

Thus what cannot be added to or excised from her poetry is mapped on to her story. Āṇṭāḷ's stories multiply, keeping pace with her growing fame and popularity, and with each new version, this troublesome and vexing female poet becomes more divine, and her love more innocent, asexual, and non-threatening.

Āṇṭāḷ's Garlands of Perfect Tamiḻ: The *Tiruppāvai* and *Nācciyār Tirumoḻi*

You were born the son of one woman

and that very night

you became the son of another,
to be nurtured in secret.

O immeasurable lord
when Kaṁsa fearing you
plotted evil things

you foiled his plans
inflamed himand burnt like a fire in his belly.

We have come to beg you:

If you give us the *paṟai*-drum

We will sing of your wealth matched only by Śrī.
We will sing of your bravery.

Our sorrows will end.
and we can rejoice.

ēl ōr empāvāy

Tiruppāvai 25

You escaped Kaṁsa's savage net
in the midst of that deep dark night
only to torture the hearts of hapless maidens
stranded here.
Yaśodā lets you stray, bold and unpunished.
O you who suckled the milk
from the breast of the deceitful demoness
Shameless one
Please return our clothes to us.

Nācciyār Tirumoḻi 3.9

The *Tiruppāvai* and *Nācciyār Tirumoḻi* are included in the first thousand verses (*mutal āyiram*) of the *Nālāyira Divya Prabandham*. Āṇṭāḷ's two compositions follow Viṣṇucittaṉ's (Periyāḻvār's) *Tiruppallāṇṭu* and *Periyāḻvār Tirumoḻi*. The *Tiruppāvai* consists of thirty eight-line verses in *kalippa* meter and describes a vow known as the *pāvai nōṉpu.*[19] Young, unmarried girls observed this vow during the month of Mārkaḻi (December–January) in order to secure a virtuous husband. In the context of the *Tiruppāvai,* the girls are the cowherd maidens of Kṛṣṇa's land of sport, Āyarpāṭi (lit cowherd town), and Kṛṣṇa himself is the desired husband. The *Tiruppāvai,* narrated in an enthusiastic plural voice, is a poem of community and documents a group of girls vigorously rousing each other to join in a festive and joyous communal endeavor. Jointly the girls approach Kṛṣṇa's house to awaken him and his family. In the poem, Āṇṭāḷ's Putuvai is transformed into the mythic world of Āyarpāṭi (Tamiḻ for Gokula/Vṛndāvana) and in the commentaries, she herself is understood as being one of the *gopī* girls. The turning point of the poem comes in the penultimate verse (*Tiruppāvai* 29), when the company of girls reject the central symbol of the quest, the enigmatic *paṟai*-drum, and instead declare that they only wish to be eternally beholden to Kṛṣṇa. Although the poem employs a plural voice, traditional interpretations insert Āṇṭāḷ into it as either as the sole protagonist or as the leader of the group of *gopīs.* The *Tiruppāvai* ends on an optimistic note, with a clear sense that the quest has successfully come to fruition.

The *Tiruppāvai* leads seamlessly into the *Nācciyār Tirumoḻi,* in that it chronologically and thematically picks up where the former poem ends. The *Nācciyār Tirumoḻi* begins in the Tamiḻ month of Tai (January–February) and opens with another vow—this one to Kāmadeva, the god of desire—undertaken as a solitary endeavor. While friends and companions make intermittent appearances in the poem, the quest in the *Nācciyār Tirumoḻi* is largely a lonely and friendless one. The poem balances a full-bodied sensuality with a savage violence, a disquieting admixture that represents a radical departure from the comforting sweetness of the *Tiruppāvai.* The erotic sentiment is not entirely absent from the *Tiruppāvai;* rather, it is ensconced in comfortable images of domesticity—Kṛṣṇa at play with his wife, Nappiṉṉai, charming allusions to Kṛṣṇa's mischievous pranks, and Yaśodā's protective indulgence. It may be said that the desire of young *gopī* girls who inhabit the *Tiruppāvai*'s imaginal world has blossomed, but not yet gone to seed. Desire in the *Nācciyār Tirumoḻi* on the other hand, is terrible, full-blown and unremitting. The experience of such a desire is essentially an isolating one, where there are neither friends nor companions to alleviate the suffering. If there are companions, be they friends, birds, clouds, or a conch, they are always positioned as antagonists, for the speaker (identified in the commentaries as Āṇṭāḷ) sees herself vying enviously with them for the position of proximity to Viṣṇu that she believes rightly belongs to her.

The *Nācciyār Tirumoḻi* is further distinguished from the *Tiruppāvai* and other similar poems composed by male poets by Āṇṭāḷ's use of shifting female voices, a dizzying non-linearity, and a strange, unsettling violence; images of profound sensuality are often jarringly juxtaposed with its violation.[20] For instance, late in the *Nācciyār Tirumoḻi*, the heroine has this to say:

> O bright *karuvai* blooms and dark *kāyā* flowers,
> you have assumed the brilliant form of my Tirumāl.
> Show me how to endure my agony.
> The master of Tirumāliruñcōlai,
> whose broad shoulders are for Śrī's pleasure
> entered my home and wrested my beautiful bangles.
> Is this right?
>
> *Nācciyār Tirumoḻi* 9.3

In the above verse, the poet uses conventional poetic tropes to sketch the contours of her/the heroine's unbearable and unfulfilled love. She sees her beloved everywhere—the dark flowers remind her of his lustrous skin; the crimson blooms of his red lips; the fragrant jasmine of his pearly teeth. But they are unable to provide any succor for her illness, because the lord of Māliruñcōlai, (literally, the lord of gardens) has not only refused her, but the union he enjoys with his eternal companion Śrī mocks the poet's (heroine's) own doomed love. While at first glance this verse might seem unremarkable within the canon of Tamiḻ *bhakti* poetry, the final assertion of physical violation done to her body—"he entered my home and wrested my beautiful bangles"—marks a substantial deviation from the ways in which these familiar *bhakti* tropes are usually deployed.[21] Instead, the common motif of the heroine growing pale and thin until her bangles slip off is inflected with a strident note of violence and violation, and the god's possession is characterized as intrusive and unwelcome.

It may well be argued that in the *Nācciyār Tirumoḻi*, violence is Āṇṭāḷ's dominant means of expressing an impossible desire and the fleeting nature of her encounter with the divine. Violence and violation are seeded throughout the poem, manifesting in unexpected places and in unexpected ways, with each occurrence building on an evocative past reference. First, there is the predicating violation that breeds all else: Viṣṇu's relentless and unsolicited violation of the heroine's person, and his cruel disregard of his word to her. The god invades the intimate space of her body and her home, overwhelms her despite her fervent and repeated refusals. In *Nācciyār Tirumoḻi* 10.9, the heroine says:

> O oceans! He entered you, churned you
> and stole your nectar from your depths.
> Just so, the cunning one entered me
> and deprived me of my life.

Such careless violation of the heroine's person by the divine beloved inevitably leads to the violence she inflicts upon herself, by denying herself food, sleep, and even thought, until she, eventually, and unforgettably, threatens self-mutilation by ripping out her useless breasts by their very roots (*Nācciyār Tirumoḻi* 13.8), an act intended to negate her femininity, her sexuality, and her desire. Nestled between these two extremes is the additional violence visited upon her by mothers, birds, and clouds, who wound either through their mocking words that pierce her like swords or with their unheeding disregard for her suffering. In certain decads and even in select verses of the *Nācciyār Tirumoḻi*, a number of these mute and callous witnesses to the heroine's misery come together to create the effect of a great, grand conspiracy designed by the absent beloved to increase her already intolerable torment. In *Nācciyār Tirumoḻi* 8.8 she says:

Dark clouds ready for the season of the rains
chant the name of the lord of Vēṅkaṭam
that one who is valiant in battle.
Tell him, like the lovely leaves that fall in the season of the rains
I waste away through the long endless years
waiting for the day when he finally sends word.

It is perhaps the combination of violence and sensuality that have prompted scholars such as Vidya Dehejia to remark on the uncomfortable and liminal place that the *Nācciyār Tirumoḻi* holds within the Tamiḻ canon of the Śrīvaiṣṇavas. However, it is also these very elements that have made the poem (at least particular sections) ritually, liturgically, and aesthetically significant, and it is in the Āṇṭāḷ hagiographic literature that the centrality of the *Nācciyār Tirumoḻi* becomes readily apparent.[22] Dennis Hudson has convincingly argued that while the *Tiruppāvai* is the more popular text, it is the *Nācciyār Tirumoḻi* that contours the Āṇṭāḷ legend.[23] Most retellings of Āṇṭāḷ's story, oral or written, are liberally interspersed with selections from this longer poem, including its more outrageous moments. For the Śrīvaiṣṇavas, Āṇṭāḷ is distinctive among the *āḻvār* poets of the *Nālāyira Divya Prabandham*, because as a woman she is considered uniquely qualified to express the peculiar disease of unrequited love for a divine beloved, and it is in the *Nācciyār Tirumoḻi* that they claim to hear that voice most clearly.

Āṇṭāḷ and the Sixteen Thousand Wives

O great and glorious conch!
Sixteen thousand women watch you
sip the nectar of Mādhava's lips.

If you do not share that which belongs to all
Why should they not quarrel with you?

Nācciyār Tirumoḻi 7.9

In both the *Tiruppāvai* and the *Nācciyār Tirumoḻi*, identities and points of view—a first-person narrator, the plural voices of a group of questing *gopī* girls, the bird's-eye view of a third-person perspective—proliferate to comment on the urgency and angst of unrequited love for an immortal beloved. In these moments of spectatorship, the poet makes a concerted effort to draw a line of distinction between herself and Viṣṇu's other consorts—be they Śrī, Bhū, or the uniquely Tamiḻ consort, Nappiṉṉai.[24] *Tiruppāvai* 18, where the group of *gopī* girls arrive at Kṛṣṇa's bedroom door and exhort Nappiṉṉai to open the door to them, presents an exemplary instance of the poet's self-conscious demarcation between devotee and consort.

Daughter-in-law
of Nandagopāla,
fierce as a rutting elephant oozing musk

our mighty chief who never flees from his enemies

Nappiṉṉai
whose hair fills the air with fragrance

Please open this door.

Listen!
The sound of crowing roosters is everywhere

Listen!
The hosts of *kuyil* coo
perched in bowers of *mātavi* creepers

O you with delicate fingers
adept at playing ball—

We are here to sing the fame of your lord.

With your lovely red hands soft as lotus petals
your wrists stacked with beautiful bangles
that clink sweetly

Open this door
and welcome us.

ēl ōr empāvāy

In this verse, the questing girls urge Nappiṉṉai to welcome them and aid them in securing their goal. The *gopī* girls express neither jealousy nor rivalry with

Nappiṉṉai. She is not the girls' rival, but is a necessary helpmate, one who can aid them in attaining their goal. Even while in a verse that follows (*Tiruppāvai* 19) the girls mildly chastise her for monopolizing Kṛṣṇa's attention, it is done so from a position of deference, where the aim is to sing the praises of her beloved and thus to be beholden to Kṛṣṇa eternally. The concluding verse of the *Tiruppāvai* conclusively demarcates the distance of the poet from the poetic situation and the characters that inhabit that world. In *Tiruppāvai* 30, the poem's final benedictory verse (*phala śruti* verse), Kōtai the poet says,

his Kōtai
  sang a garland of thirty songs in Caṅkam Tamiḻ
    about cowherd women with faces bright as the moon
    who adorned in beautiful jewels
    won the *paṟai*-drum . . .

thus making it abundantly clear that the *Tiruppāvai* is not autobiographical and instead describes an imagined reality.

It is virtually impossible to make a similar claim about the *Nācciyār Tirumoḻi*, where the boundary between poet and persona is far more permeable.[25] In the latter poem, a typical rhetorical posture is as follows:

Along time ago for the maiden of the earth
  covered in moss,
he took the shameful form of a boar
  dripping water from its filthy body.
The lord of Tiruvaraṅkam, that lustrous one
beguiled me with his words.
Now they can never be dislodged from my heart.

Nācciyār Tirumoḻi 11.8

Here the narrator belligerently recounts Viṣṇu's extravagant efforts to rescue Bhū Devī in his *avatāra* as the boar and contrasts it with his utter passivity and disinterest to her pitiable plight. While on the one hand such a rhetorical move differentiates the heroine (identified in the commentaries as Āṇṭāḷ) from the other consorts by showcasing the beloved's indifference toward her, it also curiously asserts the sameness of the experience of separation. The poet wishes to be the dependent consort only insofar as she too is rescued quickly from the slings and arrows of her unbearable love, because she suffers like any of Viṣṇu's consorts. Yet she equally recognizes the futility of such a desire, for she is in the final equation nothing like them, bound after all by the limitations of her mortality.

Of Vows, Baths, Drums, and Dolls: Central Symbols in the *Tiruppāvai*

The premise and the pretext of the *Tiruppāvai* is a ritual undertaking by a group of young unmarried maidens of Āyarpāṭi. The name of the vow, *pāvai nōṉpu,* is encapsulated both in the poem's title and in the refrain, *ēl ōr empāvāy,* that caps each of its thirty verses. The word *pāvai* is polyvalent—doll, woman, image, girl, and goddess are all in its ambit of suggestion—but in the context of this poem it becomes synonymous with a vow. In the *Bhāgavata Purāṇa* (10th century?), the *gopīs* undertake a similar ritual vow to the goddess Kātyāyanī, where they construct and propitiate her sand image on the banks of the river.[26] If one reads the *Tiruppāvai* anachronistically, then *pāvai* might refer to an image or doll, though neither this poem nor the Caṅkam poems about a comparable vow describe making sand images of the goddess.[27] In the *Tiruppāvai,* the word *pāvai* is used to refer directly to a girl (*Tiruppāvai* 13) as well as the vow (*Tiruppāvai* 2), and in the refrain (*ēl ōr empāvāy*) the word is in the vocative and perhaps can be interpreted as "O our girls." Given Āṇṭāḷ's delicate poetic touch and her dexterous play with polyvalent words in both the *Tiruppāvai* and *Nācciyār Tirumoḻi,* it is quite probable that the poem encapsulates all *three* meanings of the word *pāvai*—as girl (referring to the girls undertaking the ritual); as a vow (referring to the actual bathing rite); and finally as goddess, referring to Kṛṣṇa's consort Nappiṉṉai who acts as an intermediary in the poem, especially in *Tiruppāvai* 17–19, or as it is suggested in some commentaries, to Kāma's wife Ratī, because the *Nācciyār Tirumoḻi* opens with a vow to the god of love.[28]

The central ritual motif of the *Tiruppāvai* is an act of communal bathing in the predawn hours that is alluded to throughout the poem, but is not described.[29] It is possible that the vow described in the *Tiruppāvai* may be modeled on a bathing ritual known as *tai nīrāṭal* (lit. bathing in the month of Tai) described in several Caṅkam poems, including an extensive description in *Paripāṭal* 11. In all of these early poems, young unmarried girls undertake a ritual bath during the month of Tai (January–February).[30] While the *tai nīrāṭal* is quite likely the inspiration for Āṇṭāḷ's *Tiruppāvai,* the fact that her poem is situated in the preceding month of Mārkaḻi (December–January), raises some significant questions. Is the *tai nīrāṭal* the same as the Mārkaḻi bath of the *Tiruppāvai,* or did Āṇṭāḷ adapt the *tai nīrāṭal* to reflect an emergent devotional ethos focused on Kṛṣṇa? Norman Cutler (following Raghava Iyengar) argues that a shift in calendrical systems—from a lunar to a solar calendar—caused the *tai nīrāṭal* to be moved back into the month of Mārkaḻi, and that the vow was adapted into the new devotional culture.[31] It is equally likely that Āṇṭāḷ simply appropriated a relevant ritual for her poem and framed it within the context of Mārkaḻi, a month that holds a special significance to Vaiṣṇavas.[32] So whereas young girls in the Caṅkam poems undertook the *tai nīrāṭal* in order to secure a handsome husband or lover, in the *Tiruppāvai*, the longed-for beloved is none other than Kṛṣṇa. Any discussion of the *tai nīrāṭal* cannot exclude discussion of the version of the vow described in the *Bhāgavata Purāṇa*. In the *Purāṇa's* version, the young *gopī* girls of Āyarpāṭi awaken at the crack of dawn in the first month of winter, call out to each other, fashion a sand image of the goddess, and bathe in the Yamunā (*Bhāgavata Purāṇa* 10.22, verses 1–7).[33] While it is possible that Āṇṭāḷ was inspired by the *Bhāgavata Purāṇa*, for she was clearly aware of Kṛṣṇa mythology, I am inclined to agree with Norman Cutler that it is more probable that the regional Mārkaḻi vow was absorbed into the *Bhāgavata Purāṇa*, perhaps inspired by the popularity of the *Tiruppāvai*.[34]

In their seminal essay, "From Classicism to Bhakti," A. K. Ramanujan and Norman Cutler suggest that the reshaping of the king of Caṅkam *puṟam* poetry into that of the larger-than-life figure of the divine hero marked a great shift in the literary ethos of the Tamiḻ land. In the case of Āṇṭāḷ's poem, it is an appropriate antecedent ritual that receives new life.[35] Although the *Tiruppāvai* clearly alters the Caṅkam *tai nīrāṭal*, it nonetheless retains the central motif of bathing as a kind of purification and an efficacious means to attain one's heart's desire. The girls of the *Tiruppāvai* are required to cleave to all kinds of self-denying ascetic practices: they are obligated to awaken before the crack of dawn, bathe in the cold water, and abstain from particular kinds of food and specific kinds of behavior (*Tiruppāvai* 2). The reward for such dedicated ritual action is impressive, not only for what it promises the girls—Kṛṣṇa, eternal service to him, and the dissolution of all their past transgressions—but also for the community and the world at large: plentiful rain, an abundant harvest, and prosperity for the whole world.

Āṇṭāḷ situates the *Tiruppāvai* temporally, spatially, and ritually in the opening verse—it is the cool month of Mārkaḻi, particularly dear to Kṛṣṇa and therefore efficacious to undertake a special kind of vow. We are in the fabulous world of Āyarpāṭi, where Kṛṣṇa lurks right around the corner ready to spring into mischief. And the young and rambunctious lion cub of Yaśodā is conflated with the supreme Nārāyaṇa, and from this god who is at once accessible and transcendent the eager, the "precious" girls of Gokula are to win a mysterious *paṟai* (*Tiruppāvai* 1), a type of drum, but never clarified as such in the poem, and clearly symbolic of some abstract idea.

In the Caṅkam poems of war, various kinds of drums are sacred objects central to the battle. Each drum was played by a particular group of people. For instance, the *muṟacu*, arguably the most important drum, was a royal object, made from the tutelary tree of an enemy and invested with sacred power (*Puṟanāṉūṟu* 50). The *taṇṇumai*, a huge war drum, was manipulated by the low-caste Pāṇaṉ just before a battle commenced and was used to summon young men to battle. The *paṟai* was a versatile small drum employed to summon men to battle, to broadcast any news, and the belief was that playing it could cause the enemies' defeat.[36] Āṇṭāḷ provides neither a description of the *paṟai*, nor any details on its use. Nonetheless, it is clear from the contexts in which the word occurs that it is an actual object and not just an abstract concept. Given the communal nature of the poem, it is possible that the poet invokes the *paṟai*'s role in summoning people together, attested to in the Caṅkam corpus, although in the *Tiruppāvai* it is clearly not for a violent purpose. Despite the *paṟai*'s primary meaning in the antecedent literature as a sacred royal drum, this is an interpretation that is largely elided in commentaries of the *Tiruppāvai*, where it is conventionally interpreted as a desired objective and eternal loving servitude (*kaiṅkarya*) to Viṣṇu. At the conclusion of the poem, in *Tiruppāvai* 29, the *gopī* girls reject the all-important *paṟai* and instead ask to be eternally beholden to Kṛṣṇa.

The *Tiruppāvai* takes its name as much from the ritual event at its center, as it does from the refrain—*ēl ōr empāvāy*—that closes each of the thirty verses. The Śaiva poet Māṇikkavācakar composed a similar poem of twenty verses, the *Tiruvempāvai*, that also concludes with the same refrain. The refrain might thus be a marker of a newly emergent genre that dealt with vows, and specifically the *pāvai* vow. The meaning of the phrase *ēl ōr empāvāy* is difficult to discern, partly because of the polyvalence of the word *pāvai* (*pāvāy* is the vocative form). In the commentaries to the *Tiruppāvai*, the two words *ēl ōr* are often understood as a merely a meter filler, and thus empty of meaning. However, commentators also suggest that the phrase be interpreted as "consider this well, and perform" (for example, *ippaṭi putti paṇṇuṅkaḷ*). In keeping with its polyvalence, *pāvāy* is interpreted variously as "vow" (*nōṉpu*), "girls" (*piḷḷai*), "thoughts" (*niṉaivu*), while *ēl* is, in this context, understood as "listen" (*kēḷ*), or as "so you may consider this" (*niṉaipāyāka*).[37] Thus, the refrain could be translated roughly as "listen, consider this girls/vow." Norman Cutler renders the refrain as "Accept, Consider our Vow," which he acknowledges takes a certain liberty with the original. He suggests the above as the most plausible English version, given the shifting contexts and addressees.[38] Vidya Dehejia translates the phrase as "Fulfill, O song of our vow," making a case that because the refrain is common to all kinds of *pāvai* poems—Śrīvaiṣṇava, Śaiva, and Jain—any translation ought to be flexible and broad enough to accommodate the relevant religious contexts.[39] While Dehejia presents a persuasive argument, I have left the phrase untranslated for two main reasons. For one, it is quite likely that *ēl ōr* is empty of meaning, and thus cannot be translated. Second, and more importantly, the key word *pāvai* is ambiguous, its many meanings are all equally possible, and the richness of the *Tiruppāvai* emerges from its polyvalence. Guided by a desire to preserve as much of the poems' inherent playfulness and ambiguity, I have not translated *ēl ōr empāvāy*.

The Structure of the *Tiruppāvai*

The *Tiruppāvai* is a compact poem, with a narrative that depicts the quest of a group of nameless *gopī* girls. The poem is neatly divided into three distinct sections that trace the girls' path to Kṛṣṇa, a journey that takes them from the shared public arena of the outside world, to the inner, private chambers of their beloved. The first five verses lay out the details of the vow—when one undertakes it, what it entails, and its expected rewards. In the following set of delightful ten verses, the voices of the various girls coalesce into an indivisible chorus, vigorously rousing their neighborhood friends to join in the quest. The final section is a gradual awakening of Kṛṣṇa and his family, and the poem ends with a sense of accomplishment—that the vow has in fact been successful. The last seven verses of the *Tiruppāvai* may be understood to constitute a fourth division, which involves a lengthy panegyric to Kṛṣṇa.

The *Tiruppāvai* emphasizes the shared and public nature of worship, and this is delineated at length in the "waking up the *gopīs* section" (*Tiruppāvai* 6–15). Not only are the sleeping girls roused and pressed to join the sacred quest, but each listener/reader is invited to become a *gopī* who has slept too late and has forgotten how easy it might be to win Kṛṣṇa for herself. The poem and its characters emphasize that although the vow is for Mārkaḻi, the quest for Kṛṣṇa is itself timeless. The poem thus both describes the path to Kṛṣṇa as well as becomes the path to Kṛṣṇa. Eventually when all the girls have assembled, the *gopīs* approach Kṛṣṇa in his house to awaken him and his family. The final segment of the poem describes the confident *gopīs* boldly entering the god's inner world, until they are halted at the threshold of his bedroom, where he reclines with his wife Nappiṉṉai. The unbreakable intimacy of Kṛṣṇa and Nappiṉṉai reflects the girls' own desire; the *paṟai*, the vow, and the bath are merely pretexts to come into his presence, because the real goal of the quest is to be bound to him eternally. This special place however is not reserved for any individual girl, but is to be shared and is requested of *both* Kṛṣṇa and Nappiṉṉai. In fact, in one of the most beautiful verses of the *Tiruppāvai*, the girls say this to the happy couple, gently rebuking a sleeping Nappiṉṉai:

The lamps are ablaze.

You laze upon this bed with its stout ivory legs
and five fine qualities
your broad chest draped in garlands of flowers
rests upon the breasts of Nappiṉṉai,
her hair entwined
with heavy blossoms.

Please answer us.

O lovely woman with large eyes
darkened with kohl

How much longer
will you prevent him
from rising?

We know,
you cannot bear to be apart

from your beloved

for a single instant

But this does not befit you:
It is unfair.

ēl ōr empāvāy

Tiruppāvai 19

Medieval commentaries on this verse belabor the point that it is only via the consort that the devotee can access god, which explains Kṛṣṇa silence in the face of the girls' entreaties, until they have properly lauded his beloved wife, Nappiṉṉai. Yet, the *gopīs'* voice is not diffident, but demanding—who could know better than Nappiṉṉai the agony of separation? Her exclusive monopoly of Kṛṣṇa's attention is therefore all the more unfair to the questing girls. Given the poem's accent on shared, public worship, this verse can be read as a subtle criticism of Nappiṉṉai's individual enjoyment of Kṛṣṇa. The *gopīs'* gentle journey into the interior space of the god is as much an allegory for the devotee's journey into the self, where she finds Kṛṣṇa (and Nappiṉṉai) asleep in her heart. And when that god finally awakens, he rises majestic as a lion roused from its hibernation—recall how Āṇṭāḷ describes him as a young lioncub in the first verse of the *Tiruppāvai*—to sit upon his majestic throne, a just and benevolent king ever-ready to listen to his devotees' petitions.

With Kṛṣṇa's awakening, the *Tiruppāvai* once again moves outward and the interior world, marked by the *gopīs*' entry into Kṛṣṇa and Nappiṉṉai's intimate domain, is left behind. Kṛṣṇa, very much in the mold of a Tamiḻ king, emerges into the public external realm to enact his role as divine sovereign. The girls repeatedly petition him to fulfill just this role by granting their fondest wishes. The girls plead with Kṛṣṇa to ignore their humble lineage, to forgive their easy familiarity, and grant them their desires and the mysterious *paṟai*-drum. This move from the intimate interior world also signals a difference in their attitude to Kṛṣṇa. The boldness is replaced with deference—suddenly, the *gopīs* are not asking to share Nappiṉṉai's place; they are instead asking to be entirely dedicated to Kṛṣṇa as his servants. The *gopīs* say:

We came at the break of dawn

    to worship you
    to praise your lotus feet
        bright as gold.

Listen to the reason for our prayers:

    You were born among simple folk
    whose livelihood was tending cows

So you cannot refuse our small services.

    Know this Govinda

        We have not come here
        for the *paṟai*-drum

    For all time:
    for this birth and every birth that follows

    We are only yours.
    We serve only you.

Direct our every other desire toward you.

ēl ōr empāvāy

Tiruppāvai 29

The poem thus ends with a dramatic and unexpected twist—the *paṟai*-drum, so central a symbol in the poem, is suddenly rejected as a suitable reward and instead the *gopīs* declare that the true object of their ritual vow is and has always been eternal service to Kṛṣṇa. It concludes on a happy note with the *gopī* girls draped in rich silks, happily feasting, their desire apparently realized.

The Structure of the *Nācciyār Tirumoḻi*

The *Nācciyār Tirumoḻi* is a structurally malleable poem, although it is interpreted in commentaries and Śrīvaiṣṇava hagiographies as a linear narrative that documents the story of Āṇṭāḷ's separation and eventual union with Viṣṇu.[40] In these more conservative readings, the *Nācciyār Tirumoḻi* continues the narrative of the *Tiruppāvai* over its fourteen sections, at the end of which Āṇṭāḷ reaches her goal—union with Viṣṇu. But the poem's shifting points of view, changes in spatial orientation, and its seemingly abrupt ending challenge such tidy narrative linearity.[41]

The opening sections of the *Nācciyār Tirumoḻi* traverse terrain common in Tamiḻ Śrīvaiṣṇava *bhakti* poetry. It begins with a vow to Kāmadeva (*Nācciyār Tirumoḻi* 1), followed by two sections that describe the naughty antics of Kṛṣṇa (*Nācciyār Tirumoḻi* 2 and 3), eleven verses on divination (*Nācciyār Tirumoḻi* 4), and an appeal to a sweet little *kuyil* bird to act as a messenger to the beloved (*Nācciyār Tirumoḻi* 5). The poem then turns exactly at its halfway point, in the sixth section. Here the poet, in the first-person point of view, narrates to her friends a dream of her grand wedding to Viṣṇu. Thereafter the poem quickly gathers steam and ratchets its emotional weight and drama as the heroine's love reaches its fevered pitch in the penultimate decad, and she threatens her callous lover:

> I melt. I fray. But he does not care
> if I live or die.
> If that stealthy thief, that duplicitous Govardhana
> should even glance at me
> I shall pluck these useless breasts of mine
> from their roots
> I will fling them at his chest
> and staunch the fire scorching me.
>
> *Nācciyār Tirumoḻi* 13.8

But the eleven verses that immediately follow and conclude the *Nācciyār Tirumoḻi* do not pick up the theme of unfulfilled and unrequited desire or the terrible price it extracts from its sufferers. Instead, the poem ends with a bantering, folksy dialogue that reveals the secret that Kṛṣṇa can be found in Vṛndāvana. The heroine mocks her longed-for beloved and queries his whereabouts to an unknown and unseen audience:

> Have you seen him here
> that lord who is love
> love itself born as a bridegroom
> that one who speaks intolerable lies?
>
> We glimpsed him coming to Vṛndāvana
> flying high above
> shaded from the sun by noble Vinatā's son
> whose wings were spread like a canopy.
> *Nācciyār Tirumoḻi* 14.3

How do we make sense of this rather odd end to the anguished and tragic tone of the poem, keeping in mind that for the most part the heroine's companions have been represented as being either helpless or apathetic to her plight? On the one hand, it makes perfect sense that the unrelieved tragedy of the *Nācciyār Tirumoḻi* is assuaged in this gentle and generally optimistic tone—and this is the approach that the traditional interpreters take, suggesting that the heroine, identified with Āṇṭāḷ, is united with her beloved forever. Yet it is also equally apparent (as indicated in the verse above) that union with Kṛṣṇa, while desired, has not been fully realized. The heroine asks where one might find the naughty cowherd, and an answer in the plural (we) provides the answer—Vṛndāvana. The poem concludes ambivalently with the hint of suggestion that Kṛṣṇa may be seen in the mythical land of his childhood sports, and not with a definitive assertion of eternal union.

The final decad brings together two major symbolic streams that run through the *Nācciyār Tirumoḻi*—these are the presence of multiple poetic voices and the deft use of terrestrial, mythic, and imaginal spaces. One of the most curious aspects of the poem is the changing register of narrative perspective and the manner in which it is mapped on to specific spaces. The poem begins in the first person, but this perspective is soon discarded in favor of the plural "we" of the *gopī* girls, axiomatic of the *Tiruppāvai*. Soon this vantage too is cast aside, and the first-person point of view returns and dominates the *Nācciyār Tirumoḻi*, until both "I" and "we" come together in the poem's final section (see table 1).

TABLE 1. Voice and Place in the *Nācciyār Tirumoḻi*

Nācciyār Tirumoḻi	Voice and Number	Location of Action
Nācciyār Tirumoḻi 1: The Song to Kāmadeva	First Person Singular	Location of Action unspecified
Nācciyār Tirumoḻi 2: The Song of the Sandcastles	First Person Plural (*Gopī* Girls)	Āyarpāṭi
Nācciyār Tirumoḻi 3: The Song for the Clothes	First Person Plural (*Gopī* Girls)	Āyarpāṭi
Nācciyār Tirumoḻi 4: The Song of Divination	First Person Singular, but *phala śruti* identifies the voice as that of the *gopī* girls	Āyarpāṭi
Nācciyār Tirumoḻi 5: The Song to the *Kuyil*	First Person Singular	Location of Action unspecified
Nācciyār Tirumoḻi 6: The Song of the Wedding Dream	First Person Singular	Location of Action unspecified
Nācciyār Tirumoḻi 7: The Song to the White Conch	First Person Singular	Location of Action unspecified
Nācciyār Tirumoḻi 8: The Song to the Dark Rain Clouds	First Person Singular	Location of Action unspecified Viṣṇu specifically located in Vēṅkaṭam
Nācciyār Tirumoḻi 9: The Song in the Groves of Tirumāliruñcōlai	First Person Singular	The groves of Tirumāliruñcōlai
Nācciyār Tirumoḻi 10: The Song of Lament	First Person Singular	Location of Action unspecified
Nācciyār Tirumoḻi 11: The Song for the Conch Bangles	First Person Singular	Location of Action unspecified Addressed to Viṣṇu at Śrīraṅgam
Nācciyār Tirumoḻi 12: The Song of Sacred Places	First Person Singular	Location of Action unspecified Kṛṣṇa located in Mathurā, Vṛndāvana, Dvārakā
Nācciyār Tirumoḻi 13: The Song of Desire	First Person Singular	Location of Action unspecified
Nācciyār Tirumoḻi 14: The Song of Questions and Answers	First Person Singular and First Person Plural	Location of Action unspecified Kṛṣṇa located in Vṛndāvana

In contrast to the *Nācciyār Tirumoḻi*, the *Tiruppāvai* is presented entirely in the third-person plural and offers different challenges to the permeable boundaries of *bhakti* poetics that allow the poet to become the speaker of the poem. Though this chorus of *gopī* girl voices runs through the poetic narrative of the shorter poem and the ambiguous ending suggests an imagined poetic reality, the *Tiruppāvai* is nevertheless interpreted as documenting Āṇṭāḷ's ritual observances. On the face of it, the opening first-person narrative of the *Nācciyār Tirumoḻi* (The Song to Kāmadeva) mitigates such problems of interpretation as presented in the *Tiruppāvai*, for the veil that separates persona and poet becomes utterly sheer. In contradistinction to the concluding verse of the *Tiruppāvai*, the poet Kōtai makes no pretense about *who* has observed the vow in the final verse of the *Nācciyār Tirumoḻi*'s opening song:

> Kōtai of Viṣṇucittaṉ
> king of Putuvai
> city of towering mansions that rise like mountains
> sang this garland of sweet Tamiḻ
> to plead with Kāmadeva
> with his sugarcane bow and five-flower arrows
> to unite her with the lord. . . .
>
> *Nācciyār Tirumoḻi* 1.10

With no personae evoked and no imagined reality in which the action is situated, the *Nācciyār Tirumoḻi* thus begins much like any other similar Tamiḻ *bhakti* poem of this period. But the second, third, and fourth sections of the *Nācciyār Tirumoḻi* abruptly revert to the choir of young *gopī* girls, who like their counterparts in the *Tiruppāvai* are located in the wonderful and mythical realm of Vṛndāvana. Their child-like voices playfully chastise Kṛṣṇa for breaking their sandcastles and stealing their clothes, while also divining the future of their love for him.[42] In the poem's fifth decad, the singular voice reemerges, and remains until the final section, when the *gopī* girls once again make their appearance in Vṛndāvana. Āṇṭāḷ's alteration between "her" voice and the identity of the *gopī* girls says something significant about the ways in which she uses both female voices and the spaces in which she locates them.

The *gopī* voice is always a collective one and is the counter measure to the individual's lament that dominates the *Nācciyār Tirumoḻi*. The collective *gopī* voice invariably emerges in Āṇṭāḷ's poetry in the mythic world of Vṛndāvana, where Kṛṣṇa remains close at hand. And even when he chooses to disappear, there are those who share the pain brought by separation. The real and material world of sacred sites is lonely for one such as Āṇṭāḷ, and the decads of the *Nācciyār Tirumoḻi* express this profound loneliness by reverting to the unmediated voice of the heroine. There are no like-minded companions who can empathize with her suffering, who can make sense of an untamed and reckless love. Instead there are unheeding birds (*Nācciyār Tirumoḻi* 5), insentient clouds (*Nācciyār Tirumoḻi* 8), and groups of mothers (*Nācciyār Tirumoḻi* 10) who are all just helpless spectators of her terrible longing. It is only in the fourteenth section of the poem that both voices (I and we) come together in a dialogue conducted across space and time. While the heroine's bitter voice raises questions about Kṛṣṇa's whereabouts, a collective voice replies that he can be found only in

Vṛndāvana. It would appear that when the collective voice of the *gopī* girls emerges in the *Nācciyār Tirumoḻi*, it is to signify the possibility of union, only realized in a mythic, perhaps imaginal realm. It is a point that the poet herself makes in *Nācciyār Tirumoḻi* 12, when she/the heroine demands to be taken to the sites made sacred by Kṛṣṇa's presence: Mathurā, Vṛndāvana, the banks of the Yamunā, and Dvārakā. One bound to the material world, like the heroine of the *Nācciyār Tirumoḻi*, is condemned to a continued and endless separation, and the poem is punctuated with instances of an ephemeral and distant union embodied in the figures of the tormented or questing *gopī* girls of Vṛndāvana. When the heroine does experience that momentary union, it is either when she enters the mythical world of Kṛṣṇa's play or in the realm of dreams, where she (the heroine/Āṇṭāḷ) dreams of her marriage to Viṣṇu (*Nācciyār Tirumoḻi* 6). In the poignant section that follows, the heroine awakens only to realize that her grand wedding witnessed by the gods was but a cruel deception (*Nācciyār Tirumoḻi* 7).

The final section of the *Nācciyār Tirumoḻi* makes sense only when we map the use of space and voice in the poem. What hagiographies and commentaries read as conclusive union is in fact rather open-ended and opaque. The only certainty is that the experience of union with Kṛṣṇa is one that is shared and best achieved with a community (like in the *Tiruppāvai*), and it can be fully and permanently realized only in a mythical world. Of course, Vṛndāvana is as much a terrestrial place as Śrīraṅgam, Vēṅkaṭam, or Tirumāliruñcōlai, yet Āṇṭāḷ does not choose to end the *Nācciyār Tirumoḻi* in any of these famous sites, particularly Śrīraṅgam, where legend has it she was united with Viṣṇu. Rather, in the *Nācciyār Tirumoḻi* as in the *Tiruppāvai*, Vṛndāvana/Āyarpāṭi is a far-away magical land, a place of imagination, where the most impossible desires can be dreamed into fulfillment.

Of Conches and Conch Bangles: Recurring Symbols in the *Nācciyār Tirumoḻi*

The *Tiruppāvai* is anchored by a single central symbol—the *paṟai*—but the *Nācciyār Tirumoḻi*, true to its more supple structure, employs a variety of symbols that are nimbly layered for maximum emotive and aesthetic impact. Phrases, myths, motifs, and symbols grace the poem, heavy with meaning like the dark rain clouds the poet-heroine sends as her warrior-messengers. Often, Āṇṭāḷ achieves this effect by doing one of two things: either using a word or symbol that is inherently polyvalent or by imbuing a word with polyvalence. We see the technique already in evidence in the *Tiruppāvai* in her use of the words *pāvai* (a polyvalent word) and *paṟai* (a word imbued with polyvalence). The *Nācciyār Tirumoḻi* is replete with instances of Āṇṭāḷ's verbal dexterity; her clever use of the word *caṅku* (conch) to refer to both Viṣṇu's conch and the heroine's conch bangles is perhaps the most obvious example. One could go so far as to suggest that the *caṅku*, like the *paṟai* and *pāvai* of the *Tiruppāvai*, is the dominant symbol that holds the *Nācciyār Tirumoḻi* together.

The first instance in the *Nācciyār Tirumoḻi* where the poet plays with the dual meaning of the word *caṅku* occurs in the opening two verses of "The Song to the *Kuyil*" (*Nācciyār Tirumoḻi* 5.1 and 5.2). These two early instances of Āṇṭāḷ's play on the word *caṅku* prefigure the protracted treatment it receives in *Nācciyār Tirumoḻi* 7 (The Song to the White Conch) and *Nācciyār Tirumoḻi* 11 (The Song for the Conch Bangles).[43] The fifth section is addressed to the sweet *kuyil* bird that the poet-heroine entreats to act as her messenger to a god indifferent to her love. As we will see below, the section's opening two verses signal a rhetorical gambit that collapses the heroine's stolen bangles with the distant unattainable conch of Viṣṇu. *Nācciyār Tirumoḻi* 5 begins with the effect of Viṣṇu's possession and his subsequent abandonment of the heroine,embodied inher loose conch bangles, as a sign of her loneliness. So, we find the heroine lamenting thus in *Nācciyār Tirumoḻi* 5.1:

> Is it fair that my love
> for the eternal Mādhava
> dark as the sapphire
> greatly famed and beautiful
> adorned with his jeweled crown
> should cause me to lose my bangles of conch (*caṅku*). . . ?

In 5.2, the verse that immediately follows, she shifts her focus and offers the reason for the loss of those bangles, which is articulated not just as simple abandonment, but as forced seduction:

> My perfect lord
> who holds the spotless white conch (*caṅku*) in his left hand
> refuses to reveal himself to me.
> Instead he enters me, tortures me all day. . . .

In this early instance of Āṇṭāḷ's use of Viṣṇu's conch, she makes no direct mention of its provenance. However, her audience would have been well aware of the story of Viṣṇu's relentless pursuit of the demon Pañcācana, who became a conch in the depths of the ocean. When Viṣṇu defeated him, he claimed the demon-conch as his special emblem. By thus simply speaking of how the god entered her, *and* by evoking the conch as Viṣṇu's specific attribute, Āṇṭāḷ equates his pursuit of her with his hunt for the demon to the very depths of the ocean. But whereas Viṣṇu's conch becomes his treasured companion, the heroine is eventually abandoned. Herein lies the difference between the two conches that Āṇṭāḷ exploits fully in *Nācciyār Tirumoḻi* 11. While one is cherished and loved (Viṣṇu's conch), the other, the heroine's conch bangle, a metonomy for her very self, is rejected and unloved. What Āṇṭāḷ merely suggests in the opening two verses of *Nācciyār Tirumoḻi* 5 becomes the focus of sumptuous attention in the later sections of the *Nācciyār Tirumoḻi*, with a section devoted to each kind of conch: Viṣṇu's special symbol (*Nācciyār Tirumoḻi* 7) and the heroine's conch bangles (*Nācciyār Tirumoḻi* 11).

Āṇṭāḷ's "Song to the White Conch" (*Nācciyār Tirumoḻi* 7) is unique among the corpus of *āḻvār* poetry, for it is the only one addressed exclusively to Viṣṇu's conch. In these eleven verses, Viṣṇu's conch becomes the center of attention, where the poet lauds it for its special place of intimacy. The poet marvels that something so ordinary (*caṅku*) could become so extraordinary that it deserves its own name (Valampuri, Pāñcajanya), and simply on account of its association with her beloved. To signal this dual status, Āṇṭāḷ addresses the conch in *Nācciyār Tirumoḻi* 7 both by its generic name, *caṅku*, and by its proper name as Valampuri or Pāñcajanya.[44] *Nācciyār Tirumoḻi* 7 begins in the following way:

> Are they fragrant as camphor? Are they fragrant as the lotus?
> Or do those coral red lips taste sweet?
> I ache to know the taste, the fragrance of the lips
>   of Mādhava, who broke the tusk of the elephant.
> Tell me, O white conch from the deep sea.
>
> *Nācciyār Tirumoḻi* 7.1

In the introductory verse of the seventh section, the conch is described simply and generically as the "white conch from the deep sea" (*āḻi veṇ caṅkē*). But as the decad unfolds and the circumstances of the conch's birth revealed, she begins to address it in particular and defining terms, as Pāñcajanya (*Nācciyār Tirumoḻi* 7.2, 7.8, 7.10), referring to its birth from the demon Pañcācana, and Valampuri (7.4), referencing its rarity as a conch which curves to the right (*valam*) rather than the left. But from the frequency with which she uses *caṅku* in this section, it is clear that she favors this word over the proper names Valampuri and Pāñcajanya that speak to the conch's uniqueness. Throughout the seventh section, she uses *caṅku* in its vocative form, embellishing it adjectivally as great and beautiful conch (*kōla peruñcaṅkē*, 7.3), great conch (*peruñcaṅku*, 7.5, 7.6, 7.9), and king among conches (*caṅku araiyā*, 7.7). Āṇṭāḷ's preference for the word *caṅku* over the more specific Pāñcajanya and Valampuri highlights the conch's initially antagonistic relationship to Viṣṇu, and its rather pedestrian genealogy, rather than its sacred character. This is a significant choice, for it sets up the daring claims of the *Nācciyār Tirumoḻi*'s eleventh section, devoted entirely to the heroine's conch bangles (*caṅku*).

Nācciyār Tirumoḻi 11 is the "Song for the Conch Bangles," and begins:

> The conch (*caṅku*) he holds in his hand is dear to him.
> Aren't my conch bangles (*caṅku*) as dear to me?
>
> *Nācciyār Tirumoḻi* 11.1

This entire *Tirumoḻi* turns on the twin meanings embedded in the word *caṅku*, one of which is derivative. The word *caṅku*, connoting bangle, has long been in use, as early as Caṅkam period literature, because it denotes bangles fashioned from conch shell. And the bangle of course is a common enough trope in Indic literature, employed to signal the woman's wasting disease of longing. The empty space of the bangle acts as a metonomy for the barrenness of her womanhood, the self-made empty and useless through the heedless cruelty of the lover. But here Āṇṭāḷ turns both the mythic and the mundane into something else. In a poetic sleight of hand that juxtaposes Viṣṇu's divine conch and the heroine's rather ordinary bangles, the simple word *caṅku* becomes the window and the mirror that facilitates moving between the ordinary and the extraordinary. It is the juncture where the commonplace (bangle) is imbued with profundity and the sublime with utter ordinariness (the divine conch).

It is the wonderful seventh section in praise of the conch that sets up the daring declarations of the eleventh *Tirumoḻi* and allows that window to be thrown open. In *Nācciyār Tirumoḻi* 7 the heroine sings enviously of the conch's singular relationship with Viṣṇu. Just as she/the *gopī* girls accuse Nappiṉṉai of monopolizing her beloved's attention in the *Tiruppāvai*, in *Nācciyār Tirumoḻi* 7, she berates the Pāñcajanya for the same misdeed. But when the conch once again becomes the center of Āṇṭāḷ's lavish poetic attention in *Nācciyār Tirumoḻi* 11, the accusation of ownership is reversed and she reserves her scathing words for Viṣṇu alone. After all, it is he who bestowed upon a simple conch the honor of forever being associated with him. Similarly, her conch bangles are imbued with such gravitas because of her futile love for him. He subdued the terrible demon Pañcācana (the myth is recounted in *Nācciyār Tirumoḻi* 7) with the same single-minded ruthlessness that he loosened the bangles of conch from the heroine's wrists. In *Nācciyār Tirumoḻi* 11, she accuses Viṣṇu of hoarding wealth, including his conch and her measly conch bangles, through means both fair and foul. The lord owns the entire world, but is supremely attached to his conch, just as the heroine is attached to her conch bangles, her only wealth. In correlating *his* conch and *her* conch bangles, deeming them equally valuable, Āṇṭāḷ conjoins the mythic and the mundane and transforms the distant unattainable object into the intimate and familiar.

Enjoying Āṇṭāḷ: Commentary, Enjoyment and the King of Commentators

Śrīvaiṣṇava theologians speak of the process of commentary as *anubhava* (enjoyment) and the commentarial text as an *anubhava grantha* (text of enjoyment). Composing a commentary is not merely a cerebral act of interpretation, where the poem is made to fit a prefabricated theological agenda. Rather, the commentary is an expression of the commentator's enjoyment and relish of not just the poem, but also of the *āḻvār* poet's enjoyment of god, encoded in his/her composition. The commentary then becomes a means of accessing an *āḻvār*'s experience of the divine, while also standing witness to the commentator's own savoring of the divine as it is expressed in an *āḻvār* poem.[45] Within such a rubric, doing theology *is* an aesthetic endeavor, and arguably no one is more skilled or enthusiastic in the exegetical process than Periyavāccāṉ Piḷḷai, whose enjoyments of Āṇṭāḷ's *Tiruppāvai* and *Nācciyār Tirumoḻi* form the basis of the notes that accompany my translation.

Periyavāccāṉ Piḷḷai (b. 1228 C.E.) was the first and only medieval commentator to compose commentaries on all four thousand verses of the *Nālāyira Divya Prabandham*, which earned him the title *vyākhyāna cakravarti* or the King of Commentators.[46] This singular achievement alone is sufficient to set him apart from other medieval commentators, but the historical moment that he composed his work, and the lineage that he represented—he was the student of one of the foremost Śrīvaiṣṇava commentators, Nampiḷḷai—further compound his importance in the history of Śrīvaiṣṇavism. Periyavāccāṉ Piḷḷai's writing represents the maturation of Śrīvaiṣṇava Maṇipravāḷa discourse, and as such anticipates some of the internal philosophical differences that eventually lead to a sectarian split within the Śrīvaiṣṇava community.[47]

Piḷḷai's commentarial voice is lively and energetic. References to the *Vālmiki Rāmāyaṇa* and other scriptural sources sit comfortably beside quotations from the works of the *āḻvār* and contemporary anecdotal evidence. Piḷḷai is a thorough commentator who generates a plethora of imaginative meanings that nonetheless remain consistent with established Śrīvaiṣṇava doctrine. He makes liberal use of Sanskrit sources, both to establish equivalency, as well as to provide elucidation. Piḷḷai's great fondness for the Sanskrit *Rāmāyaṇa* manifests in his readiness to quote from it even when the concordance is not readily apparent, or perhaps even appropriate.

I have chosen to focus on Periyavāccāṉ Piḷḷai's commentary because he is the only early commentator to write on both the *Tiruppāvai* and *Nācciyār Tirumoḻi*. His commentaries on these two poems established the major contours of the commentaries that followed. In particular, Periyavāccāṉ Piḷḷai established the narrative that linked the two poems together, skillfully melding hagiography with theological discourse. In addition, he wrote at a time of significant flux in the development of Śrīvaiṣṇava traditions. His commentaries anticipate the theological schisms that developed over the next two centuries, especially as it pertains to issues of the role of the teacher, and the dependence/independence of the soul in relation to Viṣṇu. The mid-thirteenth century also witnessed the gradual apotheosis of the *āḻvār* poets, and Āṇṭāḷ in particular. Piḷḷai does not directly argue for Āṇṭāḷ's status as one of Viṣṇu's divine consorts, but he sets up consistent parallels between her and Sītā that foreshadow her eventual position as Viṣṇu's secondary consort.

The form of Piḷḷai's commentary for the *Tiruppāvai* and *Nācciyār Tirumoḻi* does not deviate from those he composed for the other *āḻvār* poems. The commentary always begins with a lengthy introduction that provides the reasons for the poem's composition. For instance, he begins the commentary to the *Tiruppāvai* by explaining Āṇṭāḷ's distinctive qualities as a devotee—that it is natural for a woman to love a man, but difficult for a man to love another man, as was the case with the other *āḻvār* poets, who had to assume the guise of women in many of their poems. He goes on to explain that Āṇṭāḷ boldly strove to awaken Viṣṇu and make her demand of him, using the vow as a mere pretext to get close to him. For the *Nācciyār Tirumoḻi*, Piḷḷai offers a general introduction to the poem and then one for each of the fourteen sections. In addition, he provides detailed explanations for each verse within any given section of the *Nācciyār Tirumoḻi*. In short, Piḷḷai offers an interpretation for all 173 of Āṇṭāḷ's verses.

The commentary for any individual verse always begins with a word gloss that can be considered the first level of interpretation. Here, a common word like *deva* (a god, divine being) may be glossed as *nityasūri* (eternally divine beings, always in service of Viṣṇu), inflecting it with a decidedly Śrīvaiṣṇava theological slant. For instance, the first occurrence of the word *paṟai* in *Tiruppāvai* 1 may be explained as *viruppam* (desire), with no mention made of *paṟai* as a sacred drum. The word gloss is followed by a phrase-by-phrase interpretation of the verse, where theology rubs shoulders with anecdotes of the delight that Śrīvaiṣṇava luminaries like Rāmānuja experienced in the compositions of the *āḻvār*.[48] In his phrase-by-phrase exegesis, Piḷḷai does not lose sight of his narrative thread and is meticulous in establishing narrative continuity, from verse to verse, section to section, and poem to poem. But for all his attention to detail, Piḷḷai is not much concerned with identifying a poem's literary allusions, even when they are readily apparent, and this is particularly true in the *Nācciyār Tirumoḻi*, where references to antecedent literary texts like the Tamiḻ epic-poem *Cilappatikāram* and the Caṅkam anthology *Kuṟuntokai* are plentiful. Piḷḷai simply ignores these in favor of a citation from, or allusion to, a relevant epic or Purāṇic source. When he does quote Tamil̲ poetry, it is invariably from the corpus of *āl̲vār* poetry. It is clear from his commentaries to other *āl̲vār* poems, such as Nammāl̲vār's *Tiruviruttam*, that Piḷḷai is aware of Tamil̲'s literary antecedents, so we cannot attribute his deliberate choices to simple ignorance, or an impulse to Sanskritize the *āl̲vār* poems. As I have argued elsewhere, the choice of Sanskrit text over secular or even Jain texts such as the *Cilappatikāram* underscores the Śrīvaiṣṇava ideal that a commentary is an *anubhava grantha*, a text of enjoyment. A commentator such as Piḷḷai therefore chooses texts—the *Vālmīki Rāmāyaṇa* being chief among them—that heighten the experience of *anubhava*, both for the author and his audience, rather than those that have great literary value, but no devotional merit.[49] In the final sum, Śrīvaiṣṇava commentary *is* a form of literary criticism. It is an uninhibited revelry in the immeasurable pleasures of the text, where the *āl̲vār* text and the commentary work in tandem to create a conduit of aesthetic experience that seeks to induce a profound mystical ecstasy.

Tiruppāvai and *Nācciyār Tirumol̲i* in Ritual

When one considers the ritual lives of the *Tiruppāvai* and *Nācciyār Tirumol̲i*, liturgical recitation, either at home or at the temple, are the most common and most widespread. The *Tiruppāvai* occupies a central place in daily Śrīvaiṣṇava temple liturgical services. Even if the poem is not recited in its entirety, a few select and important verses such as *Tiruppāvai* 29 are performed at the conclusion of morning daily *pūjas* during the waving of the camphor lamp, or even sometimes during the *abhiṣeka* (ritual ablutions). The *Tiruppāvai* and *Nācciyār Tirumol̲i* are always performed during the first ten days of the month-long Festival of Recitation in Mārkal̲i (December–January) known as the *Adhyayanotsavam*. The sixth section (Song of the Wedding Dream) of the *Nācciyār Tirumol̲i*, which recounts the heroine's wedding-dream, is recited during Śrīvaiṣṇava Brahmin marriages, where the bride is adorned as Āṇṭāḷ. Liturgical recitation of the *Tiruppāvai* and *Nācciyār Tirumol̲i* as described above are common and function as part of a larger complex of temple-based recitations of the *Nālāyira Divya Prabandham*. However, at Āṇṭāḷ's temple in Śrīvilliputtūr, both poems in equal measure are the focus of elaborate and extravagant ritual enactments that go far beyond recitation. For instance, the *śayana tirukkōlam* (The Depiction of the Attitude of Repose), an *alaṅkāra* (ornamentation) unique to the Śrīvilliputtūr Āṇṭāḷ temple, recreates *Tiruppāvai* 19.[50] In this *alaṅkāra*, Āṇṭāḷ is imagined in the role of Nappin̲n̲ai, and her consort Raṅgaman̲n̲ār is Kṛṣṇa.

During Āṇṭāḷ's Annual Bathing Festival at her temple in Śrīvilliputtūr (December–January), the *Tiruppāvai* is given special reverence and recited with the same care as the *Tiruvāymoḻi* in a tradition known as *nāḷ pāṭṭu* (Daily Song). Sections of the *Nācciyār Tirumoḻi* come to the fore in recitations and retellings of Āṇṭāḷ's story at Śrīvilliputtūr, in a ritual of divination, or in special *alaṅkāras* for Āṇṭāḷ.[51] It is beyond the scope of this introduction to discuss all of these varied and delightful ritual enjoyments and enactments of Āṇṭāḷ's *Tiruppāvai* and *Nācciyār Tirumoḻi*. In the section that follows, I present two of the most important of these ritual re-enactments at the Śrīvilliputtūr Āṇṭāḷ temple. The first deals exclusively with the *Tiruppāvai* and the other draws its inspiration from the *Nācciyār Tirumoḻi*.

Bathing in Mārkaḻi: Enacting the *Tiruppāvai* at the Śrīvilliputtūr Āṇṭāḷ Temple

Almost at the tail end of the month of Mārkaḻi (mid-January), the Śrīvilliputtūr Āṇṭāḷ temple celebrates a ten-day festival for Āṇṭāḷ called the *Mārkaḻi Nīrāṭṭa Utsavam* (Festival of Ceremonial Bathing in Mārkaḻi).[52] The festival focuses on the actual act of bathing, an event that the *Tiruppāvai* chose to leave out. In the poem, we heard Āṇṭāḷ recount the details of the vow and listened to the *gopī* girls rouse their neighborhood friends to join them in the early morning bathing ritual. Then, the poem shifted to the doorstep of the god. However in this festival, celebrated in present-day Śrīvilliputtūr and probably practiced in some form since the mid-seventeenth century, the focus is the actual bathing, which is enacted ritually in an elaborate manner.[53]

Āṇṭāḷ's daily routine during the *Mārkaḻi Nīrāṭṭa Utsavam* revolves around the bathing ritual (*nīrāṭṭam*) that is bracketed by spectacular adornments (*alaṅkāra*) twice a day. Each festival day follows the same pattern: first the beautifully decorated image of Āṇṭāḷ is brought to the gateway of the neighboring Viṣṇu temple, where she is imagined to petition Viṣṇu for his grace. Once the rituals at the gateway of the Viṣṇu temple are concluded, Āṇṭāḷ's image journeys through the streets of Śrīvilliputtūr, with only a small retinue of priests in attendance, stopping along the way at various *maṇṭapas* or halls. After several hours of journeying, the image of Āṇṭāḷ reaches her final destination, a *maṇṭapa* located by a large temple tank, where in local lore, Āṇṭāḷ is thought to have bathed when she observed the Mārkaḻi vow. At the *maṇṭapa*, an extravagant and lovely ritual known as the *eṇṇai kāppu* (Oil Anointment) is performed. This is followed by an elaborate ritual bath (*abhiṣeka*). The image of Āṇṭāḷ is then adorned sumptuously and returned in procession back to the Śrīvilliputtūr temple, where she is finally reunited with her divine husband.[54]

Āṇṭāḷ's wandering through Śrīvilliputtūr in Mārkaḻi mimics the trajectory of the *Tiruppāvai*, which also begins in the outside world—with waking up the various *gopī* girls—and ends with a gradual entry into the house of the god. The morning procession is thus meant to re-enact the "waking-up-the-girls" section of the *Tiruppāvai*, and in this regard, this festival can be understood as dramatizing the poem's rhetorical device that transforms the audience of the festival into one of the girls who have slept too late and have thus failed to uphold the strictures of the Mārkaḻi vow. In the *Tiruppāvai*, at the end of the journey is the sight of and promise of divine union in the form of Kṛṣṇa and Nappiṉṉai. In the Mārkaḻi festival, Āṇṭāḷ and her devotees traverse the same path, repeating the cycle of union and separation from the object of their desire. During the eight days of the festival, Āṇṭāḷ is both the *gopī* girl eagerly on a quest and the woman who became a goddess because her desire was so fully realized. As she moves between these personalities, to stand first at Kṛṣṇa's doorway, and then to go through that doorway, she is at once goddess and devotee, embodying both the quest for him and the fruition of her quest.[55]

Divining with Pearls: *Nācciyār Tirumoḻi* and the *Araiyar Cēvai* at Śrīvilliputtūr

The *Araiyar Cēvai* (Service of the Araiyars) is a hereditary ritual performance tradition performed by a patrilineal community of Brahmin men and is unique to the Śrīvaiṣṇava community. It survives today in three temples in Tamiḻ Nāṭu—Śrīraṅgam, Śrīvilliputtūr, and Āḻvār Tirunakari. The *Araiyar Cēvai* combines gestural interpretation with liturgical recitation and singing and has long been understood by the performers as embodying a multidimensional interpretation of the *Nālāyira Divya Prabandham*. While the Araiyars are required to perform both daily and festival ritual duties, their most elaborate performances take place in the context of temple festivals, especially during the month of Mārkaḻi. It is in the context of the *Adhyayanotsavam* (Festival of Recitation) celebrated at the temples of Śrīraṅgam, Śrīvilliputtūr, and Āḻvār Tirunakari that the *Nācciyār Tirumoḻi* becomes an integral part of the Araiyars' ritual gestural exegesis. During the first ten days of the Festival of Recitation the Araiyar performs a special ritual drama called the *muttukkuṟi* (Divination with Pearls), where the central texts are the fourth decad of the *Nācciyār Tirumoḻi* and Tirumaṅkaiyāḻvār's longer love poem, the *Tiruneṭuntāṇṭakam*.[56]

The *muttukkuṟi* is a ritual divination and is peopled with well-known stock characters—the lovelorn heroine, the anxious mother, and the wise fortune-teller. The mother is distraught to find her daughter growing thin, pale, and frail with sickness and summons the soothsayer (*kuṟatti*) to divine the cause of the girl's illness. The fortune-teller settles down to predict the girl's future, and finally reveals that her love for the "dark-hued lord" will be realized. The Araiyar recites *Nācciyār Tirumoḻi* 4.1 and 4.2 when performing the actual divination. Although in *Nācciyār Tirumoḻi* 4 it is the *gopī* girls who perform the divination, in Śrīvilliputtūr, the heroine of the *muttukkuṟi* is Āṇṭāḷ. She is both the performer of the divination (the heroine performing the divination on her own) and the recipient of the divination (the fortune-teller performing the divination on her behalf).[57] At the conclusion of the *muttukkuṟi*, the image of Āṇṭāḷ is taken in procession, and the Araiyar recites particular verses from the latter half of the *Nācciyār Tirumoḻi*—selections from *Nācciyār Tirumoḻi* 7 (Song to the White Conch), 11 (Song for the Conch Bangles), and 13 (Song of Desire). The recitation of these verses from the *Nācciyār Tirumoḻi* is unique to Śrīvilliputtūr and acknowledges the significance of the latter poem in constructing and celebrating Āṇṭāḷ at her temple.[58]

The Other Lives of Āṇṭāḷ's Poems

Āṇṭāḷ's poems, particularly the *Tiruppāvai*, are vibrantly alive in traditional modes of Śrīvaiṣṇava discourse, as well as in more recent imaginings in a wide variety of media. Āṇṭāḷ is immensely popular among diaspora Hindus, and has an almost-ubiquitous presence in Hindu temples in the United States, such as those in Atlanta, Pittsburgh, Livermore, and Malibu, which have shrines dedicated to Āṇṭāḷ rather than Bhū Devī. Lavishly illustrated e-books of the *Tiruppāvai* and *Nācciyār Tirumoḻi*, with commentary in English, and discussions on listservs (such as the "Bhakti List," on hiatus since 2003) of the *Tiruppāvai* and *Nācciyār Tirumoḻi*, especially during the month of Mārkaḻi, are common. Perhaps unsurprisingly, many of these listservs and e-books are published and maintained by diaspora Śrīvaiṣṇavas, invariably based in the United States.[59]

While Āṇṭāḷ's story has always been familiar to South Indians, the *Tiruppāvai* and *Nācciyār Tirumoḻi* were in all likelihood well known only to Śrīvaiṣṇavas until quite recently. In 1952, Ariyakudi Ramanuja Iyengar (1890–1967 C.E.), a prominent South Indian musician, set the *Tiruppāvai* to Karṇāṭak music *rāgas* and performed selections at the Śrīvilliputtūr Āṇṭāḷ temple, and then later during his concerts, usually as a concluding piece.[60] The *Tiruppāvai*, already a well-known text, soared in popularity, and it continues to be regularly performed in Karṇāṭak music concerts, especially during the Annual December Music Festival in Chennai.[61]

Parallel to the increased popularity of Āṇṭāḷ's poems in music circles in recent years is the greater visibility of her poems in the newly emergent repertoire of the South Indian neoclassical dance form, Bharatanātyam. Rukmini Arundale (1904–1986), one of the pioneers of the new hybrid theatrical form of Bharatanātyam "dance-drama," debuted *Andal Charitram* (Āṇṭāḷ's Story) in 1961, approximately thirty years after she had founded her dance school and company, Kalakshetra (est. January 1936). *Andal Charitram* liberally used verses from both the *Tiruppāvai* and *Nācciyār Tirumoḻi* to narrate Āṇṭāḷ's life story and excerpts from Periyāḻvār's *Periyāḻvār Tirumoḻi* and the Sanskrit hagiography, *Divyasūricaritram*, to depict her childhood years. The Kalakshetra *Andal Charitram* emphasized her devotion and muted the transgressive, violent, and disquieting moments of her mythologized life. The dance-drama continues to be frequently staged during Kalakshetra's annual December music and dance festival. Its popularity is largely derived from the nonconfrontational and comforting nature of its story. As presented in the Kalakshetra version, Āṇṭāḷ is a divine being, whose love for Kṛṣṇa was predestined. Kalakshetra's new retelling of an old story chose those verses from the *Nācciyār Tirumoḻi* such as the "Song of the Wedding-Dream" (*Nācciyār Tirumoḻi* 6) and the "Song to the White Conch" (*Nācciyār Tirumoḻi* 7) that do not disrupt the representation of Āṇṭāḷ as an innocent and asexual young girl. Rather, *Andal Charitram* like many of its successors strove (and by all accounts succeeded) to create a "soul-satisfying production and an elevating spiritual experience for the audience."[62]

Kalakshetra's *Andal Charitram* is only one (and possibly one of the earliest) interpretation of Āṇṭāḷ's poetry in dance that used the poems to narrate her story. Since then, Āṇṭāḷ dance-dramas have become increasingly popular both in India and in the diaspora.[63] Some focus exclusively on the *Nācciyār Tirumoḻi*, like Anita Ratnam's *Naachiyar: Mystic Search for the Divine* (2000) that claims to engage with the mature love of this later poem.[64] Dance-dramas under titles such as *Andal Kalyanam* (2002, North Carolina) are frequently staged by diaspora communities, often as fundraising for temple building in the United States and elsewhere. Still other versions bring Āṇṭāḷ's poetry and life into conversation with other female poets like Mīrā, drawing parallels between the experience of two female poets separated by time, space, and language. One such example is Jayanthi Raman's *Krishna Bhakti* (2006, Portland, Oregon), which depicts the story of Āṇṭāḷ and Mīrā using multiple forms of Indian dance including Bharatanātyam and Maṇipuri.[65] However most of these performances, following Kalakshetra's lead, are concerned primarily with presenting a dramatic hagiography for a contemporary audience. They tend to read the poems as an autobiography that confirms a well-known story. John Stratton Hawley has argued that representations of Mīrā (and other problem saints) in Indian comic books such as *Amar Chitra Katha* tend to domesticate her, where her *bhakti* (the cause of her rebelliousness) "is made consonant with her fulfillment of a woman's *dharma*."[66] Something similar happens to Āṇṭāḷ in the dance-dramas that aim to celebrate her life. Bharatanātyam dance-dramas, like comic books, address an English-educated, middle-class, global audience. Thus Āṇṭāḷ's ritual transgressions, the disturbing violence, and the frank eroticism of her poems are completely subordinated or erased in the larger cause of devotion, and her position as the god's wife makes her life worth celebrating within the framework of middle-class mores.

As the only woman among a group of eleven male *āḻvār*, and as a woman whose mythologized life was radical, Āṇṭāḷ is a vexed figure. She is revered as an incarnation of the goddess Bhū Devī, and her poems are recited and celebrated. Women in particular are attracted to her, although her life in its rejection of social norms is not emulated. As Vasudha Narayanan has pointed out, Āṇṭāḷ is a theological role model because she is one who strives for *mokṣa*, and in this regard is an exemplar for not just women, but all human beings.[67] But women in South India have found ways to make Āṇṭāḷ their own, and an excellent example is women's participation in devotional groups known as *maṇḍali* (lit. circle) that focus on Āṇṭāḷ. These *maṇḍalis* usually meet once or twice a week in private and also perform in public settings, in music festivals, temples, and on television and radio. One of the most visible of these groups is the appropriately named *Godā Maṇḍali* (Circle of Godā), which was formed in 1970 and reorganized in 1982. They perform Āṇṭāḷ songs on television, radio, and for various temple functions, and although the women of this group perform the songs of the other *āḻvār*, their emphasis is on Āṇṭāḷ, on her poetry, and her ability as the consort of Viṣṇu to act as an effective mediator.[68] Given that only Brahmin men are allowed to recite the *āḻvār* songs, including the *Tiruppāvai* and *Nācciyār Tirumoḻi*, in the context of temple and festival worship, groups such as the *Godā Maṇḍali* represent a thoroughly modern means for women to participate in public worship and empowering religious activities.

About the Translation

Vidya Dehejia's *Āṇṭāḷ and Her Path of Love* is the sole academic translation of both the *Tiruppāvai* and *Nācciyār Tirumoḻi*. This work, published over a decade ago locates Āṇṭāḷ in the milieu of Tamiḻ *bhakti* and introduces her as "Woman, Poet, and Mystic." The brief introduction discusses the Caṅkam antecedents of Āṇṭāḷ's poetry, the rhythm and metrical structures of her verses, and prominent motifs such as the history of the *pāvai* vow. The accompanying notes function to clarify specific myths, particular names, and flora and fauna, but do not explicate the verses or situate them in their ritual, performative, or commentarial contexts. This book is an excellent basic introduction to Āṇṭāḷ, but it is also limited by its format and cannot explore any of the aforementioned themes in depth. One of the problems in its approach is that the book posits a dichotomy between the *Tiruppāvai* and *Nācciyār Tirumoḻi*, saying, "... the *Nācciyār Tirumoḻi* is lesser known and is not chanted in temples or at religious festivals."[69] But as I have discussed at length in this introduction, both the *Tiruppāvai* and *Nācciyār Tirumoḻi* have active ritual and performative lives. While the *Tiruppāvai* is certainly better known and more accessible to a lay, non-Śrīvaiṣṇava public, it is the *Nācciyār Tirumoḻi* that is central to asserting Āṇṭāḷ's grand passion for Viṣṇu within the oral and written hagiographic traditions. One of my main aims in this translation of Āṇṭāḷ's two poems is to demonstrate the significance and the interlinked nature of the *Tiruppāvai* and *Nācciyār Tirumoḻi* through a detailed discussion of the lives of both poems and the accompanying notes.

Any translation of the *Tiruppāvai* and *Nācciyār Tirumoḻi*, and indeed any *bhakti* poem, carries a double burden. The first is what Hank Heifetz referred to as Indologese, the laboring, heavy Victorian diction that hampers the majority of English translations of Indic texts.[70] The genealogy of Indologese and its impact on South Asian literary studies has subsequently been explored comprehensively by Steven Hopkins in *Singing the Body of God*[71] and in his sensitive translations of Vedānta Deśika's poems in *An Ornament for Jewels*,[72] and I refrain from rehearsing those issues here. Suffice it to say, these Indologese translation are often haunted by the desire to convey the weight and the canonicity of the poem with evocations of Shakespearean thou's and archaic language. In addition, these translations are wedded to Tamiḻ syntax, either in terms of word order or in the language's tendency to stack adverbial and adjectival participles, drop off the endings of nouns, and leave the finite verb until the final line of the verse. In the *Tiruppāvai*, there is no finite verb that ends each verse. Rather an adverbial participle such as *makiḻntu* (having rejoiced) leads into the refrain, *ēl ōr empāvāy*, making it impossible to translate into clear English. To adhere to Tamiḻ syntax with slavish fidelity is a losing proposition and would undoubtedly create a translation that is not only labored, but also more important, one that is unintelligible.[73]

The thirty verses of the *Tiruppāvai* are composed in eight concise lines of *koccaka kalippa* meter, while the *Nācciyār Tirumoḻi* employs five different metrical structures in line length ranging from four to eight. I have not endeavored to duplicate either Āṇṭāḷ's compact metrical and rhythmic style, or the eight-line/four-line verse format of either poem. Instead, I have attempted to convey her lucid imagery, her ability to paint "word-pictures," and her embedded poetic style through a translation approach that makes visual Āṇṭāḷ's craft as a poet. Wherever possible, I have retained the order of the lines, metaphors, and images. When I have indented an image and/or metaphor from the body of the verse it is to indicate that it is embedded. For example I translate the final lines of *Tiruppāvai* 8 as follows:

> If we sing of him
> and we attain the *paṟai*-drum
>
> If we go to him,
>   who ripped open the beak of the bird
>   who destroyed the terrible wrestlers
>   that god of gods
>
> he will listen intently and grant us grace.

In my translation, I indent the two lines starting with, "who tore open the beak. . . ." while lining up the final two lines, "He will listen intently and he will give us grace" to convey that both the stacked and embedded qualifiers apply to him,—here, Kṛṣṇa. The above verse also highlights an important choice I have made as a translator. While technical vocabulary and foreign words can hamper a translation, I have chosen to retain those words that do not have a workable English equivalent—this is especially true of the vast range of flora and fauna, birds and animals that make their appearance in Āṇṭāḷ's poetry. I indicate these terms in italics within the verses themselves and explicate them in the glossary. Sometimes a foreign word becomes self-explanatory within the context of the verse. For instance, a line such as "the *ceṅkaḻunīr* blossoms have opened their purple lips/and the *āmpal* flowers have closed their dark petals." despite the strange words, sufficiently conveys that these are two kinds of flowers, one of which blooms during the day, while the other is night blooming. In some cases, I have chosen to use a familiar Indic equivalent over an English word for some Tamiḻ words. The most obvious example of this decision is *tulasī* (*tuḻāy* in Tamiḻ). In addition to being cumbersome, to translate *tulasī/tuḻāy* as "sacred basil" is to eject a reader who only knows basil as a fragrant herb used in cooking out of the text. As discussed earlier in the introduction, I have also chosen not to translate words such as *paṟai* or the refrain *ēl ōr empāvāy* for their great rhetorical impact emerges from their ambiguity. In the former case, I half translate *paṟai* as *paṟai*-drum, so as to suggest that it refers to something both specific and nebulous. The phrase *ēl ōr empāvāy* is the poem's refrain and generates a mantra-like quality. I have left it untranslated because it is impossible to have it make grammatical sense while also retaining the inherent ambivalence of the word *pāvai*.

These translation choices lead me to the second concern that has troubled translations of Tamil̲ *bhakti* literature. For centuries, these poems have been read, appreciated, and enjoyed primarily as devotional texts. This approach has translated itself into how academics, whether trained in the Western academy or not, have regarded these poems.[74] The Tamil̲ *bhakti* poems—and the *Tiruppāvai* and *Nācciyār Tirumol̲i* are no exception—are rooted in the idiom of religious literature, and any translation strives to convey the gravity worthy of a text that seeks to convey metaphysical knowledge. Within the context of this worthy endeavor, the literary value of the poem is not only secondary, but also marginal. As early as the great Śrīvaiṣṇava theologian Periyavāccāṉ Piḷḷai one can adduce the tendency to reconfigure what is aesthetically pleasing in a poem, be it the *Tiruppāvai* or the *Tiruvāymol̲i*. Even though Āṇṭāḷ's poems brim with allusions to Caṅkam poems, there is little acknowledgment of this literary past. The literary culture of the Caṅkam period has negligible relevance for Śrīvaiṣṇava theologians, who are redefining aesthetic pleasure in terms of a poem's efficacy in distilling and producing a devotional affect.[75]

Āṇṭāḷ's poems and the commentaries that accompany them are rich with mythic allusions and are filled with evocative epithets for Viṣṇu. I have discussed the significance of some of these divine names in the notes to the poems. Where appropriate, I have also provided a gloss of unfamiliar terms that occur in the commentaries or in the poems in the notes that accompany the relevant verse or section. However, in order to keep the notes as lean as possible, appendix 2 provides a synopsis of the major myths that occur in the *Tiruppāvai*, *Nācciyār Tirumol̲i*, and the commentaries, while appendix 3 provides an index of all the myths and Viṣṇu's epithets employed in the two poems. In addition, I have provided a glossary for all un-translated Tamil̲ and Sanskrit words that occur in the *Tiruppāvai* and *Nācciyār Tirumol̲i* and in the accompanying commentaries.

Within the Śrīvaiṣṇava communities, each verse of the *Tiruppāvai* is referred to by its opening line, and not by its number. Similarly, the decads that comprise the *Nācciyār Tirumol̲i* are cited by the first line of its first verse, and not by where the *Tirumol̲i* occurs in the poem. Therefore, most Śrīvaiṣṇava scholars will reference *Tiruppāvai* 27 as *kūṭārai vellum*, rather than by its verse number, while *kaṇṇaṉ eṉṉum*, the first line of the penultimate *Tirumol̲i*, guides the reader/listener to *Nācciyār Tirumol̲i* 13. I have integrated this emic way of citing the text by including the opening phrase of the verse and the relevant number for each of the thirty verses of the *Tiruppāvai* in both the translation and in the notes. For the *Nācciyār Tirumoḻi*, I have provided a title for each decad (for example, The Song of Desire), which is not used in the traditional interpretations of the poem. In addition, I have also incorporated the opening Tamiḻ phrase of the decad in question (for example, *kaṇṇaṉ eṉṉum*) and the translation of that phrase (*kaṇṇaṉ*, my dark lord). To avoid confusion, I have not included the Tamiḻ texts, and their translations to headline the notes to each section of the *Nācciyār Tirumoḻi*. Instead, they occur under the title for each decad with the relevant *Tirumoḻi* number listed beside it, like so: 13. The Song of Desire.

I have not encountered any significant discrepancies in either the published or liturgical versions of the *Tiruppāvai* and *Nācciyār Tirumoḻi*. Therefore, my translation choices have not been influenced by the various text and commentary versions that I have consulted over the years. My primary references were the versions of the *Tiruppāvai* and *Nācciyār Tirumoḻi* in the *Nālāyira Divya Prabandham* published by the Annangarachariar Press (1972) and by Krishnaswamy Iyengar's Srinivasa Press.

In these translations of the *Tiruppāvai* and *Nācciyār Tirumoḻi*, I have attempted versions that are both accurate and poetic. I have been guided by the desire to produce a work that acknowledges equally the literary and the theological. After all, what does it mean to translate a *bhakti* text in its entirety, given the vibrant lives of these poems in commentary, temple and lay ritual, and contemporary performance traditions of music and dance? My translations are meant to evoke Āṇṭāḷ's extraordinary poetic virtuosity, the introduction brings the poems alive in their performative dimensions, and the appended notes highlight the art of the commentator and the theological significance of these poems. In the final sum, a translation is an interpretation, whatever claims toward fidelity to the text one might make. The translator, the commentator, the priest, the performer, all have translated these lovely poems into their own special languages, be they of words, ritual, or theology. Here, I have brought in multiple interpretive voices, so that the poet's words cross over alongside the equally important lives of those words.

Although Āṇṭāḷ is revered primarily today as a goddess, it is her poetry—both the *Tiruppāvai* and *Nācciyār Tirumoḻi*—apotheosized into revealed texts that is the vehicle of the expression of her spiritual process. Āṇṭāḷ often evokes the metaphor of the garland to describe the *Tiruppāvai* and *Nācciyār Tirumoḻi*. Sometimes, her verses are garlands of songs (*pāmālai*) and sometimes they are garlands of flowers (*pūmālai*), bound together by a shared symbolic world of a singular savoring of the divine. As the title of the book *The Secret Garland* implies, the *Tiruppāvai* and *Nācciyār Tirumoḻi*, linked through richly layered and detailed imagery, moored by the spectacular interpretive worlds that they have spawned, exemplify a cohesive entity that is at once obvious and enigmatic.

Notes

1. This is a quote from *Nācciyār Tirumoḻi* 1.4 that is included in all retellings of the Āṇṭāḷ story. In the hagiographies (oral and written), it is considered the moment that impresses upon Viṣṇucittaṉ the steadfastness of Āṇṭāḷ's goal.

2. My retelling of the Āṇṭāḷ story is an amalgamation of several oral and written hagiographic accounts, but includes all the salient points. There are a number of subtle and obvious differences between the many versions of the Āṇṭāḷ story. I have discussed these differences at length in Venkatesan, Archana. "The Āṇṭāḷ Story." *Journal of Vaishnava Studies*, 189–206; and in "Āṇṭāḷ and Her Magic Mirror: Her Life as Poet in the Guises of the Goddess," 42–117.

3. The poet Kōtai is known by several names. Godā (Sanskrit for Kōtai), *cūṭikkoṭutta nācciyār* (the woman who gave what she had worn) and Āṇṭāḷ are the best known. Of these, Āṇṭāḷ is the most common, regardless of whether it is used to refer to her as the author of the *Tiruppāvai* and *Nācciyār Tirumoḻi* or in her capacity as the divine consort. For reasons of familiarity and to avoid confusion, I use Āṇṭāḷ throughout this book, except in places where her other names have special significance.

4. For a discussion of *phala śruti* verses, please see the note for *Tiruppāvai* 30. Also, refer to Cutler, Norman. *Songs of Experience: The Poetics of Tamil Devotion*, 27–29.

5. This town is identified with contemporary Śrīvilliputtūr, a town about seventy-five kilometers south of Maturai.

6. For a discussion of Viṣṇucittaṉ's relationship to Āṇṭāḷ as her teachers, see Hudson, Dennis. "Āṇṭāḷ's Desire." *Vaiṣṇavī: Women and the Worship of Krishna*, 177–79.

7. For a detailed discussion of Viṣṇucittaṉ/Periyāḻvār, including issues relating to dating, see Ate, Lynn Marie. *Periyāḻvār Tirumoḻi: A Bālakṛṣṇa Text from the Devotional Period in Tamil Literature.*

There have been attempts to date Āṇṭāḷ on the basis of the astronomical evidence of her two poems, specifically the *Tiruppāvai*. However, such dating is extremely unreliable for several reasons. First is that several dates correspond to any given astrological conjunction. The *Tiruppāvai*, which forms the basis for these astrological calculations, is a poem predicated on the creation of a mythical landscape. We cannot definitively know that Āṇṭāḷ observed the vows she describes, and even if she did, it is impossible to distinguish her vivid world of poetic imagination from the ninth century day-to-day life she led. For a concise discussion of these astrological calculations, see Dehejia, Vidya "Introduction." *Āṇṭāḷ and Her Path of Love: Poems of a Woman Saint from South India*, 2–3.

8. Here, I refer to the Āṇṭāḷ temple of Śrīvilliputtūr, which was probably built around 1571 C.E., under the direction of the Nāyakars of Maturai. Branfoot, Crispin. "'Expanding Form': The Architectural Sculpture of the South Indian Temple, ca 1500–1700." p. 197.

9. Narayanan, Vasudha. "The Realm of Play and the Sacred Stage." *Gods at Play: Līlā in South Asia*, 177–204.

10. Tharu, Susie, and K. Lalitha. *Women Writing in India: 600 BC to the Present*, 68.

11. Cutler, Norman. *Songs of Experience*, 118.

12. Cutler, Norman. *Songs of Experience*, 120.

13. For further discussion on the significance of Āṇṭāḷ's marriage to Viṣṇu within the Śrīvaiṣṇava hagiographic traditions, see Venkatesan, Archana. "Who Stole the Garland of Love: Āṇṭāḷ Stories in the Śrīvaiṣṇava Tradition" and "Āṇṭāḷ and Her Magic Mirror: Her Life as Poet in the Guises of the Goddess," 42–117.

14. Ramanujan, A.K. "On Women Saints." *The Divine Consort: Rādhā and the Goddesses of India*, 323.

15. Hawley, John Stratton. *Three Bhakti Voices: Mirabai, Surdas and Kabir in Their Times and Ours*, 118.

16. See appendix 1 for a translation and brief discussion of the *taṉiyaṉ* verses to the *Tiruppāvai* and *Nācciyār Tirumoḻi*.

17. Hawley, John Stratton. *Three Bhakti Voices: Mirabai, Surdas and Kabir in Their Times and Ours*, 118.

18. Hawley, John Stratton. *Three Bhakti Voices: Mirabai, Surdas and Kabir in Their Times and Ours*, 118.

19. Tamiḻ poetic meters have three constituent elements: the foot (*cīr*), the manner in which the metrical feet are connected (*talai*), and the line (*aṭi*). The fundamental component of a foot (*cīr*) is the *acai* (metrical syllable), which in turn comprises combinations of long syllables (*nēr*) and two short syllables (*niṟai*). While a metrical foot can be made of a single syllable, as the smallest metrical unit, a two-syllable *acai* is far more common. Such an *acai* is referred to as *akavacīr*. A *veṉcīr* is the next longest, consisting of four *akavacīr* and ending in a *nēr*. The *kalippa* meter uses both the *akavacīr* and the *veṉcīr*, though it is the latter that is more common. Hart, George, L. *The Poems of Ancient Tamil: Their Milieu and Their Sanskrit Counterpart*, 97–211.

20. This technique of juxtaposing images of violence with those of sexual desire is common in the Tamiḻ Caṅkam poems. The following example from the *Puṟanāṉūru* illustrates the point beautifully:

> The chaste trees, dark-clustered,
> blend with the land
> that knows no dryness;
> the colors on the leaves
> mob the eyes
>
> We've seen those leaves
>   on jeweled women
>   on their mounds of love.
>
> Now the chaste wreath lies slashed
> on the ground, so changed, so mixed
> with blood, the vulture snatches it
> with its beak,
> thinking it raw meat.

We see this too
just because a young man
in love with war
wore it for glory.

Puṟanāṉūṟu 271
Trans. AK Ramanujan, *Poems of Love and War.* p. 186.

21. See Venkatesan, Archana. "A Woman's Kind of Love." *Journal of Hindu Christian Studies,* 16–24, for a detailed discussion on the ways in which three *āḻvār* poets—Āṇṭāḷ, Nammāḻvār and Tirumaṅkai—utilize the voice of the female beloved. For a perspective discussing love and longing in the Northern Indian *bhakti* traditions, see also Hawley, John S. "Krishna and the Gender of Longing." *Three Bhakti Voices,* 165–78, and Hawley John S. "The Damage of Separation: Krishna's Loves and Kali's Child," 369–93.

22. I discuss the one of the most important uses of the *Nācciyār Tirumoḻi* in the context of temple-based ritual in the section below on the ritual lives of Āṇṭāḷ's poems. For further informationon the ritual and aesthetic lives of Āṇṭāḷ's poems, refer to Venkatesan, Archana. "Āṇṭāḷ and Her Magic Mirror," 118–240.

23. Hudson, Dennis. "Āṇṭāḷ Āḻvār: A Developing Hagiography." *The Journal of Vaishnava Studies,* 27–61.

24. For a detailed discussion on the identity of Nappiṉṉai see Hudson, Dennis. "Piṉṉai: Krishna's Cowherd Wife," 238–61.

25. For a detailed discussion on the poetics of *bhakti* and *bhakti* poetry as a genre see Cutler, Norman. *Songs of Experience: The Poetics of Tamil Devotion.* Chapter 1, which focuses on the relationship between poet/persona, god and audience (19–29) and chapter 3 "The Poetics of Bhakti" (57–77) are particularly useful for the guided readings and analysis of several important *bhakti* verses.

26. As Edwin Bryant points out, there is no consensus regarding the date of the *Bhāgavata Purāṇa,* particularly in its final version. Dates for the *Bhāgavata Purāṇa* range from the Gupta period (280–550 C.E.) to the ninth through the thirteenth century C.E., with many Western scholars suggesting that it is the latest of the eighteen *Purāṇas.* Bryant, Edwin. *Krishna: The Beautiful Legend of God (Śrīmad Bhāgavatam Book X).* p. xvi. For a detailed discussion on the dating of the *Bhāgavata Purāṇa,* see Bryant, Edwin. "The Date and Provenance of the Bhāgavata Purāṇa and the Vaikuṇṭha Perumāḷ Temple" and Rukmani, T. S. *A Critical Study of the Bhāgavata Purāṇa.*

I am of the opinion that Āṇṭāḷ drew her influence for the bathing ritual in the *Tiruppāvai* from the Caṅkam corpus and not the *Bhāgavata Purāṇa.* Dennis Hudson is of the opinion that the bathing ritual was incorporated into the South Indian Kṛṣṇa tradition, and that Āṇṭāḷ probably was inspired by its presence in the *Bhāgavata Purāṇa,* which scholars generally accept was composed in South India. See Hudson, Dennis. "Bathing in Krishna: A Study in Vaiṣṇava Hindu Theology," 539–66.

27. For a detailed discussion of the vow and the use of sand images, refer to Reynolds, Holly Baker. "To Keep the Tāli Strong: Women's Rituals in Tamilnad, India," 406–7.

The Śaiva poet Māṇikkavācakar, roughly a contemporary of Āṇṭāḷ, also composed a *pāvai* poem known as *Tiruvempāvai*. His poem, similar to that of Āṇṭāḷ's, consists of twenty verses and describes a similar vow undertaken by a group of unmarried girls. The biggest difference between the *Tiruppāvai* and *Tiruvempāvai* is the focus on the bathing ritual in the latter poem. For a translation and discussion of both *Tiruppāvai* and *Tiruvempāvai*, see Cutler, Norman. *Consider Our Vow: Translation of Tiruppāvai and Tiruvempāvai*.
For a discussion of the *pāvai* vow in these two poems see Reynolds, Holly Baker. "To Keep the Tāli Strong," 401–13.

28. For instance, see Srinivasa Iyengar Swami's commentary *Tiruppāvai Vyākhyāṉam*, 40.

29. I discuss bathing as a metaphor for sexual union in the commentary section that accompanies this translation. Refer in particular to the commentary for *Tiruppāvai* 1 and 20. I will simply note here that commentators do not shy away from the sexual implications of the metaphor of bathing and, in fact, explicate it in detail. For another perspective on the significance of bathing in the *Tiruppāvai*, see Dennis Hudson's "Bathing in Krishna: A Study in Vaiṣṇava Hindu Theology." His analysis is also based on Periyavāccāṉ Piḷḷai's commentary to the *Tiruppāvai*.

30. Caṅkam poems that discuss the *tai nīrāṭal* are *Naṟṟiṇai* 80, 82, *Kalittokai* 59, and *Aiṅkuṟunūṟu* 24. It is employed as a simile in *Naṟṟiṇai* 22 and 84. The most detailed description of the vow is in *Paripāṭal* 11. For a comprehensive discussion of the *tai nīrāṭal* in Caṅkam poems, refer to Reynolds, Holly Baker. "To Keep the Tāli Strong," 392–98. Also see, Cutler, Norman. *Consider Our Vow*, 6–9.

31. Cutler, Norman. *Consider Our Vow*, 8–11.

32. See Notes to *Tiruppāvai* 1 for the significance of Mārkaḻi to Vaiṣṇavas.

33. The *Bhāgavata Purāṇa* version of the *gopīs'* vow leads directly into the episode of Kṛṣṇa stealing their clothes. This episode becomes the focus of *Nācciyār Tirumoḻi* 3, but Āntāl's version makes no mention of a vow.

34. Cutler, Norman. *Consider Our Vow*. p. 11. The commentators do not refer to the *tai nīrāṭal* as a possible source for the vow described in the *Tiruppavai*. They only reference the *Bhāgavata Purāṇa* version and in their comments present Āntāl as imagining herself as one of the *gopīs* described in that text.

35. Ramanujan, A.K., and Norman Cutler. "From Classicism to Bhakti," 232–59.

36. For examples of the use of the *muṟacu* see *Puṟanāṉūṟu* 50. For examples of the use of the *taṇṇumai* see *Puṟanāṉūṟu* 289. For further examples of the use of drums in Caṅkam poetry see Hart, George L. *Poets of the Tamil Anthologies: Ancient Poems of Love and War*, 15–16 and 32–33. For discussion on the *paṟai* in particular, refer to page 32 of *Poets of the Tamil Anthologies*.

37. For example, see Srinivasa Iyengar Swami. *Tiruppāvai Vyākhyanam*, 40.

38. Cutler, Norman. *Consider Our Vow*, 22n3.

39. Dehejia, Vidya. *Āṇṭāḷ and Her Path of Love*, 20.

40. For instance, Nammāḻvār's *Tiruvyāmoḻi*, composed in the tightly woven *antāti* format, lends itself to a reading that maps the poet's unfolding mystical process. On the other hand, the *Nācciyār Tirumoḻi* is bound by a malleable internal coherence.

41. For a reading of the *Nācciyār Tirumoḻi* according to the phases of the moon, see Hudson, Dennis. "Āṇṭāḷ's Desire." *Vaiṣṇavī: Women and the Worship of Krishna*, 171–209.

42. *Nācciyār Tirumoḻi* 4 is presented in the first person singular. The *phala śruti* (4.11) to this section clarifies that it represents a scenario of various *gopī* girls divining their future. The poet says: "Kōtai of Viṣṇucittaṉ/sang a song about the lovely maidens of Āyarpāṭi/of their quarrels and friendships, their intimacy and bickering/ of long waits and a *kūṭal* game."

43. The word *caṅku* (conch) occurs in the following verses of the *Nācciyār Tirumoḻi*: 1.5, 5.1, 5.2, 5.7, 5.9, 6.6, in all of section 7, 8.5, 8.7, 9.9, in all of section 11, and 14.8. In 1.5, which is the first instance of the word's occurrence, it is mentioned as Viṣṇu's attribute (*āḻi caṅku uttamar*: the lord who holds aloft the discus and the conch). In 6.6, the word conch is mentioned in the context of the heroine's dream wedding, but refers to ordinary conches sounded to celebrate the wedding: "The drums throbbed and great white conches resounded."

44. Āṇṭāḷ does not evoke the conch as frequently in the *Tiruppāvai*. When she evokes Viṣṇu's conch, it is always by its proper name, either Valampuri (*Tiruppāvai* 4) or Pāñcajanya (*Tiruppāvai* 26). When she speaks of conches in general, as in *Tiruppāvai* 6 and 14, she uses the generic word, *caṅku*.

45. For a discussion of aesthetics and *anubhava*, see Venkatesan, Archana. "Āṇṭāḷ and Her Magic Mirror, " 139–43.

46. The earliest Śrīvaiṣṇava commentataries were composed for Nammāḻvār's *Tiruvāymoḻi*. Piḷḷāṉ (b. 1161 C.E.) was the first commentator on the *Tiruvāymoḻi*. He was followed by Nañjīyar (1182–1287 C.E.), Nampiḷḷai, and Periyavāccāṉ Piḷḷai (b. 1228). Only the last of this illustrious group composed commentaries on the entire *Nālāyira Divya Prabandham*.

47. Maṇipravāḷa, literally gems and coral, is a specialized Tamiḻ prose form that combines Tamil and Sanskrit vocabulary. For a detailed examination of Śrīvaiṣṇava Maṇipravāḷa literature, see Venkatachari, K. K. A. *The Maṇipravāḷa Literature of the Śrīvaiṣṇava Ācāryas*.

48. See notes to the poems for examples of anecdotes that recount the savoring of the *Tiruppāvai* and *Nācciyār Tirumoḻi* by important figures like Rāmānuja.

49. For a discussion of Śrīvaiṣṇava commentary as an aesthetic experience, see Venkatesan, Archana. "Double the Pleasure: Reading Nammāḻvār's *Tiruviruttam*."

50. For a detailed discussion and the multiple interpretations of the *śayana tirukkōlam*, see Venkatesan, Archana. "Āṇṭāḷ and Her Magic Mirror," 160–67.

51. An example of the *Nācciyār Tirumoḻi* and *alaṅkāra* concerns an apocryphal narrative attached to *Nācciyār Tirumoḻi* 9.6. In that verse, the heroine (Āṇṭāḷ) promises Viṣṇu several pots of sweet rice if he comes to claim her. Rāmānuja, the foremost of the Śrīvaiṣṇava preceptors, is said to have honored Āṇṭāḷ's vow at the temple of Aḻakar, and when he arrived at Āṇṭāḷ's temple in Śrīvilliputtūr, she is believed to have manifested from her icon and run toward him, calling him "Aṇṇā!" (Older Brother). This event is marked in two ways at Śrīvilliputtūr. First, to honor this moment, the festival images of Āṇṭāḷ, her consort Raṅgamaṉṉār, and the divine bird, Garuḍa are permanently placed in the foreground of the Āṇṭāḷ temple *garbha gṛha*. Second, on the

final day of the December Festival of Bathing, the image of Rāmānuja is brought into the *garbha gṛha* and placed beside Āṇṭāḷ to commemorate this moment. For further discussion of this episode and its use in *alaṅkāra* at the Āṇṭāḷ temple, see Venkatesan, Archana. "Āṇṭāḷ and Her Magic Mirror," 118–22.

52. Asimilar festival called the *Eṇṇai Kāppu Utsavam* is also celebrated for the goddess Mīnākṣī of Maturai. The name, which translates as "The Festival of the Anointing of Oil," refers to the elaborate preliminaries observed prior to the actual ritual bath. In Maturai, the text used during the *Eṇṇai Kāppu Utsavam* is Māṇikkavācakar's *Tiruvempāvai*. For a discussion of the two festivals see Venkatesan, Archana. "Āṇṭāḷ and Her Magic Mirror," 217–19. For a discussion of the *Eṇṇai Kāppu Utsavam* at Maturai, see Fuller, C. J. *The Camphor Flame: Popular Hinduism and Society in India*, 187.

53. Venkatesan, Archana. "Āṇṭāḷ and Her Magic Mirror," 219–20.

54. Venkatesan, Archana. "Āṇṭāḷ and Her Magic Mirror," 219–20.

55. For a further information on the *Mārkaḻi Nīrāṭṭa Utsavam*, please see Venkatesan, Archana. "Āṇṭāḷ and Her Magic Mirror," 167–82. For a list of Āṇṭāḷ's *alaṅkāras* during the festival see 427–28.

56. Tirumaṅkaiyāḻvār composed the *Tiruneṭuntāṇṭakam*, a poem of thirty verses. The poem describes the love-sickness of a young girl in love and the lamentations of her mother. The poem's first eleven verses are central to the performance of the Araiyar's *muttukkuṟi*.

57. Venkatesan, Archana. "Āṇṭāḷ and Her Magic Mirror," 220–39.

58. For a detailed discussion of the function of *Araiyar Cēvai* and *muttukkuṟi* in Āṇṭāḷ lore, see Venkatesan, Archana. "Āṇṭāḷ and Her Magic Mirror," 220–39, and Venkatesan, Archana. "Divining the Future of A Goddess: The Araiyar Cēvai as Commentary at the Śrīvilliputtūr Āṇṭāḷ Temple," 19–51.

59. The archives for the bhakti list can be found at http://www.Rāmānuja.org/sv/bhakti/about.html. The database is searchable, and queries on Āṇṭāḷ, Tiruppāvai, and Nācciyār Tirumoḻi yield numerous results. The e-books of Nācciyār Tirumoḻi with commentary can be found at http://www.sundarasimham.org/e-booksS2.htm, and Tiruppāvai at http://www.sundarasimham.org/e-booksS3.htm. A commentary for Vedānta Deśika's Godā Stuti (Praise to Godā) can be found at http://www.sundarasimham.org/e-books.htm.

60. Sriram, V. *Carnatic Summer: Lives of Twenty Great Exponents*, 10–14.

61. In recent years, select verses from the *Nācciyār Tirumoḻi* such as 7.1 (The Song to the Conch) have gained a following both among Karṇāṭak musicians and their audiences.

62. Sarada, S. "Andal Charitram." *Kalakshetra Rukmini Devi: Reminiscences by S. Sarada*, 138.

63. Examples of dance dramas in the diaspora and in India featuring either Āṇṭāḷ's story, her poems, or both, are Malathi Iyengar's (California, USA) *Kodhai's Dream* (2006); Jayanthi Balachandran's (North Carolina, USA); *Andal Kalyanam* (2002); Adyar K. Laksman's (Chennai, India) *Godha Govindam* (2004); and Priyadarshini Govind's (Chennai, India) varnam "Ātkoḷḷa Vēṇṭum Aiyaṉē," (2002).

64. http://www.arangham.com/repertor/nachiyar/nachiyar.html.

65. http://www.jayanthiraman.com/Productions/productions.htm.

66. Hawley, John Stratton. *Three Bhakti Voices: Mirabai, Surdas and Kabir in Their Times and Ours*, 142.

67. Narayanan, Vasudha. "Brimming with Bhakti, Embodiments of Shakti: Devotees, Deities, Performers, Reformers and Other Women of Power in the Hindu Tradition," 45.

68. Narayanan, Vasudha. "Brimming with *Bhakti*, Embodiments of Shakti: Devotees, Deities, Performers, Reformers and Other Women of Power in the Hindu Tradition," 43–44.

69. Dehejia, Vidya. *Āṇṭāḷ and Her Path of Love*, 4.

70. Heifetz, Hank, trans. *Origin of a Young God: Kālidāsa's Kumārasambhava.*

71. Hopkins, Steven Paul. *Singing the Body of God: The Hymns of Vedāntadeśika in Their South Indian Tradition*, 15–21.

72. Hopkins, Steven P. *An Ornament for Jewels: Love Poems for the Lord of Gods by Vedāntadeśika.*

73. P. Sundaram's translation, *The Poems of Andal*, is accurate, but is weighed down by some of the issues discussed in the section on translation.

74. Norman Cutler in *Songs of Experience* explores the shift in rhetorical strategies in Tamil̲ *bhakti* poetry from those in evidence in Caṅkam corpus, placing as much emphasis on the religious content of the poems as their literary form. See chapter 3, 61–70 in particular.

75. Śrīvaiṣṇava commentators such as Periyavāccāṉ Piḷḷai do not point out Caṅkam references—even obvious ones—in their commentaries. For instance, although *Nācciyār Tirumoḻi* 13.8 alludes to the *Cilappatikāram*, no commentators deem this a suitable point of reference. This is not to say that these commentators were unaware of their Caṅkam literary past, or were incapable of aesthetic appreciation. Rather it indicates a fundamental shift in the understanding of what constitutes pleasure and experience (*anubhava*) and how that might be created and replicated in the context of doing theology. In order to accomplish the last of these, the commentators looked to a different corpus of texts, foremost amongst which was the *Vālmiki Rāmāyaṇa*, to heighten the devotional mood. A key idea in Śrīvaiṣṇava commentary was that of *anubhava* experience and a commentary as a text of experience (*anubhava grantha*). See Venkatesan, Archana."Āṇṭāḷ and Her Magic Mirror" for a detailed discussion of Śrīvaiṣṇava commentary as *anubhava*. Also see Hopkins, Steven. *Singing the Body of God*, 136–65.

Tiruppāvai

Thirty Verses for the Drum of Māl

1. Mārkaḻi Tiṅkaḷ

It is the month of Mārkaḻi
the moon is full and the day auspicious.

Come to bathe
you precious girls, richly adorned
    dear to Āyarpāṭi,
        land of abounding prosperity.

The son of Nandagopa
    fierce with his sharp spear,
the youthful lion-cub of Yaśodā
    woman of matchless eyes,

dark-hued and lotus eyed
his face, is both the sun and the moon
that Nārāyaṇa alone can give us the *paṟai*-drum.

Undertake this vow
And the whole world will rejoice.

ēl ōr empāvāy

2. Vaiyattu Vā<u>l</u>vīrkāḷ

All you people of this world,
consider the rituals of our *pāvai*-vow:

We sing the praises of the supreme one
who rests silently
upon the ocean of milk.

We eat no ghee and drink no milk
and daily, we bathe before the dawn.

Kohl does not darken our eyes
and flowers do not adorn our hair.

We do nothing that is wrong
and speak nothing that is evil

Instead, we give freely
and offer alms to those in need

We live joyously,
trusting that all this will liberate us.

ēl ōr empāvāy

3. Ōṅki Ulakaḷanta

Singing the names
    of the perfect one who
    spanned the worlds with his feet
    and measured them

we bathe at the break of dawn
and proclaim:

If we undertake this vow

  our land will be free from evil

  rains will fall three times a month
  and the *kayal* will leap agilely
  amidst the thick, tall, red grain

  the spotted bee will sleep
  nestled in the *kuvaḷai* bloom.

  and when we clasp their heavy udders.
  the great, generous cows
  will fill our pots ceaselessly.

limitless wealth is certain to abound.

ēl ōr empāvāy

4. Āḻi Maḻai Kaṇṇā

Beloved rain, withhold nothing from us.

You scoop up the ocean and rise up replete and full:
your body dark

as the form of the primordial lord:
supreme in the final deluge.

Flash like the flaming discus
Resound like the *valampuri*

held aloft in the hands of Padmanābha,
whose shoulders are broad and beautiful.

Rain without delay
like a shower of arrows
released from his *śārṅga*.

Rain, so we may bathe in the month of Mārkaḻi
so we may live in this world
and rejoice.

ēl ōr empāvāy

5. Māyaṉai Maṉṉu

O enigmatic Māyaṉ
king of eternal Mathurā of the North
lord who plays
by the great unsullied waters of the Yamunā
radiant beacon
of the cowherd clan,
Dāmodara
who brightened his mother's womb—

We are pure and
come to you
with these fresh flowers.

we sing of you.
we think of you.

So let all our past misdeeds
and even those still to come

burn

and turn to ash.

O, sing of him!

ēl ōr empāvāy

6. Puḷḷum Cilampiṉa Kāṇ

Listen: even the birds are chirping.
Can you not hear

the vibrant sound of the white conch
from the temple of Garuḍa's lord?

Wake up, child!

The one
who sucked poison
from the breast
of the demoness

The one
who raised his foot
and destroyed
cunning Śakaṭa

That primordial lord
who rests on his serpent
upon the ocean of milk . . .

Sages and ascetics rise gently
and place *him* in their hearts.

The immense sound

"Hari"

is everywhere

It enters our minds
and we are cooled.

ēl ōr empāvāy

7. Kīcu Kīcu

Can you not hear
the pervasive
screech and chatter
of the *āṉaiccāttaṉ*?

Witless ghost of a girl
do you not hear

the clink of long necklaces
and the jangle of ornaments,
as the women of Āyarpāṭi
whose hair is fragrant,
swish and turn their churning rods
in the curd?

O you who are our leader
how can you just lie there
even as we sing of Keśava
the essence of Nārāyaṇa?

O beautiful maiden
come now—open your door.

ēl ōr empāvāy

8. Kīḻvāṉam Veḷeṉṟu

As the eastern sky brightens into dawn
the buffaloes let lose for a short while
spread out to graze.

All the girls eager to go, have not gone
but wait for you.

We have come to rouse you
spirited girl

Wake up now.

If we sing of him
and we attain the *paṟai*-drum

If we go to him,
    who ripped open the beak of the bird
    who destroyed the terrible wrestlers
    that god of gods

he will listen intently and grant us grace.

ēl ōr empāvāy

9. Tūmaṇi Māṭattu

In your mansion,
studded with immaculate gems
surrounded by glowing lamps
and filled with fragrant frankincense

You continue to sleep upon your soft bed
O cousin
won't you unlock your jeweled door?

Māmi, wake her!

Is your daughter mute or deaf?
Perhaps, she is simply weary
or entranced into a deep sleep.

We are here singing
"O great, elusive Mādhava!"
"Great lord of Vaikuṇṭha!"

Join us and sing his many names.

ēl ōr empāvāy

10. Nōṟṟuccuvarkam

Dear friend, who wishes to enter heaven
through rituals and vows
Why won't you answer us?

Open your door now.

We praise Nārāyaṇa
whose dark curls are fragrant with *tulasī*
the immaculate one
who will give us the *paṟai*-drum

A very long time ago
Kumbhakarṇa defeated

fell

into the gaping jaws of death.

Did he then gift
his great undisturbed sleep to you?

O listless maiden, rarest of gems

Shake off your sleep
and open this door.

ēl ōr empāvāy

11. Kaṟṟukkaṟavai

O golden creeper
    of the faultless cowherds
    who milk their herds of cows
    and battle their enemies until they are destroyed

O you with an *alkul*
    like the hood of a snake
    still in its pit

O wild peacock
    Come and join us.

    Even though
        all your friends and relatives are here
        and await you in your courtyard
        singing the praises of the one,
            dark as a rain cloud

you neither move nor speak.

O precious girl
what is the use of such sleep?

ēl ōr empāvāy

12. Kaṉaittiḷaṅ Kaṟṟerumai

The udders of the buffaloes overflow
merely thinking of their tender calves,
and wet the floors of your home with milk.

Dear sister of such impeccable fortune

The mist falls lightly upon our heads
and still we clasp your front door
as we sing
    of the one whose anger, aroused
    destroyed the king of Southern Laṅka

    that Lord sweet to the heart.

Yet you still do not open your door.

At least wake up now! What great sleep is this?

But know that everyone else is here.

ēl ōr empāvāy

13. Puḷḷiṉvāy Kīṇṭāṉai

He split apart the beak of the bird.
He severed the heads of the cruel *rākṣasa*
and killed him.

We sing of his glory.

All the young girls have entered the *pāvai* fields
Venus has arisen and Jupiter has slept
Listen to the chatter of birds

O you
whose eyes are dark as the bees
nestled into the petals of a bud

Friend,
you have still not entered the cold water
and instead remain sleeping
on this auspicious day.

Push aside such apathy
and join us.

ēl ōr empāvāy

14. Uṅkaḷ Puḻaikkaṭai

In the garden-ponds of your backyard
the *ceṅkaḻunīr* blossoms have opened their purple lips
and the *āmpal* blooms have closed their dark petals.

Ascetics with brilliant white teeth and brick-colored clothes venture out
to blow the conch in their temples.

O beautiful girl,
who promised to rouse us first!

Wake up!

O shameless one!
O sweet-talking girl!

Come now,

sing of the one
who holds aloft the conch and discus
in his broad hands

sing of that lotus-eyed one.

ēl ōr empāvāy

15. Ellē Iḷaṅkiḷiyē

You girl, delicate as a parrot
are you still asleep?

Oh, do not clamor so shrilly
I am coming.

Enough of these false promises
We know all your old excuses.

Ah, you are the clever ones
but can you not just let me be?

Come *now*. What else is there to do?

Has everyone else gathered?

Yes! *everyone* is here—
join us and count them for yourself.

Come sing,

of the mighty one
who killed the rutting elephant
the one who destroys
the malice of his enemies

the enigmatic Māyaṉ
who is unsurpassed.

ēl ōr empāvāy

16. Nāyakaṉai Niṉṟa

Guardian of the mansions
of our master, Nandagopa

You who guard his gates
where banners and flags fly high

Unlock these jeweled doors.

Just yesterday,

the enigmatic Māyaṉ
dark and lustrous
as a sapphire

promised us
the innocent girls of Āyarpāṭi,

the resounding *paṟai*-drum

so we are here,
pure and unsullied

to awaken him
with our singing.

Do not bar our way at the outset.

Please open these doors.

ēl ōr empāvāy

17. Amparamē Taṇṇīre

Nandagopāla,
    generous master who gifts us
    with clothes, fresh water and rice

Awaken!

Yaśodā,
    radiant light of the cowherds,
    immaculate as a new leaf

Arise!

God of gods,
    you sliced apart the sky
    and spanned the worlds

Do not sleep
but wake up now!

Beloved Baladeva
    whose red feet are adorned
    with splendid gold anklets

We cannot allow your brother and you
to sleep any longer.

ēl ōr empāvāy

18. Untu Mata Kaḻiṟṟaṉ

Daughter-in-law
of Nandagopāla,
fierce as a rutting elephant oozing musk

our mighty chief who never flees from his enemies

Nappiṉṉai
whose hair fills the air with fragrance

Please open this door.

Listen!
The sound of crowing roosters is everywhere

Listen!
The hosts of *kuyil* coo
perched in bowers of *mātavi* creepers

O you with delicate fingers
adept at playing ball—

We are here to sing the fame of your lord.

With your lovely red hands soft as lotus petals
your wrists stacked with beautiful bangles
that clink sweetly

Open this door
and welcome us.

ēl ōr empāvāy

19. Kuttu Viḷakkeriya

The lamps are ablaze.

You laze upon this bed with its stout ivory legs
and five fine qualities
your broad chest draped in garlands of flowers
rests upon the breasts of Nappiṉṉai,
her hair entwined
with heavy blossoms.

Please answer us.

O lovely woman with large eyes
darkened with kohl

How much longer
will you prevent him
from rising?

We know,
you cannot bear to be apart

from your beloved

for a single instant

But this does not befit you:
It is unfair.

ēl ōr empāvāy

20. Muppattu Mūvar

Defender
of the thirty-three million celestials

Protector
who allays their fears

Abandon your sleep.

Impartial, invincible lord!
O immaculate one
terrifying to your enemies

Abandon your sleep.

Gentle Nappiṉṉai
woman with soft breasts shaped like copper pots
lustrous red lips and slender hips
O Śrī

Abandon your sleep.

Give us the fan and the mirror
and command your beloved

to bathe us, this very instant.

ēl ōr empāvāy

21. Ē<u>r</u><u>r</u>a Kalaṅkaḷ

Son of that generous Nandagopa
    whose great cows yield their milk
    without pause
    even as the pots spill over.

Awake!

Supreme unknowable lord
who appeared in this world
as a brilliant flame

Abandon your sleep.

Like your enemies
    who lose their strength,
    seek refuge at your door and surrender at your feet

We have come to sing your praise.

ēl ōr empāvāy

22. Aṅkaṇmā Ñālattu

We are assembled here

like the great kings
of this wide beautiful world

who tamed their pride
to gather beside your bed.

Won't you glance at us?

Open your red eyes just a little:
half-open lotuses
that are like the mouths of *kiṅkiṇi* bells.

If you gaze on us

with the moon and the sun:
your two beautiful eyes

All of our worries, our sorrows
will certainly be destroyed.

ēl ōr empāvāy

23. Māri Maḻai Muḻañcil

A fierce lion asleep
in a mountain cave
for the season of the rains
comes awake:

He opens his fiery eyes
shakes himself
and his fragrant mane flies in all directions.

He stretches slowly
roars
and sets out.

Just so, O lord
　　dark as the *pūvai* blossoms
come out from your palace
and bless us with your presence—

Seated upon your splendid lion-throne
consider our prayers
and bestow your grace upon us.

ēl ōr empāvāy

24. Aṉṟivvulakam

That time long ago you measured these worlds
We praise your feet.

You went there and razed southern Laṅka
We praise your strength.

You kicked Śakaṭa and killed him
We praise your fame.

You threw that calf, broke him like a twig
We praise your anklets.

You lifted the mountain as an umbrella
We praise your virtue.

We praise the triumphant spear held in your hand
that ravages your enemies.

In all these ways we praise your mighty deeds
And we are here now to ask for the *paṟai*-drum

Please, O lord, show us compassion
now.

ēl ōr empāvāy

25. Orutti Makaṉāy Piṟantu

You were born the son of one woman

    and that very night

you became the son of another,
to be nurtured in secret.

O immeasurable lord
    when Kaṁsa fearing you
    plotted evil things

    you foiled his plans
    inflamed him and burnt like a fire in his belly.

We have come to beg you:

If you give us the *paṟai*-drum

We will sing of your wealth matched only by Śrī.
We will sing of your bravery.

Our sorrows will end
and we can rejoice.

ēl ōr empāvāy

26. Mālē Maṇivaṇṇā

O great one, the color of a dark gem

If you ask us what we need
for this ancient Mārkaḻi vow, performed even by our ancestors

Listen, these are it:

conches
like your *pāñcajanya*, white as milk
that makes the world shudder with its deep sound
a large magnificent *paṟai*-drum
chanters singing the *pallāṇṭu*
beautiful lamps, canopies, banners.

Lord who floats upon a banyan leaf

bless us with all this.

ēl ōr empāvāy

27. Kūṭārai Vellum

O splendid Govinda,
    who defeats all your enemies

we sang your praise
and received the *paṟai*-drum.

The world marvels at our rewards.

Now we adorn ourselves
with bangles, bracelets, earrings, ear-studs, anklets
and much more.

Finally we drape ourselves in fine silk
sit down for the rice steeped in milk
smothered in so much butter
that it drips down our elbows.

And in this way we come together
and we are cooled.

ēl ōr empāvāy

28. Kaṟavaikaḷ Piṉ Ceṉṟu

We follow our cows to the forest
eat beside them, roam with them.

And even though we are simple cowherds
with little wisdom

we are blessed
    for you were born
as one of us.

    O faultless Govinda,
    neither you nor we, can ever destroy the bond between us.

We are just artless children
who out of love called you names.

Do not hold that against us

    O lord!

Please give us the *paṟai*-drum.

ēl ōr empāvāy

29. Ciṟṟañciṟukālē

We came at the break of dawn

    to worship you
    to praise your lotus feet
        bright as gold.

Listen to the reason for our prayers:

    You were born among simple folk
    whose livelihood was tending cows

So you cannot refuse our small services.

    Know this Govinda

        We have not come here
        for the *paṟai*-drum

    For all time:
    for this birth and every birth that follows

    We are only yours.
    We serve only you.

Direct our every other desire toward you.

ēl ōr empāvāy

30. Vaṅkakkaṭal

The priest of beautiful Putuvai
who wears a garland of pure, cool lotuses
his Kōtai
sang a garland of thirty songs in Caṅkam Tamiḻ

about cowherd women with faces bright as the moon
who adorned in beautiful jewels
won the *paṟai*-drum,

worshiping

Keśava, that very Mādhava
who churned the ocean
with its many waves

and those who flawlessly recite these verses
will instantly earn the reward
of the grace of our beloved Tirumāl
whose eyes and face are radiant
whose four shoulders are like four dark mountains.

and having received all this
they will be joyful forever.

ēl ōr empāvāy

Commentary and Notes to the *Tiruppāvai*

If one were to evoke classical Tamiḻ poetic paradigms of the interior (*akam*) and exterior (*puṟam*), then the *Tiruppāvai* moves from the external worlds inhabited by the *gopīs*, pausing at the threshold of their homes, but not quite entering there. That voyage into the interior, into the heart as it were, is reserved for Kṛṣṇa's mansion (verses 16–30), where Āṇṭāḷ (in the *gopī* persona, according to various commentators) and her companions make a tantalizing journey into the very interior of Kṛṣṇa's home. But the *Tiruppāvai* seems to assert that the bold entry into the heart of the matter as it were can only be accomplished with companions, even if some of them are less than eager to wake up at the crack of dawn and venture to bathe in the freezing waters of the local pond. The "waking up of the *gopīs*" section of the *Tiruppāvai* in essence is addressed not to just the characters of the poem. Each listener/reader becomes a *gopī* who has slept too late and has forgotten how *easy* it might be to win Kṛṣṇa for herself; or is too absorbed in Kṛṣṇa and has forgotten the importance of fellow devotees, an interpretation that dominates the exegetical discourse around the *Tiruppāvai*, beginning with Periyavāccāṉ Piḷḷai in the thirteenth century. Curiously, despite being anachronistic, later commentarial traditions identify each of the sleeping *gopīs* of this section with a particular *āḻvār* (or alternately, *ācārya*). For example, in verse 7 Pēyāḻvār is imagined as being awakened because the girl is addressed as *pēypeṇṇē* (refer to the note for *Tiruppāvai* 7 for a listing of the *āḻvār* verse concordances in the text).

Although the vow in the *Tiruppāvai* takes place in Mārkaḻi (December–January), the quest for Kṛṣṇa is presented as timeless, and the poem describes the path to Kṛṣṇa as well as becomes the path to Kṛṣṇa. When finally all of the girls have been gathered, the *gopīs* (and all the audience of the poem imagining themselves as *gopīs*) approach Kṛṣṇa in his house to awaken him and his family there. The last section of the poem is a gradual and provocative entry into the god's inner world—one might almost imagine, entering a temple, moving past the door—guardians (*dvārapālas*), and the directional deities (*dikpālas*), until one reaches the sacred womb—where the great god awaits. Here, the *gopīs* pause at the very threshold of Kṛṣṇa's bedroom, peering in, asking to be let in. When they finally do gaze upon Kṛṣṇa, it is to witness a moment of profound intimacy: Kṛṣṇa is with his wife Nappiṉṉai, the woman for whom he subdued the seven bulls. It is *this* intimacy, and it is just such a special place that the *gopī* girls desire, and indeed boldly claim in the penultimate verse of the *Tiruppāvai* (29).

In the general introduction to each o f the three sections of the poem, I discuss Āṇṭāḷ's use of the categories of *akam* (interior) and *puṟam* (exterior) in the *Tiruppāvai*. In the *Nācciyār Tirumoḻi*, time (for example, dream time, mythic time, poetic time) and space (for example, interior/exterior, mythic, geographic) constantly intersect and collide to create a fluid, non-linear and, in many ways-disorienting narrative. In the introduction, I have unpacked the play of interior and exterior places/time, mythic and dream spaces/time, contrasting their use in the *Tiruppāvai* and *Nācciyār Tirumoḻi*.

The *Tiruppāvai* has a rich and very deep history of Śrīvaiṣṇava commentary, rivaling that of Nammāḻvār's *Tiruvāymoḻi*. The most significant of the *Tiruppāvai* commentaries, composed in the hybrid commentarial prose language Maṇipravāḷa, are Periyavāccāṉ Piḷḷai's *Mūvāyirappaṭi*, the *Ārāyirappaṭi* of Aḻakiya Maṇavāḷa Perumāḷ Nāyaṉār, the *Nālāyirappaṭi* and the *Īrāyirappaṭi*. In addition, Raṅgarāmānuja composed an important Sanskrit commentary to the *Tiruppāvai*. Several contemporary traditional scholars of the two major Śrīvaiṣṇava schools have added to this collection of *Tiruppāvai* commentaries. These include Uttamur Veeraraghavachariar and Annangarachariar, among others. In addition, one can find any number of *Tiruppāvai* explications composed in Tamiḻ and English by lay practitioners who have a lifelong love for this text.

Similar to other *āḻvār* poems, traditional commentaries identify two layers of meaning in the *Tiruppāvai*. The first layer is referred to as *anyāpadeśārtha* (literal meaning), while the second meaning is known as *svāpadeśārtha* (esoteric meaning). According to this framework, to grasp just the *anyāpadeśa* meaning of a poem is to miss the point. In unpacking a poem's esoteric meanings, the commentator skillfully incorporates into his interpretations the qualified non-dualist philosophy (*viśiṣṭādvaita*) of Rāmānuja, especially as it pertains to the role of the teacher or other mediators in guiding one's surrender to god, the nature of god's grace, and what the very act of surrender constitutes.

The recitation of the names of Viṣṇu (*Hari nāmasaṅkīrtana*) is a central theme in the *Tiruppāvai* and is referred to in verses 2–3, 5–8, 11–16, and 25. The commentators also stress the efficacy of this mode of worship and offer a few detailed comments on the idea in *Tiruppāvai* 2. The commentaries to the *Tiruppāvai* are rich in allusions to epic and Purāṇic sources, namely the *Rāmāyaṇa*, the *Bhagavad Gītā*, and the *Bhāgavata Purāṇa*. In addition, the commentators also reference other *āḻvār* poets like Nammāḻvār. Allusions to and quotations from any other Tamiḻ literary sources are quite rare.

These notes are meant to offer a taste of the craft of Śrīvaiṣṇava exegesis. They are not a translation of any single commentary. Rather, they represent a synthesis of the major interpretations associated with the *Tiruppāvai* verses, while still pointing out differences in interpretation. I have relied on the following commentators who wrote in Maṇipravāḷa and Tamiḻ—Periyavāccāṉ Piḷḷai, Uttamur Veeraraghavachariar, Annangarachariar, and Srinivasa Aiyyankar Swami. In English, I have relied on C. Jagannathachariar and Oppiliappan Sri Varadachari Sathakopan. In the notes below, I clearly indicate where I follow the commentators by referring to them individually or as a group. Where there is no such marker, the interpretation is my own.

Note: In the notes below I have used Kṛṣṇa and Viṣṇu-Nārāyaṇa interchangeably. In the *Tiruppāvai*, Āṇṭāḷ does not make a clear distinction between these two forms and in fact frequently equates the two. The commentators follow her lead and use Kṛṣṇa and Viṣṇu-Nārāyaṇa as synonyms.

Tiruppāvai 1–5: A General Introduction

The first five verses of the *Tiruppāvai* are referred to as *pāyiram* (preface) or *mahāpraveśam* (grand entry). In these introductory stanzas, the poem introduces the *pāvai nōṉpu*, the vow the young *gopī* girls of Āyarpāṭi are about to undertake. As such, it lays out the time of the year that this vow is practiced, the goal of this vow, its requirements, and its benefits (see introduction for a discussion of the *pāvai* vow and its literary antecedents in the Tamil̠ Caṅkam literary corpus).

These opening verses call out to the *gopī* girls of Āyarpāṭi to join in the quest for the *paṟai*-drum. While *paṟai* literally means drum, the Śrīvaiṣṇava *ācāryas* interpret it variously. It can refer to *puruṣārtha* (the goals of life), *kaiṅkarya* (loving service), goal, divine grace, favor, and intimacy. Outside of the Śrīvaiṣṇava doctrinal universe, the *paṟai* plays with several registers of meaning including sacred power, sacred time, and of course its Caṅkam association with the king and his all-important drum. I half-translate it as *paṟai*-drum, foregrounding its literal meaning, while allowing its multiple (theological) meanings to resonate.

In each of the five verses that comprise the *pāyiram*, Śrīvaiṣṇava commentators read each of Viṣṇu's names mentioned there in and its attendant quality (*guṇa*) as central. In verse 1, he is referred to as Nārāyaṇaṉ, in verse 2 as Paramaṉ, in verse 3 as Uttamaṉ, in verse 4 as Padmanābhaṉ and finally in verse 5 as Dāmodaraṉ.

Tiruppāvai 1 (Mārkaḻi Tiṅkaḷ)

The first song of the *Tiruppāvai* establishes the locale: it transports the audience to Āyarpāṭi (Sanskrit: Gokula) the mythical world of Kṛṣṇa. Though the transparent poetics of *bhakti* (discussed by Norman Cutler in *Songs of Experience*) allow one to insert Āṇṭāḷ into the poem, specifically as the leader of the retinue of questing girls, it is actually unclear where the poet has positioned herself in the poem. That is, has Āṇṭāḷ (as the final verse seems to indicate) imagined a situation where *gopī* girls undertook such a quest? Or is she imagining herself as one of the questing girls? Or is she describing a vow that she actually undertook? Yet, despite the poem's deep ambiguity, oral narratives, hagiographies, and the ritual culture of Āṇṭāḷ's temple in Śrīvilliputtūr, understand the *Tiruppāvai* to recount and authentically report a real *pāvai* vow undertaken by Āṇṭāḷ in order to win her lord. Still, it would be disingenuous to suggest that commentators beginning with Periyavāccāṉ Piḷḷai are unaware of the poem's rhetorical complexity. Periyavāccāṉ Piḷḷai frames the question of voice and the *Tiruppāvai*'s authenticity in terms of caste, wondering how a Brahmin girl like Āṇṭāḷ (for she was the foster daughter of the Brahmin garland maker, Viṣṇucittaṉ) could practice a vow meant for cowherds. He answers his self-imposed query—no doubt anticipating his medieval interlocutors—saying that Āṇṭāḷ simply imagined herself as a *gopī*, because her love for Kṛṣṇa was so profound. According to Piḷḷai and the commentators that follow, Āṇṭāḷ's imagination was so fertile, and her transformation complete, that she began to smell of milk and curds, like "real" cowherds.

Mārkaḻi, the first word of the *Tiruppāvai*, is of great import for it situates the poem not only temporally in the month that falls between December and January in the Tamiḻ calendar, but also embeds it within its very specific ritual associations. This month, the ninth month of the Tamiḻ calendar, is considered especially favored by Viṣṇu/Kṛṣṇa, as specified in *Bhagavad Gītā* 10.35 ("I am the great ritual chant,/the meter of sacred song, the most sacred month [Mārgaśirṣa] in the year, the spring blooming with flowers.").[1] The reason for the particularity of Mārkaḻi (Tamiḻ form for the Sanskrit month Mārgaśirṣa) is that it too like Viṣṇu is neither too hot, nor too cold. In conjunction with the ritual weight of Mārkaḻi, the poem asserts the auspiciousness of the full moon. The evocation of the moon resonates on multiple levels. The *gopīs* are imagined as having faces bright and beautiful as the full moon. Further, it anticipates the final lines of this opening verse, where Kṛṣṇa's face reconciles duality, being described as both the sun and the moon. As the commentators frequently point out, while Viṣṇu is like fire to enemies, his love for his devotees is cool as moonlight.

The quest of the *Tiruppāvai* is a communal one and the opening verse stresses this idea. It is not sufficient to approach god individually, but one must do so in the company of like-minded beings. Here the like-minded are the crowd of *gopī* girls, who are exhorted to bathe during the auspicious hours of the *brahmamuhūrta*, which occurs approximately two hours prior to sunrise. The word *nīrāṭa* (infinitive, to bathe) is used in this verse to signify both a literal bath and a figurative one. Taking their cue from similar usage Caṅkam *akam* poems, commentators interpret *nīrāṭa* in the poem to mean union, specifically, sexual union, or in theological terms *kṛṣṇānubhavam* (the enjoyment of Kṛṣṇa) or *kṛṣṇasaṁśleṣa* (union with Kṛṣṇa). Alternately, bathing in the cool waters with the chill of the early dawn still in the air can also be understood as damping the fire of separation that burns these questing *gopī* girls. I have translated *nīrāṭa* as bathe to convey both the literal and figurative meanings. The word *nīrāṭa* literally means to play (*āṭa*) in the water (*nīr*).

The opening verse of the *Tiruppāvai* constantly juxtaposes images of fire with those of coolness, realized most fully—as mentioned above—in the description of Kṛṣṇa as one whose face is both the sun and the moon. The verse relishes other kinds of juxtapositions as well, particularly in its description of Kṛṣṇa's foster-parents: Nandagopa and Yaśodā. Nandagopa is described as the "one with a sharp spear," while Yaśodā is the lady with matchless eyes. Commentaries understand the above description to allude to the fierce love that protects Kṛṣṇa in Gokula. Nandagopa, terrifying as any Tamiḻ warrior, holds enemies at bay with his terrible weapon. But for Yaśodā, her eyes, sharp as spears (in Tamiḻ poetry, women's eyes are often compared to spears), are her defense against all adversity that might touch her son. The commentators note that these eyes are matchless because they gaze continually upon the lovely form of Kṛṣṇa.

For the commentators, the penultimate line of this first verse (*nārāyaṇaṉē namakkē paṟai taruvāṉ:* Nārāyaṇan alone can give us the *paṟai*-drum) holds the key to the entire *Tiruppāvai*. I briefly sketch below their reasoning. Even on a literal level, the line above encapsulates the reward for the vow (the *paṟai*-drum) and from whom the girls receive that reward (Nārāyaṇa). Rather than choose any of the thousand names of Viṣṇu, Āṇṭāḷ begins her poem by addressing the supreme lord (*sarveśvara*) as Nārāyaṇa. Nārāyaṇa is both the one who contains all sentient things (*nāra*), as well as the refuge (*ayana*) for all sentient things (*nāra*). Thus, the name itself distills for the Śrīvaiṣṇava commentators one of the key ideas of *viśiṣṭādvaita* philosophy (qualified nondualism). That is, Viṣṇu-Nārāyaṇa is both what is desired (*prāpya*) and the means to that desire (*prāpaka*). That is, he is both the way (*upāya*) and the goal (*upeya*). Finally, the commentators note that Āṇṭāḷ has placed an emphasis on two very significant words in this line—*Nārāyaṇaṉē*: (Nārāyaṇa alone) and *namakkē* (for us alone), suggesting both the supremacy of Viṣṇu-Nārāyaṇa, and the uniqueness of the devotee who has surrendered to him.

Mārkaḻi: The winter month that falls between December 15–January 15.
Āyarpāṭi: Land of the cowherds. The place of Kṛṣṇa's childhood.

Tiruppāvai 2 (Vaiyattu Vāḻvīrkāḷ)

If the opening verse locates the poem temporally and spatially in the month of Mārkaḻi and in the mythical world of Āyarpāṭi, the second verse acts as a veritable guide to the actual performance of the vow. The verse alternates between two lists of ritual obligations that index both what the girls must do and what they must avoid to ensure the successful completion of their quest. They must sing Viṣṇu's praises; they must abstain from ghee or milk. They must bathe daily, but refrain from adorning themselves in any way. They must not gossip or speak ill of anyone and instead ought to give alms to those in need. The verse ends on a positive note, asserting once again the significance of singing the praises of Kṛṣṇa in a community of devotees. In its final lines encouraging charity, the commentators note that Āṇṭāḷ draws a distinction between *aiyam*—understood as generosity to deserving people—and *piccai*, which is specifically *bhikṣa* (alms) given to Brahmins and *sannyāsis* (renunciants).

Any vow requires renunciation, and the *pāvai nōṉpu* is no exception. Periyavāccāṉ Piḷḷai and others points out that a vow such as this one undertaken to achieve union with Kṛṣṇa requires that one renounce (*vairāgya*) worldly objects that intoxicate the senses, in order to obtain the incomparable intoxicant (*paramabhogya*) that is god. Nevertheless, in verse 27 of the *Tiruppāvai* these very relinquished objects—milk, ghee, and adornment—are actively sought and understood as integral to achieving Kṛṣṇa's grace. The *Tiruppāvai* plays with the tension between the desires of this world and those associated with eternal union with Viṣṇu. The quest for Kṛṣṇa *is* the quest for a drum, a symbol that is eventually rejected in the final verses of the *Tiruppāvai* as a suitable reward. It is also a vow undertaken for the prosperity of the land made manifest in plentiful rain, but also expressed as the desire for eternal service to Kṛṣṇa.

In *Tiruppāvai* 2, Viṣṇu is addressed as *paramaṉ* (The Supreme One). If the first verse figured Viṣṇu as the transcendent, inaccessible lord in his heaven, Vaikuṇṭha, this verse places him on the ocean of milk (*pāṟ kaṭal*), where he manifests, according to the commentators, out of his desire to help sentient beings. Vaikuṇṭha is far away, while the ocean of milk is somehow closer. As he reclines on his thousand-headed serpent on the ocean of milk, Viṣṇu practices a profound *yoga nidra* (meditation), contemplating all the ways that he can help those who need him. So, although he is without comparison (*paramaṉ*), he is also accessible and immanent.

Tiruppāvai 3 (Ōṅki Ulakaḷanta)

This third verse develops several central themes laid out in the opening two verses. It focuses primarily on the rewards from the observance of the vow. These blessings are manifest in *laukika* (worldly) things: plentiful rain, unstintingly generous cows, and an abundant harvest. At the center of the observance of the vow is the ritual bath at the break of dawn, and the communal singing of Viṣṇu's glories. These glories however are expressed not through reliving his wondrous deeds, but by remembering Viṣṇu's *names* (*uttamaṉ pēr pāṭi*: singing the names (*pēr*) of Uttamaṉ). Periyavāccāṉ Piḷḷai stresses the point that reciting Viṣṇu's names is utterly egalitarian, available to one and all, regardless of gender, birth, or caste.

The poem begins with an allusion Viṣṇu's *avatāra* as Vāmana, evoked through the use of the adverbial participle *ōṅki* (stretching/spanning). This word is echoed later in the poem in the adjective, *ōṅku* (tall) to describe the copious harvest. Periyavāccāṉ Piḷḷai's commentary explicates that the poet chooses to describe the grain as tall to drive home the *gopīs'* single-minded devotion to Kṛṣṇa in his form as Vāmana; everywhere they look, they witness his great deeds.

In *Tiruppāvai* 3, Viṣṇu is addressed as *uttamaṉ* (lit. excellent one). Periyavāccāṉ Piḷḷai and others following his lead explicate the use of this name in the following ways. First, they contextualize *who* qualifies as an *uttamaṉ*. Following well-established guidelines in Sanskrit treatises for categorizing men according to their behavior and actions, the commentators identify an *uttamaṉ* as one who performs good deeds without expecting a reward. This is unlike an *adamātmaṉ*, who does evil things in return for the good that is done to him; or the *atamaṉ*, who does nothing in return for a service done for him; or the *madhyamaṉ*, who only does what is required of him in response to any aid he is given. The commentators further assert, even the first level of interpretation—the word gloss—that Viṣṇu is not just an *uttamaṉ*, but Purṣusottamaṉ (Supreme/most excellent among men).

kayal: A carp fish, *Cyprinus fimbriatus*.
kuvaḷai: Indian purple water lily.

Tiruppāvai 4 (Āḻi Maḻai Kaṇṇā)

Tiruppāvai 4 is exemplary of Āṇṭāḷ's dexterity as a poet. It focuses on an extended simile that compares the gathering rain (god of rain) to the body of god. Usually, as in verse 1 of the *Tiruppāvai*, Viṣṇu's body is compared to the dark rain clouds, but here that comparison is reversed. Both logic and poetic theory demand that a known object (*upamāna*) is employed to describe an unknown entity (*upameya*). Therefore god (Viṣṇu/Kṛṣṇa) who is indescribable and unknowable is usually described as dark as the rain clouds. In this verse, Āṇṭāḷ reverses this correspondence, such that Kṛṣṇa is the *upamāna* and the landscape (here, the rain clouds) is the object to be described (*upameya*). *Tiruppāvai* 4 is not the only instance of Āṇṭāḷ's use of this particular rhetorical technique; it occurs frequently in the *Nācciyār Tirumoḻi*, most notably in that poem's tenth decad, where various plants, flowers, and birds are chastised for assuming the form of the heroine's divine lover.

This verse begins with a vocative, where the lord of rain is addressed with the endearment *kaṇṇā*. Because, *kaṇṇā* is also the Tamiḻ version of Kṛṣṇa, commentators interpret the line to indicate that for the *gopīs* god is everywhere. Ultimately, then this is no simple simile; the landscape is not just a suggestion of embodiment, but is itself the embodiment of divinity. Paradoxically, the speaker(s) of the poem also scold the clouds for *trying* to imitate god. The commentators elaborate the above point as follows: while the clouds can turn dark *like* Kṛṣṇa, and the sky can thunder like his conch, and lightning can flash like his *cakra*, the rain can never be full of love like god. To illustrate the point of Viṣṇu's unwavering love when one takes refuge in him, Periyavāccāṉ Piḷḷai draws a lovely comparison. Unlike the plants that look to the sky, dependent on rain for their nourishment, a devotee who has taken refuge in him is like the field through which a river runs, unbidden.

In this verse Viṣṇu is described as *ūḻi mutalvaṉ padmanābhaṉ* (Padmanābha who is the cause/first of all time). The word *mutal* means both cause and first. The commentators gloss the phrase as the lord who is the eternal cause of all things, parsing *ūḻ* (lit. a very long time; the final deluge, final destruction) as the one who exists eternally. As the commentators note, describing Viṣṇu as Padmanābha *and* as the primordial cause of the world is particularly effective. He is the cause of time (*ūḻi*) and stands beyond time as the primordial one. He is the cause (*mutal*) of the final destruction, but as the foremost divinity (*mutal*) is also the one who protects the world in his belly in the final deluge. And then, through Brahmā, who rises from the lotus that emerges from his belly, he creates that world once again.

Commentators argue that the *svāpadeśārtha* (esoteric meaning) equates the rain clouds to the great teachers of the Śrīvaiṣṇava lineage. In this interpretation, the rain/rain clouds are the teacher's (*ācārya*) compassion (*dayā*) and knowledge (*jñāna*), which guide the devotee to Viṣṇu.

valampuri: lit. right turning. The name of Viṣṇu's conch.
śārṅga: the name of Viṣṇu's bow.

Tiruppāvai 5 (Māyaṉai Maṉṉu)

This is the final verse of the *pāyiram* and like *Tiruppāvai* 3 and 4, describes the benefits of undertaking the *pāvai* vow. It also represents a turn away from the worldly rewards that the *gopīs* requested in the previous two verses. Instead, Kṛṣṇa is enjoined to burn away all of the *gopīs'* past misdeeds and in a sense prepare them for eternal service to him.

Much of the commentary for this verse focuses on the word *tūya*, "pure," which Āṇṭāḷ uses to describe the Yamunā, the *gopī* girls, and the flowers that they bring to Kṛṣṇa as an offering. According to the commentators, the Yamunā attains its purity for several reasons. First, she parted of her own volition on the night of Kṛṣṇa's birth, so that Vasudeva might cross her and spirit the child Kṛṣṇa to safety. Second, she had the unique privilege of touching and being touched by Kṛṣṇa, because he bathed and played in her waters during his childhood in Gokula. To further stress the unrivaled purity of the Yamunā, the commentators offer a contrast, with an explication of an episode taken from the *Rāmāyaṇa*. Here, they allude to an episode in *Rāmāyaṇa* where Sītā, abducted by Rāvaṇa, beseeched the river Godāvarī to report it to Rāma. The river, fearing Rāvaṇa's wrath, failed to do so. The Yamunā, on the other hand, was fearless of Kaṁsa's wrath, though she flowed right beside his dominion and aided Vasudeva and saw Kṛṣṇa to safety.

The commentators begin a meditation on "purity" in order to explain how the *gopī* girls claim such a state, especially when they have yet to bathe. Their rhetorical question asserts that the purity referred to here is not ritual purity, but the purity of intent and love for god. To drive home the point, the commentators offer several paradigmatic examples. In the *Rāmāyaṇa*, Rāvaṇa's brother Vibhīṣaṇa's did not bathe before surrendering (*śaraṇāgati*) to Rāma. In the *Mahābhārata*, Kṛṣṇa's great friend and disciple Arjuna did not bathe before he heard the *Bhagavad Gītā* from Kṛṣṇa. And finally Draupadī, the *Mahābhārata*'s heroine, sought Kṛṣṇa's aid when she was menstruating.

The commentators elucidate that Āṇṭāḷ describes the flowers as pure (*tūmalar*) because their final destination is Kṛṣṇa's feet. Just as the Yamunā attained her purity through association with Kṛṣṇa's divine body, and just as the *gopī* girls are purified by their abiding love for Kṛṣṇa, so too are ordinary flowers transformed by the intent of their worshippersand their use in the service of Kṛṣṇa.

In this verse, Kṛṣṇa is addressed as Dāmodara (the one who bears the [scar] left by the rope). The name refers to an episode from the childhood days of Kṛṣṇa, when his foster-mother Yaśodā bound him to a grinding stone with a rope (Dāma) as a punishment. This name, perhaps above all, serves as an eternal reminder of Kṛṣṇa's love for his devotees, and the commentators understand it to encapsulate Viṣṇu's attribute as *āśrita paratantra* (devotion to his devotees).

Māyaṉ: lord of mystery, cunning one. A name of Kṛṣṇa.

Mathurā of the North: the city of Kṛṣṇa's birth. Āṇṭāḷ refers to it as such to distinguish it from the southern city of Maturai.

Tiruppāvai 6–15: General Introduction

The next ten verses comprise the *tuyileṭai* (waking-up) section of the *Tiruppāvai*. In each verse the *gopī* girls rouse a friend and encourage her to join their quest. This rhetorical strategy is successful in asserting the inherent superiority of a communal devotion to god. The community of questing girls embodies the principle of loving god in the company of good, like-minded people. Though each of the awakened girls is eventually absorbed into the ubiquitous group, each of them in their role as the sleeping girl retains a distinctive personality, most clearly in evidence in the fifteenth verse that closes the section.

These ten verses also signal the beginning of the journey into the interior that reaches its fruition between verses 16–20 of the *Tiruppāvai*. The girls call out to their friends poised on the threshold of their homes; they never actually enter their houses, but stand on the porch, the threshold or the doorway. This reticence to engage spatially the inner space of the devotee suggests that it is a privilege reserved for the private, but joint, enjoyment of Kṛṣṇa in his home.

In an anachronistic reading, Vanamamalai Jiyar and other later Śrīvaiṣṇava commentators have argued that each of these ten verses alludes to the awakening of one of the other eleven *āḻvār*. The correspondences are as indicated in table 2:[2]

TABLE 2. Tiruppāvai Verse and Āḻvār Concordance

Verse	Āḻvār
Verse 6	Poykai or Periyāḻvār
Verse 7	Pēy or Kulaśekara
Verse 8	Pūtam or Nammāḻvār
Verse 9	Tirumaḻicai
Verse 10	Kulaśekara or Pēy
Verse 11	Periyāḻvār or Pūātam
Verse 12	Toṇṭaraṭippoṭi or Poykai
Verse 13	Tiruppāṇāḻvār or Toṇṭaraṭippoṭi
Verse 14	Nammāḻvār or Tiruppāṇāḻvār
Verse 15	Tirumaṅkai

There is an additional tradition that associates each of these verses with one of the ten *ācāryas* in the order listed in the Śrīvaiṣṇavas' *ācārya paramparā* (lineage of teachers).

The commentaries for many of these next ten verses are interspersed with lively and imagined dialogue between the *gopī* girls and the sleeping friends, though only one verse (verse 15) in the *Tiruppāvai* takes that form. In the notes below, I have replicated the dialogic format only for the opening phrase of

Tiruppāvai 6 in order to give a sense of the commentaries' form. It must be noted that this kind of imagined dialogue is a regular feature of Śrīvaiṣṇava commentary. Sometimes the dialogue is introduced to provide context for a particular theological exposition. In other cases, it is interjected in response to a silent question asked by an imaginary audience, and occasionally, the commentator provides both the question and the answer.

Tiruppāvai 6 (Puḷḷum Cilampiṉa Kāṇ)

The verse inaugurating the second section of the *Tiruppāvai* aptly begins with the chirping of birds to signal the dawn and the subsequent arrival of the dawn. The urgency of the moment is conveyed through the addition of the particle *puḷḷ(um)*—even the birds are awake. But when the girl who was already supposed to be awake remains slumbering and refuses to acknowledge the signs of dawn, the group of girls roundly scold her thus:

> "Were you not supposed to be awake at the crack of dawn? Why are you still asleep?"
> "O, but it is not dawn as yet."
> "No, it is already morning."
> "So, what is the proof that it has in fact dawned? I can't accept that it is morning simply because you say it is so."
> "Isn't it enough that we have experienced it?"
> "The rest of you just don't sleep. So, how do *know* it is dawn?"

It is to this final question that the girls answer:

> "Listen, even the birds are chirping."

The dialogue continues in much the same vein as the *gopī* girls try various arguments to cajole their reluctant friend out of bed. They allude to Kṛṣṇa suckling at the breast of the demoness Pūtanā, in the hope that fear for the safety of the child will hasten the girl out of sleep. Next, they gesture to the exemplary *muni* and *yogi* (translated as sages and ascetics) who always hold Viṣṇu in their hearts. Here the commentaries take note of the fact that the poet appears to make a distinction between *muni* (sages) and *yogi* (ascetics), a distinction which is similar to the different kinds of charity and philanthropy (*aiyam, piccai*) that Āṇṭāḷ alludes to in *Tiruppāvai* 2. In this case, the commentators explain that the former (*muni*) are those who continuously contemplate Viṣṇu, while the latter are those, like Rāma's brother Lakṣmaṇa, whose austerity (*yogābhyāsa*) is to be in god's eternal service. The implication of the commentators' interpretative move is that the girls who remain asleep are the *muni*, and those who hasten to awaken them in order that they too may join the quest are like the *yogi*. While both kinds of spiritual activity are valued and necessary, the commentators subtly suggest that loving service (*kaiṅkarya*) such as that of the exemplary Lakṣmaṇa is preferable.

Finally, when all these arguments fail to rouse the girl, her friends gathered together outside her door remind her that the "great sound Hari" (*pēraravam*) reverberates through the morning air, beckoning devotees toward contemplation. The phrase *pēraravam* (great sound) is used to describe both the sound of the conch *and* the sound of the name of god. Given the *Tiruppāvai*'s emphasis on the recitation of god's names, it is no surprise that the first verse in the poem's second section evokes this central rite of Viṣṇu worship.

Garuḍa: the divine eagle, Viṣṇu's vehicle.
Śakaṭa: the demon who assumed the form of a cart.

Tiruppāvai 7 (Kīcu Kīcu)

For the commentators, the theological implication of this verse is located in the figure of the still-sleeping girl, who is described in contradictory terms. In the verse's opening lines, her friends call out to her as "*pēy peṇṇē,*" which literally means "ghost (*pēy*) girl." As the verse reaches it conclusion, these same friends address her as *nāyaka peṇ piḷḷāy*, literally, "the girl who is the leader." The word *pēy* has connotations of possession, and according to traditional interpretations, indicates that the girl has been taken over by Kṛṣṇa and has lost all associations with this world. Yet, there is also a keen sense that the girl is still *sleeping* and haunts the realm of dreams. It is for this reason that I have chosen to translate the phrase as "witless girl ghost of a girl" to connote the insensate state of sleeping as well as possession.

According to Periyavāccāṉ Piḷḷai and other commentators, the latter phrase *nāyaka peṇ piḷḷāy* suggests that the girl is well versed in mystical knowledge. The juxtaposition of these two diametrically opposed descriptives implies that it is unbecoming of a girl who has experienced Kṛṣṇa (Viṣṇu-Nārāyaṇa) to continue to sleep. This is a line of reasoning that the retinue of *gopī* girls continually employ in the "waking-up-the-girls" section of the *Tiruppāvai.* We can also interpret the mild insult dealt to the sleeping girl to argue for the primacy of loving god with a community of devotees as opposed to individually. This certainly is in keeping with the general theme of the *Tiruppāvai.*

In the *Tiruppāvai,* Kṛṣṇa is often identified or collapsed with Viṣṇu-Nārāyaṇa; in this verse, Kṛṣṇa is referred to as *mūrti* (embodiment) or *avatāra* of Viṣṇu. The phrase - *nārāyaṇaṉ mūrti* is interpreted in the commentaries to indicate both Viṣṇu's embodiment as Kṛṣṇa and his form as the god who dwells in all sentient things (*antaryāmin*). The feats of Kṛṣṇa alluded to in the above verse are understood to signify specific attributes of god. In his defeat of the demon Keśi, Kṛṣṇa demonstrates unhesitating and maternal protection (*vātsalya*) for his devotees; in his descent as Kṛṣṇa, he demonstrates his limitless compassion, as well as his immaculate nature (*sauśīlya*).

āṉaiccāttaṉ: King crow.

Tiruppāvai 8 (Kīḻvāṉam Veḷeṉṟu)

Each verse in this section of the *Tiruppāvai* can be read as marking the gradual progression of the dawn. In the previous verse, one can imagine that the sky is still dark and the still, crisp early-morning air is broken by the piercing calls of birds. This verse opens with the beginnings of first light. A line of light on the horizon breaks the darkness of the sky; the buffaloes have begun to stir. The buffaloes have been let out to graze for a short time in a contained area (*ciṟu vīṭu*), prior to being allowed to roam freely late in the day, a practice common among cowherds. Periyavāccāṉ Piḷḷai suggests that Āṇṭāḷ's use of this detail is evidence of her complete identification with the cowherding community, contrary to her status as a Brahmin girl. In exegetical moments such as these the ambiguity of the speaker of the poem and the poet comes to the fore. The commentators not only insert Āṇṭāḷ into the poem, but also collapse the plural voices of the *gopī* girls to Āṇṭāḷ's singular voice. In a sense—and paradoxically so—a poem that exalts communal worship becomes reflective of a particular and individual experience.

Tiruppāvai 8 builds on the significance of approaching Kṛṣṇa accompanied by fellow devotees. The girls insist that they wait for their still-sleeping friend, demonstrating the importance of communal devotion toward Viṣṇu. The act of *going* to god is itself understood as consequential. To illustrate this point, the commentators offer a reference to Akrūra, one of Kṛṣṇa's devotees, who was sent as a messenger to Kṛṣṇa by the evil Kaṁsa. The significance of this allusion is that Akrūra's devotion, and the very act of journeying toward Kṛṣṇa, even if on a nefarious mission, is sufficient to elicit Viṣṇu's grace.

The *gopīs'* single-minded goal of going to Kṛṣṇa implies that they are not content to wait passively for their beloved to return to them; rather, they have seized the initiative to make him accept them. Periyavāccāṉ Piḷḷai interprets this act of *going* (*ceṉṟu*) to Kṛṣṇa to emphasize the intimacy of the bond between god and devotee. He says that the girls go to Kṛṣṇa to display their bodies grown emaciated from their separation from him. Up until this point, each girl has experienced Kṛṣṇa internally, individually, and in secret. This is suggested by how the girls have been addressed thus far: *nāyaka peṇ piḷḷāy* (leader among the girls), *kōtukalam uṭaiya pāvāy* (joyous girl), *pēy peṇ* (witless ghost of a girl). Now, the opportunity, under the pretext of the *pāvai* vow, to experience Kṛṣṇa publicly, with no secrecy, and in the company of fellow devotees presents itself and each girl is urged not to squander it.

The sleeping girl (*pāvāy*) in *Tiruppāvai* 8 is described as joyous (*kōtukalam uṭaiya*), which the commentators attribute to her having already experienced and enjoyed Kṛṣṇa. But this in itself is not sufficient in their minds to merit such an extravagant description. They opine that she is joyous because she is dear to Kṛṣṇa. Alternately, the word *pāvāy* is interpreted as encapsulating a rhetorical question: will you also be like the great lord who does not understand the suffering of women?

Tiruppāvai 9 (Tūmaṇi Māṭattu)

In the concluding *phala śruti* verses of the *Tiruppāvai* and *Nācciyār Tirumoḻi*, Āṇṭāḷ constantly stresses the wealth and prosperity of Putuvai (lit. New Town, identified with contemporary Śrīvilliputtūr), a city crowded with resplendent, towering mansions, beautiful women, and perfect priests. Some of the grandeur of Āṇṭāḷ's Putuvai infiltrates her dense description of the slumbering maiden's home. The sleeping girl's mansion is studded with gems that the commentaries assert are naturally pure and without blemish: for them it is a mansion fashioned after Āṇṭāḷ's own home in Śrīvilliputtūr. The brilliant gems so refract the light of the single lamp inside her home that it seems to the girls standing outside that her home is filled with lights. It is in such a spectacular setting that the girl continues to sleep despite her companions' entreaties. Her bed is so luxurious that it coaxes even one who has no wish for rest into a deep slumber. The girls are nevertheless baffled: after all, how can one continue to sleep, when the anguish of separation from Kṛṣṇa makes it seem a bed of fire or of thorns? Simply put, sleep is antithetical to the experience of love, especially when separated from one's beloved. Therefore, how can this girl continue to sleep? The above is the context commentators provide for the question the *gopīs* address to the girl's mother:

> "Is she mute that she cannot answer our summons? Even if she cannot respond, can she not *hear* us calling? Or is she bewitched by the enchanting name of Kṛṣṇa?"

Nācciyār Tirumoḻi 2.1, spoken in the voice of young *gopīs* building sandcastles, expresses and expands on a similar notion. The young girls tormented by a mischievous Kṛṣṇa who insists on kicking down their fragile sandcastles say:

> O Nārāyaṇa! Praised with a thousand names!
> O Nara! Raised as Yaśodā's son!
> We are unable to escape the troubles
> you inflict upon us.

In *Nācciyār Tirumoḻi* 2.4, these same girls insist that they are entranced by Kṛṣṇa despite themselves, and despite his many torments:

> Lord, dark as the rain clouds
> your charming words hold us in a thrall,
> your endearing ways captivate us
> your face bewitches us like an incantation.

In *Tiruppāvai* 9, Kṛṣṇa is addressed by three names: Māmāyaṉ, Mādhavaṉ, and Vaikuṇṭhaṉ, which are interpreted in the commentarial traditions as reflecting Viṣṇu's essential qualities (*guṇas*). Māmāyaṉ (lit. Great Mysterious One) signifies the lord's *saulabhya* (accessibility), for he deigned to descend to earth, mingle with his devotees, and astonish them with his wondrous feats. The name Vaikuṇṭhaṉ (lit. Lord of Vaikuṇṭha) indicates his *paratva* (transcendence), for this supreme lord (*paradevata/jagatsvāmin*) is the one who resides in Vaikuṇṭha surrounded by the *nityasūris* (eternal beings), *bhaktas* (devotees), and *bhāgavatas* (those who worship Viṣṇu). Mādhavaṉ is interpreted to indicate his inseparability from Lakṣmī (Mā), who as Sītā, Rāma's wife in the *Rāmāyaṇa*, was compassionate even to the *rākṣasas* that enforced her imprisonment in Laṅka and tormented her for sport.

Tiruppāvai 9 also ends with a call to the slumbering girl to join the questing group of *gopīs* in singing the many names of Viṣṇu.

Māmi: lit. Aunt.

Tiruppāvai 10 (Nōṟṟvuccuvarkam)

The girl in this verse is addressed in the vocative as the girl who wishes to enter heaven (*cuvarkam/svarga*) through the observance of rituals and vows (*nōṉpu*). While this is a laudable goal, it remains unrealized because she continues to sleep and does not join her friends. In the commentaries, this opening line is also interpreted to imply that it refers to a girl who enjoys the uninterrupted pleasure of Kṛṣṇa (*kṛṣṇānubhavam*) both in her sleep and through the observance of her vows. Certainly, in the latter interpretation one is expected to read the waiting girls' praise as sarcastic, so that the poet and the commentators may once again assert the importance of undertaking the vow jointly.

According to the commentators, the girl is chastised for two reasons. First, she did not wait to observe the vow along with her friends and second, she enjoys Kṛṣṇa privately. In either interpretation, *cuvarkam* (Sanskrit *svarga*) is understood to refer to the enjoyment of Kṛṣṇa (*kṛṣṇānubhavam*) or more generally as the enjoyment of god (*bhagavat-anubhavam*).

How the traditional commentaries unfold for the rest of the verse hinges on the opening line discussed above and attempts to answer the questions: why does the girl continue to sleep? Is she asleep or simply immersed in the experience of Kṛṣṇa? The answer to both questions emerges in the commentators' meditation on the phrase: "Nārāyaṇa/whose dark curls are fragrant with *tulasī* (*nāṟṟattuḻāy muṭi nārāyaṇaṉ*)." The commentators develop a delightfully imaginative scenario to explicate this phrase. First, they point out that the questing *gopīs* describe Viṣṇu as "one whose dark curls are fragrant with *tulasī*" only after arriving at the young girl's door. Why is this, the commentators wonder? They suggest an ingenious answer: that the fragrance of *tulasī* must still hang in the air, causing the girls to speculate that Kṛṣṇa had visited the sleeping girl on the previous night. This then leads the *gopīs* to wonder how long the fragrance of the *tulasī* entwined in Kṛṣṇa's hair actually lasts. Finally, the *gopīs* conclude that since the fragrance of *tulasī* is so heady, Kṛṣṇa must actually still be inside with their friend in her bedroom. And to these imagined arguments from her friends, the sleeping girl of *Tiruppāvai* 10 is (according to the commentators) thought to respond, "How is it possible that he came here, when you have all been standing guard at my door since before daybreak? But, it is true," she continues, "He was here several days ago and he embraced me then. It is the fragrance of the *tulasī* from his visit so long ago that still lingers."

While the aforementioned interpretation suggests that the girl is immersed in Kṛṣṇa, commentators also accommodate the irony and humor inherent in this verse. The latter understanding of the opening line that the girl cannot fulfill her desire to enter heaven (here: the enjoyment of Kṛṣṇa/god) because she continues to sleep is taken up in the exposition of the line where she is compared to Rāvaṇa's brother Kumbhakarṇa who slept six months of the year. In another apocryphal conversation, the *gopīs* say, "While Kumbhakarṇa's sleep was merely sleep (*tuyil*), yours is a great sleep (*peruntuyil*). We have no further need to proceed to Kṛṣṇa's house to awaken him, for your sleep is so deep that it may as well be that we are waking him."

tulasī: Indian basil, *Ocimum sanctum*.

Tiruppāvai 11 (Kaṟṟukkaṟavai)

In this verse, the group of questing *gopīs* describe their sleeping friend in three distinctive ways: she is a golden creeper (*poṟkoṭi*), she is a peacock (*puṉamayil*) and finally she is precious (*celva-p-peṇṭāṭṭi*). For the commentators each of these descriptives indicates her exemplary status both in the community of cowherds and as a devotee (*poṟkoṭi*), her extraordinary beauty (*puṉamayil*), and her immaculate virtue (*celva-p-peṇṭāṭṭi*). If Kṛṣṇa is the light of the cowherd clan (*Tiruppāvai* 1), this girl is the golden creeper of the cowherds (*kōvalar poṟkoṭi*). If this girl is a lovely peacock, then Kṛṣṇa is the one dark as the rain clouds (*mukil vaṇṇaṉ*). She is Kṛṣṇa's equal in every way. And just as men become women so that they may enjoy Kṛṣṇa, her beauty is so profound that even women wish to become men so that they may enjoy it. Nonetheless, her chastity remains unsullied—her *alkul* (mound of Venus) is like a cobra still in its pit, indicating that it is untouched by the grime of the outside world. According to the commentators, just as a peacock lends beauty to a garden, so too would this girl enhance their group if only she would awaken and join the girls on their quest for Kṛṣṇa.

The girl's lineage is also emphasized as the cowherds are fearless, seeking out the enemy or routing them when they seek to conquer them. To illustrate the above point, the commentators turn to the *Rāmāyaṇa*. The commentators compare the girls to Rāma, who when provoked went to Laṅka to vanquish Rāvaṇa. The enemies of the cowherds are anyone who wishes ill on Kṛṣṇa, just as Rāvaṇa who was Rāma's enemy became an enemy to the monkey-prince Aṅgada.

The adverbial participle *ceṉṟu* (having gone/going) is used to describe the cowherds' fearless nature. Just like the *gopīs* in verse 8, who boldly grabbed the initiative to present themselves before Kṛṣṇa, the cowherds too do not docilely wait for someone to make war on them. Instead they destroy those who would seek to harm them and Kṛṣṇa.

The girl is finally addressed as "precious girl" (*celva-p-peṇṭāṭṭi*) to indicate that she possesses the greatest wealth: the enjoyment of Kṛṣṇa. Furthermore, she is also the wealth of the cowherd clan, for she embodies the *gopīs'* desire fully realized.

alkul: the mound of Venus, which is often compared to the hood of a snake in Tamiḻ literature.

Tiruppāvai 12 (Kaṉaittiḷaṅ Kaṟṟerumai)

This verse begins with a striking image—the buffaloes, hearing the hungry cry of its calf, unhesistatingly produce an abundance of milk. The commentators interpret this image in two ways. On the one hand the image conveys causeless maternal love (*vātsalya*). Alternately, the image raises a question on the nature of duty. That is, had the cows been milked in a timely fashion, the floors of the homes would not be drenched with milk, which is for these traditional interpreters an oblique way of asking the question: is it better to do one's duty (milk the cows in a timely manner) or is it better to act in the service of god and forget everything else (*bhagavat kaiṅkarya*)? The exegetical conclusion is of course that loving service to god is a superior form of action.

Such commentarial gymnastics aside, buffaloes, cowherding and milking figure prominently in the *Tiruppāvai*, set as it is, in the imagined world of Kṛṣṇa and his *gopīs*. The cows and buffaloes most often are used to signal abundance, prosperity and generosity, as in this case, where the generosity of the mother buffaloes is mapped on to the sleeping girl's household. The unstinting and spontaneous production of milk is like that of the rain clouds that had scooped up the sea (*Tiruppāvai* 4), and thus nourish the earth.

But unlike these buffaloes that feed their hungry calves, the *gopīs* accuse their friend in her refusal to awaken, of lacking even this compassion; they are after all standing outside her door with the cold morning dew drenching them. At the end of the verse, the *gopīs* exclaim that their friend continues to sleep. Periyavāccāṉ Piḷḷai and commentators following his lead suggest that there are two kinds of sleep: a worldly sleep and meditative sleep (*yoga nidrā*). It is clear to the *gopīs* that their friend's is a dense, worldly sleep. The commentators develop this idea further by wondering how it is that when Viṣṇu can be roused from his profound *yoga nidrā* to run to the aid of his devotees, his devotee can continue her mundane sleep, even when her friends eagerly call her to join their quest.

Viṣṇu is characterized in two important and distinct ways in this verse, both of which illustrate his profound love for his devotees. First he is praised as Rāma, who because of his terrible anger at Rāvaṇa for abducting Sītā destroyed him (*ciṉattiṉāl . . . kōmāṉai ceṟṟa*: lit. because of anger, destroyed the king [Rāvaṇa]). Viṣṇu's (as Rāma) anger is not without proper cause or reason, but is aroused on behalf of the devotee, here Sītā.

As the verse ends, the poet employs a radically different image to invoke a similar theme. Viṣṇu who in his anger destroys those who dare endanger his devotees, is described as sweet to the heart (*maṉattukku iṉiyāṉ*). To the *gopīs* he is akin to the cool breeze, to the moon, to sandalwood. He is the lord who makes women suffer, only to eventually remove that suffering with his presence.

Tiruppāvai 13 (Puḷḷiṉvāy Kīṇṭāṉai)

The verse begins with allusions to two of Viṣṇu's heroic feats undertaken in his *avatāras* as Kṛṣṇa and Rāma. The first is a reference to Kṛṣṇa's defeat of the stork-demon Bakāsura, whom he vanquished by splitting open his beak. The second, builds on the reference to Rāvaṇa in the previous verse, and obliquely evokes him with the phrase *pollā arakkaṉ*: cruel *rākṣasa*. While the aforementioned generic phrase could apply to any number of Viṣṇu's many demon antagonists, according to the commentators, only Rāvaṇa, who separated Sītā from Rāma could be condemned in such stark terms. To further stress this point, they marvel that Rāvaṇa's unforgivable and terrible deed left even one with Āṇṭāḷ's poetic virtuosity bereft of words.

The commentators provide an additional explication for the phrase *pollā arakkaṉ* (cruel *rākṣasa*), beginning by posing the question: "Are not all *rākṣasas* cruel?" Why does Āṇṭāḷ describe *rākṣasa* as cruel? Once again, they turn to the *Rāmāyaṇa* to provide an answer. Not all demons are cruel or evil—Vibhīṣaṇa, Rāvaṇa's brother is the exemplar in this regard; despite being a demon he surrendered to Rāma and was therefore redeemed.

The girls who are already gathered and who have made their way to the banks of the pond are described as *piḷḷai* (young girls/children). This description is interpreted in the commentaries as an attempt to shame the sleeping girl into wakefulness: "even the young girls that you were supposed to wake up, have already begun the vow. Yet, you continue to sleep!"

Āṇṭāḷ uses a beautiful image in this verse to describe the sleep girl, addressing her as *pōtarikkaṇṇiṉāy*, a phrase that can be interpreted multiple ways. It can be read as, "she whose eyes (*kaṇṇi*) are like the deer (*ari*) and the *kuvaḷai* flower" (*pōtu*: lit. bud); "she whose eyes are like the bee (*ari*) nestled in the *kuvuḷai* flower (*pōtu*)"; lastly as, "she whose eyes exceed the beauty of flowers." Regardless of which of these interpretations one favors, in the final sum, for the questing *gopīs* the purpose of her beautiful eyes, are that they might act as a snare to capture Kṛṣṇa.

A phrase *puḷḷum cilampiṉakāṇ* (listen, the birds are chirping) is repeated from *Tiruppāvai* 6, which begins with this very phrase. While this repetition could be read as poetic redundancy, it is worth noting that in this instance, the phrase is creatively juxtaposed with this verse's opening words, *puḷḷiṉvāy kīṇṭāṉai* (he who rent open the mouth of the bird), referring of to Kṛṣṇa's defeat of the stork-demon Bakāsura. Furthermore, the second occurrence of the word *puḷ* (bird) in the verse is at the exact mid-point of the eight-line stanza (line 5) and is paired with the lovely image *pōtarikkaṇṇiṉāy*, discussed above. The repetition is ultimately ingenious, for it becomes loaded and polyvalent, invoking on the one hand terror and god's heroism, and on the other, a sense of urgency and camaraderie for fulfilling the vow. The commentators also assert—to absolve Āṇṭāḷ of the blemish of repetition—that the chirping of birds in *Tiruppāvai* 6 signaled the dawn, but in this case, the chirping suggests that the birds are foraging for food. As such it marks the passage of time, making the point that the sleeping girl has already slept far too long.

This verse is unique in the "Waking Up the Girls" section of the *Tiruppāvai*, because it provides the only reference to the site of the ritual bath. Unlike its Śaiva counterpart, *Tiruvempāvai*, the *Tiruppāvai* does not focus on the central ritual action of the vow: the bath. However, the poem is littered with references to the bath, to bathing and to being bathed. Here, the actual site of the bath is referenced as a means to mark the passage of time—all the girls have already entered the bathing pond (*piḷḷaikaḷ ellārum pāvaikkaḷam pukkār*). It is the only mention of the actual act of bathing *at* the site of the vow in the entire poem.

The thirteenth verse includes an astronomical reference, which has been used to determine that Āṇṭāḷ's lived in the mid-eighth century. The speculation (discussed in detail by Vidya Dehejia in *Āṇṭāḷ and Her Path of Love*) centers on two lines in the *Tiruppāvai*. The fourth line of this verse states, "Venus (*veḷḷi*) has risen and Jupiter has slept (*viyāḻaṉ*)," and the opening line of the *Tiruppāvai*, states that it is the full moon in the month of Mārkaḻi. According to astronomical calculations, the planets Jupiter and Venus align in Mārkaḻi as described in the poem on a number of occasions, three of which provide possible dates for Āṇṭāḷ: 731 C.E., 850 C.E., or even 1205 C.E. (Dehejia 3). For a detailed discussion of dating Āṇṭāḷ, please see the introduction to this book.

rākṣasa: demon.

Tiruppāvai 14 (Uṅkaḷ Pu̱laikkaṭai)

In this verse, fresh images to invoke the dawn are introduced to augment the chirping birds and slowly brightening horizon. The chirping birds of *Tiruppāvai* 6 and 13 are left behind, and instead the *gopīs* announce that the conches resound everywhere, the temple doors have been opened and that sages and ascetics have begun their ritual day. These ascetics (*tavattavar*) are described as wearing brick red garments (*ceṅkal poṭikkūṟai*) and having bright white teeth. Commentators take this specific description *and* the othering of their ritual activity—going to *their* temple (*taṅkaḷ tirukkōyil*)—to imply that these renunciants are devotes of Śiva. Furthermore, the sound of the conch stands for the beginning of all ritual activities of the day. For the commentators, the *gopī* girls evoke these as markers of the passage of ritually efficacious time. The commentators imply that when even Śaiva ascetics have begun their ritual day, it is unbecoming for a girl immersed in Kṛṣṇa to continue to sleep.

For the *gopīs,* the evidence of the encroaching dawn and the sleeping girl's reluctance to awaken is found in her very backyard. Parallel to the planetary references of the previous verse, here two flowers are employed to signal the passage of time. The girls announce that the morning flowers (*ceṅkaḻunīr*) have bloomed, while the night-flowering *āmpal* has closed its petals. But when the *gopīs* announce that the dawn had arrived because the flowers have bloomed, the still-sleepy young girl is imagined to retort that they have mistaken their own eyes for the flowers, and that she cannot be fooled with clever punning. The commentaries' unique interpretation of the motif recalls the metaphor used to describe the sleeping girl in the previous verse (*pōtarikkaṇṇiṇāy*). It would appear that the drowsy protagonist of this stanza appropriates the metaphor in order to steal a few more precious moments of rest!

Like in *Tiruppāvai* 11, the girl in this verse is described in three distinct ways: as *vāy pēcum naṅkāy* (woman who speaks well), *nāṇātāy* (one without shame) and *nāvuṭaiyāy* (eloquent one). The first and the last description of the girl stress her eloquence as well as what is perceived to be her "forked" tongue. On the other hand, her felicity of speech is interpreted as the girl whose words and actions are contrary. This is the girl that claimed that she would be the first to be up, but instead she continues to sleep and has therefore gone back on her word. She continues to sleep shamelessly, heedless of her friends who wait outside calling to her and providing all the necessary evidence of daybreak.

ceṅkaḻunīr: a kind of red/purple water lily, *Nymphaea odorata*
āmpal: Water lily, also known as *alli, Nymphaea lotus.*

Tiruppāvai 15 (Ellē Iḷaṅkiḷiyē)

This verse is singular in the *Tiruppāvai* for its lively and almost colloquial dialogue between the recalcitrant girl and her waiting *gopī* companions. While the previous verses only supply the *gopīs'* insistent questions, here we are privy to the answers as well, which the sleeping girl often cleverly phrases as a question.

On account of her great love Kṛṣṇa, the girl in this verse is distinguished by her desire to see *all* her fellow devotees assembled outside her door. It is for this reason that she asks in the verse, "Has everyone gathered?" The commentators provide the following context for this verse. Hearing the previous song that described Kṛṣṇa as holding aloft the conch and the discus, this girl is believed by her friends to have succumbed to his beauty. In ecstasy, she joined the girls' chorus, and hence she is first addressed, as "Parrot," to attest to the sweetness of her voice. But the girl absorbed in enjoyment of Kṛṣṇa finds her friends' summons a harsh interruption and retorts cuttingly saying, "I am coming, do not call so shrilly." Though her friends appear to recognize her special relationship to Kṛṣṇa, they also serve to remind her that private and individual service to the lord is only secondary to communal devotion. This devotion expresses itself in song and through the recitation of the names of god. The girls extol Kṛṣṇa, who killed the elephant sent by Kaṁsa (Kuyalayāpīḍa) but rescued another (Gajendra). This very Kṛṣṇa who ruthlessly destroys his enemies allows himself to become beholden to his devotees, in this instance, the *gopī* girls.

Tiruppāvai 16–29: General Introduction

The first five verses that comprise the next section of the *Tiruppāvai* are devoted to awakening Kṛṣṇa and his family (16–20), and they artfully play off similar metaphors from the preceding section. Unlike Māṇikkavācakar's *Tiruvempāvai*, the *Tiruppāvai* skips a description of the bath crucial to the successful observance of the Mārkaḻi vow. The girls arrive at Kṛṣṇa's doorstep having already completed the requisite rituals. Commentators read the absence of a description of the bath in the *Tiruppāvai* as an indication that the girls did not complete the ritual bath. They offer the explanation that the *gopīs* in their eagerness to see Kṛṣṇa failed to observe this ritual activity. Though Āṇṭāḷ does not exploit the full potential of bathing as a metaphor for sexual union as Māṇikkavācakar does in his *Tiruvempāvai*, she alludes to it in *Tiruppāvai* 20 when the *gopīs* request the ritual accessories necessary to complete the vow from Kṛṣṇa. The metaphor of union with god as sexual union is embodied in the intimacy shared between Kṛṣṇa and Nappiṉṉai, which is the poem's focus in verses 17–20.

If the preceding set of ten verses stress the importance of communal worship, theologically, these set of verses emphasize the necessity for the intermediary figure (*puruṣakāra*) to facilitate one's union with god. While the gatekeepers Yaśodā, Nandagopāla and Balarāma have a place in guiding the girls' quest, pride of place is reserved for the beloved consort Nappiṉṉai, who, because of her cherished relationship, has a special accessibility to Kṛṣṇa. Such an interpretation is not unique to this set of verses in the *Tiruppāvai*; it is already introduced as a possible exegesis for *Tiruppāvai* 4, where the rain is understood as being the grace of the *ācārya* (teacher). However, it is only in these five verses that the idea receives a sustained exposition in the commentaries to the *Tiruppāvai*.

Not only do these verses emphasize the significance of the intermediary, known as the *puruṣakāra*, they also accentuate the importance of approaching Kṛṣṇa in a group of like-minded devotees, a theme that is not new to the *Tiruppāvai*. In this section, all the distinctive sleeping girls of the preceding ten verses have been happily subsumed into a questing collective "we," who assertively demand entrance into Kṛṣṇa's home. In this last regard the *Tiruppāvai* is fundamentally different from the *Nācciyār Tirumoḻi*, which especially in its latter sections expresses a firmly individual and lonely path to Kṛṣṇa. While intermediaries do make their appearance in the *Nācciyār Tirumoḻi* in the form of birds, clouds, and conches, god is often addressed, scolded, chastised, and scorned directly, and usually in a singular voice (except *Nācciyār Tirumoḻi* 2, 3, 4, and 14).

In these next several verses of the *Tiruppāvai*, Āṇṭāḷ fully exploits the spatial and poetic categories of *akam* and *puṟam*. In the previous verses, the girls stand at the threshold of their friends' homes and attempt to awaken them. Often the commentary will insert Kṛṣṇa's presence *inside* the girl's house, which is understood as the implied reason for her desultory state. In the section that follows, which can be read as "the attainment of the goal/fruit of the vow," the girls, *en masse* seek permission to enter Kṛṣṇa's home. It is a communal move from the external world of vows and public sentiment to the internal world of love, intimacy, and loving service. This idea—the centrality of the genre of love and the interior world (*akapporuḷ*)—is embodied in the inseparability of Kṛṣṇa and his consort Nappiṉṉai. It is finally at the threshold of their bedroom that the girls pause and make a bold request to not just be allowed in, but to actually share in the special intimacy of Kṛṣṇa and Nappiṉṉai.

While verses 16–20 celebrate the inner world, verses 21–29 of the *Tiruppāvai* are entirely devoted to Kṛṣṇa as a king, dispensing justice, ruling with compassion and grace. In these final verses, as Kṛṣṇa awakens from his slumber and emerges from the embrace of Nappiṉṉai, he simultaneously enters the external and public world. In *Tiruppāvai* 23, Āṇṭāḷ makes this outward movement literal. She uses the verb *puṟappāṭu* (to set out) to describe a lion rousing itself from its sleep and compares Kṛṣṇa to the same. Kṛṣṇa here is figured as the Tamiḻ king of the Caṅkam poems, and the *gopīs* are much like the wandering bards of those poems, singing the praises of the king in order to secure their future. While in those early secular Tamiḻ poems, the bards received patronage, and gifts in gold and kind, in the *Tiruppāvai*, the *gopīs'* desired reward for singing the divine king's praise is the symbolic *paṟai*-drum and the immeasurable blessing of eternal service.

Tiruppāvai 16 (Nāyakaṉai Niṉṟa)

This verse is addressed to the gatekeepers of Nandagopāla's mansion, whom the commentators point out are blessed to serve Kṛṣṇa even though they are only guarding his father's house. But for the commentators, the question inevitably arises as to why god who is the *nāyakaṉ* (leader/lord) of the entire universe requires a guard. Furthermore, why does the poet address him as the guard of Nandagopa's mansion rather than that of Kṛṣṇa's? The commentators answer both questions by pointing to god's immense love for his devotees. Viṣṇu who is lonely in his *svātantriya* (quality of independence) in Vaikuṇṭha, enjoys the pleasure of his dependence on his devotees in Āyarpāṭi. Next, though god is omnipotent, he nevertheless indulges his devotees' love for him and allows himself to be protected from Kaṁsa's evil demons. In *Tiruppāvai* 1, the phrase "Nandagopa with his sharp spear" is interpreted similarly to indicate both god's dependence on his devotees and Nanda's fierce guardianship of Kṛṣṇa.

In this verse, the girls identify themselves as the young girls of Āyarpāṭi (*āyarpāṭi ciṟumiyarōm*), which in the commentaries is interpreted as the young *and* innocent girls of Āyarpāṭi. The commentators offer this reading for several reasons. First, they point out that the girls desire to distinguish themselves from the demons that Kaṁsa might send to harm Kṛṣṇa. They thus seek to convince the gatekeeper to allow them entry on the basis of their youth and their obvious sincerity. But, in yet another imagined conversation, the gatekeeper reminds the *gopī* girls of the actions of the demoness Pūtanā, who disguised herself as a beautiful cowherdess in order to infiltrate Kṛṣṇa's home. It is to this query that the girls assure the watchmen that they are too young and naïve (*āyar ciṟumiyarōm*) to assume a disguise or to plot such evil designs against their beloved Kṛṣṇa.

Tiruppāvai 17 (Amparamē Taṇṇīre)

In this verse, three intermediaries—Nandagopāla, Yaśodā, and Baladeva—are awakened and obliquely exhorted to aid the girls in their quest for Kṛṣṇa. In the previous verse, the girls begged the guard "Please open these doors." Presumably, their entreaties were answered and they have won entry into Nandagopa's home. Rather than devote a verse each for Kṛṣṇa's parents and his brother, they are all awakened together. Nandagopa is roused first, then Yaśodā, and finally Baladeva, in the order in which, according to the commentaries, the *gopīs* encounter them.

In the commentaries, each of the three characters of the poem is interpreted as embodying a particular quality that highlights their relationship to Kṛṣṇa. Like in *Tiruppāvai* 1, Nandagopa stands guard over Kṛṣṇa, however not in fear of Kaṁsa's demons but in concern that the *gopī* girls overcome by his son's beauty might abduct him. To illustrate that Nandagopāla's concern is not unwarranted, the commentators offer the example of Kṛṣṇa's grandson Aniruddha, who was abducted by a lovesick maiden. In the verse, Nanda is praised as one who practices a king's most important *dharma* (*aṟam*) of gifting clothes (*amparam*), water (*taṇṇīr*) and food (*cōṟu*) to his dependents. The implication is that such a just and noble leader has no cause to remain asleep and hinder the *gopīs'* quest, and in fact must wake up in order to protect his name.

While Nandagopāla guards Kṛṣṇa, Yaśodā protects the virtue of the cowherds. The girls address her as our lady/our "queen" (*emperumāṭṭi*) to assert her alliance with their cause. As a woman, she can fully appreciate the pain of separation and will undoubtedly aid them on their quest. Moreover, she is the guardian of the cowherd clan's good fortune and steadfastness. Yaśodā is therefore also described as "immaculate as a tender leaf," because—as the commentators are quick to point out—if a plant is sick, it is always the fresh leaf that withers first.

Baladeva, Kṛṣṇa's brother, is awakened next, through the use of the vocative, *celvā*. Much of the commentary centers on unpacking and providing reasons for why Baladeva is addressed as *celva(ṉ)*. He is both wealthy and dear (*celvā*) for it is his great fortune to be of eternal service to Kṛṣṇa. The commentators turn to the *Rāmāyaṇa* for an appropriate parallel that also exemplifies this idea. Lakṣmaṇa, Rāma's younger brother, stood resolutely by his elder brother, even going into exile along with him. Just so, in the Kṛṣṇa *avatāra*, though older, Baladeva nonetheless serves and watches over Kṛṣṇa. Like Lakṣmaṇa, Baladeva is considered an *aṁśa* (emanation) of Ādiśeṣa, Viṣṇu's thousand-headed serpent. The commentators inject a bit of humor, as they envisage the girls teasing

Baladeva by saying that while it is usual for one to sleep on a bed, it is surprising that the bed (Baladeva as Ādiśeṣa) is itself asleep!

Despite the girls' entreaties to these three intermediaries, Kṛṣṇa remains silent and unmoved, which gestures toward the significance of his consort to the successful completion of their vow. The next two verses are devoted to Nappiṉṉai, Kṛṣṇa's wife, who plays a role similar to Viṣṇu's other exemplary consorts—Lakṣmī, Rukmiṇī, and Sītā. According to Śrīvaiṣṇava theology, god's love is like that of a father's and is characterized by "divine justice." On the other hand, the goddess, embodied here in the figure of Nappiṉṉai, is like a mother, and represents divine compassion. It is this fundamental trait along with her inseparable closeness to Viṣṇu that makes her such an effective mediator or *puruṣakāra*.

Tiruppāvai 18 (Untu Mata Kaḻiṟṟaṉ)

The next two verses are addressed to Nappiṉṉai, though the girls in their eagerness to be with Kṛṣṇa forget themselves and call to him directly first. When their direct appeal fails, they recall themselves and entreat her, focusing on the relationship she shares with Kṛṣṇa, symbolized by their sexual union. It is, after all, poised at the threshold of their bedroom that the girls eventually find themselves (*Tiruppāvai* 18 and 19).

The girls call to Nappiṉṉai in the vocative—"O Nappiṉṉai whose hair fills the air with fragrance"—to point out that she cannot pretend to be absent from the room, for her hair's unmistakable fragrance gives her away. This interpretation is similar to the argument that the group of girls makes to one of their sleeping recalcitrant friends, accusing her of having, the previous night, enjoyed Kṛṣṇa for herself (*Tiruppāvai* 10). When this tactic fails, they once again rehearse the arguments for the evidence of daybreak (for example, the birds are singing, the cows are out grazing) and urge Nappiṉṉai to no longer linger in bed.

In order to assert the interdependency of Kṛṣṇa and his consort, the commentators focus on the description of Nappiṉṉai as one who is "adept at playing ball." Nappiṉṉai is imagined to have defeated Kṛṣṇa in a game of ball throwing; in actual point of fact, Kṛṣṇa, out of his abiding love for his beloved, allowed himself to be so defeated. Periyavāccāṉ Piḷḷai elucidates this notion further, suggesting that Kṛṣṇa is meant to be enjoyed both through Nappiṉṉai and by Nappiṉṉai. As the goddess, she is in the enviable position of holding both the contained (*nāram*; here the ball) and the container of all things (*Nārāyaṇa*). Nappiṉṉai is described as wearing beautiful bangles, which indicates her inseparability from Kṛṣṇa. Because she is always with Kṛṣṇa, she never needs to grow frail from lovesickness, causing her bangles to grow loose around her wrists. Though Lakṣmī is the foremost *puruṣakāra* (*pradhāna puruṣakāra*), in the *Tiruppāvai* Nappiṉṉai occupies that place, because in the *kṛṣṇāvatāra*, especially in Āyarpāṭi, *she* is his beloved and inseparable consort.

It is both the motif of Nappiṉṉai with her lotus-like hands and that of her wrists adorned with bangles that become crucial in an important apocryphal story associated with this verse. Rāmānuja, who was known as Tiruppāvai Jīyar, is the chief actor in this famous narrative, which Śrīvaiṣṇavas often retell to impress his particular attachment to the Tamiḻ *āḻvār* poems in general, and the *Tiruppāvai* in particular. It is impossible to prove the validity of this story. In keeping with his lively style, Periyavāccāṉ Piḷḷai's commentaries are filled with many such anecdotes, which he often evokes to illustrate the power of a particular a verse, or a famous Śrīvaiṣṇava personage's intense enjoyment of an *āḻvār* poem. The Rāmānuja story associated with this verse goes something like this.

Rāmānuja was begging for alms while contemplating the verses of the *Tiruppāvai*. As he was reciting the eighteenth verse, he found himself outside the closed door of his teacher, Periya Nampi. When he uttered the line *centāmarai kaiyāl* . . . (with your lovely lotus hands . . .), the door was opened suddenly by Nampi's daughter Attuḻāy. Rāmānuja was so immersed in the beauty of the *Tiruppāvai* verse he imagined Attuḻāy to be Nappiṉṉai and fainted. When Rāmānuja's strange reaction was reported to Periya Nampi, he identified it at once as the verse that began with the words, *untu mata kaliṟṟaṉ* (one fierce as a rutting elephant, referring to Nandagopa).

mātavi: a type of tropical creeper, *Hiptage benghalensis.*

Tiruppāvai 19 (Kuttu Viḷakkeriya)

In the commentaries, another imagined scenario provides the context for this verse, which is generated in response to the question: why does Nappiṉṉai not open the door immediately? If Nappiṉṉai is compassion itself, and the ideal mediator, why do the girls need to plead with her again? And more importantly, why do the girls forget Nappiṉṉai's role as the mediator and approach Kṛṣṇa directly?

Verse 18 ends with the girls pleading with Nappiṉṉai to open the door, and hearing their entreaties she is ready to open the door. However, Kṛṣṇa is hesitant to allow Nappiṉṉai to be the one to grant them their wish and detains her. It is for this reason, the commentators explain, that the *gopīs* turn to Kṛṣṇa once again, abandoning the requisite appeal to the consort. But Nappiṉṉai, unhappy with Kṛṣṇa's interference in her role, asserts her authority and disallows him from opening the door, thereby forcing the girls to once again turn to her for assistance in their quest.

This verse stresses the inseparability of Viṣṇu and his consort, here Nappiṉṉai, and more specifically, the importance of approaching god through the consort, contending that no good can come of the devotees' attempts to circumvent her. The commentators provide several examples to prove this point. It is no surprise, especially where Periyavāccāṉ Piḷḷai is concerned, that the examples are from his beloved *Rāmāyaṇa*. He offers the instance of the demoness Śūrpaṇakhā, who suffered mutilation because she not only desired Rāma, but also sought to harm Sītā. Rāvaṇa abducted Sītā, committing the awful deed of separating Viṣṇu from his beloved. Kākāsura, the terrible "crow-demon," was saved because Rāma and Sītā were together during his ill-conceived attack on Sītā.

The inseparability of Kṛṣṇa and Nappiṉṉai is emphasized in the lovely image of Kṛṣṇa who rests with his head on Nappiṉṉai's breast (*nappiṉṉai koṅkai mēl vaittu kiṭanta malarmārpā*). The image thus beautifully reverses conventional iconography that locates Śrī on Viṣṇu's chest, a rhetorical move that exalts Nappiṉṉai to a place of prominence and as the agent of action. That is, rather than Viṣṇu who contains all things including Śrī, here through this innovative reversal, it is Nappiṉṉai who holds the lord close to her. It suggests his dependency on his consort and provides a reason for her preeminence as a *puruṣakāra*. It must be noted that the same phrase (*nappiṉṉai koṅkai mēl*) is also glossed in the commentaries as "the lord reclines with Nappiṉṉai's breasts pressed to his chest," though it is clear from the explication of the phrase that it is the former meaning that is preferred.

In the verse Nappiṉṉai and Kṛṣṇa recline on a bed described ambiguously as resting on a *pañca cayaṉam*. This phrase can be interpreted in a number of ways. It can refer to a bed possessed of five fine qualities (beauty, coolness, whiteness, softness, and fragrance), a bed made of cotton (*pañcu*), or a bed composed of the five suitable substances (leaves, flowers, cotton, soft wool, and silk). In the commentaries, the bed is a metaphor for the *līlā vibhūti*—the material world of play—and its four legs are the four *puruṣārthas* (the goals of life), which guide one to Viṣṇu. The bed may also be understood as the *artha pañcaka* or the five truths that seek to explain the form of god, the form of the soul, and the means to reach god.

In the previous verse, Nappiṉṉai's inseparability from Kṛṣṇa was marked in the bangles that tightly encircle her wrists. In this verse that same theme is emphasized through the motif of her eyes encircled with kohl. While the questing girls have eschewed any form of personal adornment (*Tiruppāvai* 2), Nappiṉṉai, always with Kṛṣṇa, does not need to undertake any such vow; her beauty remains unfaded because her beloved remains a constant companion. The verse ends with the girls mildly chastising Nappiṉṉai for keeping them from Kṛṣṇa. They assert that this is without merit or precedence and is unbefitting of Nappiṉṉai's *svarūpa*, nature/status, as the intermediary or *puruṣakāra*.

This verse is the focus of an elaborate adornment (*alaṅkāra*) at the Āṇṭāḷ temple in Śrīvilliputtūr. The *alaṅkāra* is called the *Śayana Tirukkōlam* (The Sacred Attitude of Repose), and takes place annually on the seventh night of the Śrīvilliputtūr temple's festival in the month of Āṇṭāḷ (mid-July–mid-August). The *alaṅkāra* is staged so that the bronze festival image of Āṇṭāḷ is seated, while the image of Viṣṇu's reclines with his head resting on her lap—hence the name *Śayana Tirukkōlam*. While there are certainly number of possible interpretations for this *alaṅkāra*, it is clear that it is meant to allude to this particular verse of the *Tiruppāvai*, while more overtly it is said to enact the incident of the crow-demon Kākāsura's attack on Sītā.

Tiruppāvai 20 (Muppattu Mūvar)

The commentaries for this verse begin with an imaginative prologue that provides its "missing" context. The girls end their previous appeal to Nappiṉṉai (*Tiruppāvai* 19) by chastising her reluctance to share Kṛṣṇa with them. The *gopīs* assume that she failed then to act on their behalf because she was hurt by their unfound accusations, namely that her actions do not befit her nature or her stature (*Tiruppāvai* 19). So in this verse the *gopīs* once again begin pleading with Kṛṣṇa in a lengthy panegyric directly addressed to him. The young girls assert their utter dependence on Kṛṣṇa for grace, and suggest that while he was completely willing to save the gods (*devas*), he remains unmoved by the plight of innocent, young girls. However, Kṛṣṇa continues to remain unmoved by their pleas, angry now on Nappiṉṉai's behalf. This requires the girls to redouble their efforts toward winning Nappiṉṉai's favor. According to the commentators, it is for this reason that Nappiṉṉai becomes the focus of the *gopīs'* appeal in the latter half of the verse (lines 5–8).

In this verse Nappiṉṉai is addressed with the epithet *Tiruvē* (Skt. Śrī), which the commentators interpret in a number of ways. It indicates that Nappiṉṉai is possessed of *śrītvam* (the character of Śrī), she is equal to Śrī, or is an embodiment of Śrī. She is also the one who lends auspiciousness (Śrī) to Kṛṣṇa. Nappiṉṉai is also blessed by the auspiciousness that can only come from union (*sambhoga*). The *gopīs* use this final meaning (eternal union with Kṛṣṇa) for the vocative *tiruvē* to argue that Nappiṉṉai cannot remain asleep like Kṛṣṇa who as a man cannot understand the suffering of women.

If Nappiṉṉai is addressed as Śrī in this verse, Kṛṣṇa is extolled using a string of four powerful vocatives (*kaliyē, ceppam uṭaiyāy* , *tiṟal uṭaiyāy*, and *vimalā*). Each of these words are read in the commentaries to indicate the central attributes of Viṣṇu, the very attributes that make him the god of gods (*sarveśvaraṉ*).

The first name is *kaliyē*, which is glossed by commentators as "Kṛṣṇa of great strength," because he anticipates the fears (*kappam*) of the thirty-three crore gods (*muppattu mūvar amarar*), and quells their shivers (*kappam*).

The second phrase is *ceppam uṭaiyāy* (lit. one who is impartial) indicates Viṣṇu's impartiality in rescuing all those who are dependent on him.

The third phrase, *tiṟal uṭaiyāy*, literally means "one who has strength." I have translated it as invincible—to highlight the adjective Āṇṭāḷ uses in the previous lines to denote the awesome power of Viṣṇu as well as to foreshadow what is to come in the following line.

The last phrase, *ceṟṟārkku veppam koṭukkum vimalā* (immaculate one who terrifies enemies), is a delicate counterpoint to the opening line of the verse, which portrays the gods quaking with fear, presumably because of the harassment from some unknown (or known) demon. Here, it is the enemy that is terror-struck. The commentators note that in this instance, it does not refer to Viṣṇu's enemies, but to the enemies of his devotees.

Both Nappiṉṉai and Kṛṣṇa are urged to awaken with the use of the refrain *tuyil eḻāy*, which I have translated as "abandon your sleep." The phrase occurs several times in the *Tiruppāvai*, notably in the preceding verse (in reference to Nappiṉṉai) and in the verse that follows *Tiruppāvai* 21, where it is used in reference to Kṛṣṇa.

At this point, the commentators provide further context to assert that Nappiṉṉai has indeed heeded the girls' request. At the girls' fervent calls, Nappiṉṉai announces that she is awake and ready to hear their entreaties. The girls then request from her two ritual implements—the fan and the mirror—that are necessary for the completion of their vow. In addition to these ritual objects, the girls also petition Nappiṉṉai to beseech Kṛṣṇa, on their behalf, to bathe them.

The act of bathing is an important component of the vow itself, though any description of the ritual act is absent from the poem. In addition, bathing (*nirāṭutal*), from as far back as the Caṅkam poems, is clearly a metaphor for sexual union. Here sexual union becomes a further metaphor for union with god. The verb *nīrāṭal* (bathing) is used several times in the *Tiruppāvai*, most notably in verses 1, 2, and 3, and is interpreted in the commentaries in each of these instances as symbolic of immersion in Kṛṣṇa (*kṛṣṇānubhavam*). But *Tiruppāvai* 20 is the only instance that it occurs in relation to Kṛṣṇa in so direct a manner.

The commentators also put forth other possible interpretations for *nīrāṭal* in this instance. The phrase "command your beloved to bathe us . . ." may be directed at Nappiṉṉai, who is asked to bathe Kṛṣṇa with the sweetness of her words, thereby dispelling his anger towards the girls. It is also read as "bathe us in the grace that *both* of you shower upon us." The request is for a collective union (*emmai*: us), indicating that there is no differentiation once the girls have arrived at Kṛṣṇa's doorstep. While they may have been individual (*pēypeṇṇē, poṟkoṭiyē, nāyaka peṇ piḷḷāy*, etc.) when being awakened, in their quest for Kṛṣṇa, suffering the pangs of separation, manifesting in their emaciated bodies, they are all equal. The girls are at death's door and only union with Kṛṣṇa can save them.

Periyavāccāṉ Piḷḷai understands the metaphor of bathing as clearly signifying sexual union. He compares Nappiṉṉai's role as the intermediary (*uṉ maṇāḷaṉai*: your groom/your beloved) to that of a priest in a wedding ceremony, who accrues the merit for performing the ritual. Though it is Kṛṣṇa who ultimately fulfills the *gopīs'* desires, Nappiṉṉai is credited with their success because she intercedes on their behalf.

Tiruppāvai 21 (Ēṟṟa Kalaṅkaḷ)

Tiruppāvai 21 may be read as inaugurating a fourth section of the *Tiruppāvai*, one devoted solely to Kṛṣṇa's praise. With this shift one can assume (as the commentators do) that Nappiṉṉai heeded the girls' appeal and acceded to their wishes. In fact the commentators go so far as to assert that overcome with benevolence, which is after all Nappiṉṉai's nature, she insists that as a woman she too join the *gopīs* in awakening Kṛṣṇa. This suggests that her role is more than just allowing access to her beloved, but that she is actively invested in securing the girls his favor.

With the above context established in the commentaries, it is understood that the *gopīs* have an unmediated access to Kṛṣṇa. In this section of panegyric verses (*Tiruppāvai* 21–29), the relationship between Kṛṣṇa and the *gopīs* undergoes a fundamental change. Spatially the poem moves outward again and Kṛṣṇa, quintessential Tamiḻ lover of the interior landscape (*akam*), is portrayed in the last series of verses as also the quintessential Tamiḻ king, watching over his domain (*puṟam*), protecting his subjects, and guaranteeing his generosity. The relationship between the *gopīs* and Kṛṣṇa therefore subtly alters; the intimacy signaled by the metaphor of bathing/sexual union is replaced with a more direct demand to be beholden to him in eternal service.

In the verse that inaugurates this section, Kṛṣṇa is characterized as having descended from Vaikuṇṭha to earth in order to help his devotees. But his unhindered sleep is contrary to such a promise. The *gopīs*' initial belligerence at Kṛṣṇa's recalcitrance is replaced with a deep reverence. In this verse, Viṣṇu is described variously as the lord who is unknowable (*ūṟṟam uṭaiyāy*), supreme (*periyāy*), and [brilliant as] a flame (*cuṭar*).

The first phrase (*ūṟṟam uṭaiyāy*) is glossed in the commentaries as the god spoken of in the Vedas and yet is beyond them. He is foundational to the world, yet embodies himself through his *avatāras* for the sake of his devotees.

The second descriptive (*periyāy*) is interpreted to suggest that Viṣṇu is beyond thought, and beyond knowing. He is larger than the *antarīkṣa* (the heavens), and the *devaloka* (the world of the gods), although he nevertheless resides in the heart of all sentient things as an *antaryāmin* (in-dweller).

In elucidating the implications of the epithet *cuṭarē* (lit.O Flame), the commentators turn to Kṛṣṇa's unshakable devotion to his devotees. The first demonstration of this love is that he takes birth in this world as Rāma and Kṛṣṇa. They turn to the *Rāmāyaṇa* to provide another instance of Viṣṇu's unstinting love for his devotee. It deals with Vibhīṣaṇa's surrender to Rāma. When several of Rāma's most trusted allies warned Rāma of Vibhīṣaṇa's *rākṣasa* antecedents, he ignored their advice, arguing that he could not reject even an enemy in the guise of a friend, if he had sought his protection. It is this love (*vātsalya*) that gives Viṣṇu his radiance (*cuṭar*), and he demonstrates his *āśritapakṣapādam* (impartial protection), appearing brilliant as a flame (*tōṟṟum cuṭar*) in this lowly world that even the ordinary people loathe. His protection is not just limited to devotees, but he is equally cognizant of enemies like Rāvaṇa of the *Rāmāyaṇa*, and Duryodhana of the *Mahābhārata* and Śiśupāla of the *Bhāgavata Purāṇa*.

The commentators' evocation of *vātsalya* (maternal love) in the context of this verse is particularly appropriate, because it begins with a description of the great, generous cows of Āyarpāṭi. Kṛṣṇa like the cows that he tends is full of unhesitating, spontaneous, and causeless love (*nirhetuka kṛpā*) for his devotees. It is such a love that prompts his birth into the endless world of *saṁsāra*, for example, as Kṛṣṇa in Āyarpāṭi, among the humble cowherds. This last interpretation is of special significance to the *Tiruppāvai*, because it is precisely his embodiment as a cowherd in Āyarpāṭi that is the focus of the final verses of the poem.

Tiruppāvai 22 (Aṅkaṇmā Ñālattu)

If in the previous verse, Kṛṣṇa vanquished even his enemies who surrendered to his protection, here it is the kings of the world who humble themselves before him. The *gopīs* request that Kṛṣṇa glance at them, and thus destroy all their sorrows. In doing so, the commentaries assert, the *gopīs* declare themselves *ananyārha śeṣa bhūtas*, beings who are exclusively devoted to Kṛṣṇa.

Beginning with this verse, Kṛṣṇa is firmly placed in a *puṟam* context, wherein he enacts his role as king. Although the verse only refers to the kings of the beautiful, vast earth (*aṅkaṇ mā ñālattu aracar*), in the commentaries, the phrase is interpreted as referring to Kṛṣṇa's divine sovereignty over both gods and men. The kings from every corner of the world congregate at Kṛṣṇa's feet, suppressing their pride, because their dominion over a small area might beguile them into delusions of grandeur. As the commentators are quick to point out, the pitfall of kingship is that it exaggerates one's sense of self-importance (*ahaṁkāra*). As a result, kings—despite their lofty social position—are in fact the lowliest creatures. Several, recurrent births are needed to erase the stain of such self-delusion. However, the mere glimpse of Kṛṣṇa absolves these kings, who arrive surrendering their arrogance (*apimāṉa paṅkamāy vantu*) of such a painful punishment.

So, why is it that the *gopīs* compare themselves to these great kings? Commentators point out that they do so to emphasize the supremacy of their quest. While these kings only abandon their pride, the *gopīs* in seeking Kṛṣṇa out boldly and directly have surrendered their - *strītvam* (womanly nature); while these kings seek Kṛṣṇa as a final refuge, the *gopīs* desire to be of eternal service to him. Thus, in all regards, these simple *gopīs* are in fact superior to the great kings of yore, who only surrendered their pride.

The poetic and commentarial center of the verse lies in a striking simile used to describe Kṛṣṇa's half-closed eyes: half-open lotuses shaped liked *kiṅkiṇi* bells (*kiṅkiṇi vāy-c-ceyta tāmarai-p-pū-p-pōlē*). The first implication of the simile is that the *gopīs* simply wish to enjoy the beauty of his eyes, these eyes that brim with *vātsalya*.

In analyzing the comparison, the question arises as to *why* Kṛṣṇa's eyes are half-open/closed, which in turn gives rise to a number of rich interpretive possibilities. First, the commentator suggests that Kṛṣṇa's independence (*svātantriya*) prevents him from opening his eyes at the devotees' pleas. But, he cannot resist the gentle persuasion of Nappiṉṉai who intercedes on their behalf and is finally forced to open his eyes. While the devotees' many transgressions make him close his eyes, his compassion (*kṛpā*) also impels him to open them.

The girls urge him to open his eyes slowly, not all at once, for they cannot bear the full force of his divine gaze. In yet another imagined dialogue generated by the commentator, Kṛṣṇa forestalls the *gopīs'* request saying, "You have already attained your goal and should therefore have no regrets." The girls quickly respond, "Yes, we may have reached you, but we have yet to enjoy the fruit of the experience of attaining you. Give *that* to us." It is in this context, then, that Kṛṣṇa is urged to open his eyes and glance at them.

In *Tiruppāvai* 1, Kṛṣṇa's eyes are described as the sun and the moon, which is interpreted as bringing the heat of the sun to burn the residues of their past actions away (*cāpam*), while the coolness of the moon comforts the girls. The poem ends with the phrase *cāpam iḻantu* (which literally means forfeiting/losing an imprecation or curse (*cāpam*, Skt. *śāpa*). In the commentaries *cāpam* is interpreted as transgressions, and specifically those associated with living through the endless cycles of birth and death (*saṁsāra*). This interpretation is certainly a derivative meaning, because living in *saṁsāra* is a curse, which produces unending sorrow. Taking my cue from the commentaries, where *cāpam* is glossed as *tukkam* (Skt. *duḥkha*, sorrow), I have rendered it as "sorrow" in my translation.

kiṅkiṇi: small bells that adorn anklets or an ornament worn around the waist.

Tiruppāvai 23 (Māri Malai Mulañcil)

Much of this verse is an extended metaphor that compares Kṛṣṇa to a hibernating lion that has just come awake. It begins with an extravagance of alliterative "m" sounds (*māri malai mulañcil*) coupled with alternating hard and soft sounds (*manni-k-kiṭantu uraṅkum*) that convey both the gentleness of the rain as well as the fiery nature of the awakening lion. His full-throated roar shatters the stillness of the surrounding forests, while his fiery gaze is fixed on the horizon. The opening image of the lion is striking and evocative and is then carried over to the end of the verse, where Kṛṣṇa is imagined seated on a lion throne (*ciṅkācanam*). This comparison also recalls the opening metaphor of the *Tiruppāvai*, where Kṛṣṇa is described as Yaśodā's young lion cub (*ilañ ciṅkam*). Here, however, he is full-grown and no longer the mischievous boy playing tricks, but a virile king dispensing justice, compared to a majestic lion (*cīriya ciṅkam*). The word *cīriya* (*cīrmai*) is glossed in the commentaries as bravery and virility, but—in a stretch—also as that which is possessed of *śrī* (auspiciousness).

The literary move from the interior world of love and intimacy (*akam*) to the external realm (*puram*) of justice is marked spatially. The leonine Kṛṣṇa is bid to leave the mountain cave (understood in the commentaries as Nappinnai's breasts—*Tiruppāvai* 19) and seat himself as a king on the lion-throne. The young lion cub of *Tiruppāvai* 1 doted upon by his parents is imaged in this verse as a fully grown and fully capable king.

Therefore the girls feel obliged to awaken their divine king before he is derelict in his obligations to them. After all, during the cold winter months when animals retreat to hibernate, the girls have awakened at the crack of dawn, bathed in the cold waters of their local pond, and have seriously undertaken their quest. To emphasize the stupor-inducing effects of the cold winter months, the commentators turn to the *Rāmāyaṇa*. They cite the example of Rāma's monkey ally Sugrīva, who was devoted to Rāma, but forgot himself and his duties because of the unbearable cold.

The season of the rains also characteristically celebrates the meeting and union of lovers; so too is it with Kṛṣṇa. The *gopīs* believe that captured in the blissful embrace of Nappinnai he forgot his duties to his devotees. Āṇṭāḷ uses the rain (and the season of the rains) extensively in her poetry. In *Tiruppāvai* 4, the rain is compared to Kṛṣṇa (addressed with the endearment Kaṇṇā, which is also the Tamil version of his name). In that verse the rain brings good fortune and abundance to the cowherds and is urged to do so for *its* form is like their beloved lord. Theologically, in that instance, the rain is a metaphor for the grace and intervention of the teacher. In the eighth section of the *Nācciyār Tirumoḻi*, the rain and, more specifically, the rain clouds are summoned as messengers and the opening verse accuses the "lord of Vēṅkaṭam" of having destroyed her womanhood (*peṇ nīrmai*).

> O clouds, spread like blue cloth
> across the vast sky—
> Has Tirumāl my beautiful lord
> of Vēṅkaṭam, where cool streams leap
> come with you?
> My tears gather and spill between my breasts
> like waterfalls.
> He has destroyed my womanhood.
> How does this bring him pride?
>
> *Nācciyār Tirumoḻi* 8.1

pūvai: the flowers of a kind of hardy evergreen tree that produces very dark flowers. *Memecylon edule.*

Tiruppāvai 24 (Aṉṟivvulakam)

This verse can be seen as ushering in what we can argue is the final section of the *Tiruppāvai*. If the previous verse moves spatially from the *akam* to the *puṟam*, this verse is framed temporally. The verse's opening line begins with *aṉṟu* (then) while the last line begins with *iṉṟu* (here/now). *Aṉṟu* indexes Kṛṣṇa's feats undertaken on behalf of his devotees over the course of time. It commences with a reference to his *avatāra* as Trivikrama—rendered here as the one who measured this world (*aṉṟivvulakam aḷantāy*). But the focus is not on his action, but the instrument of the action—Viṣṇu's feet, which are singled out for praise. Rather than take the line as straightforward praise of Viṣṇu's feet, the commentators imagine that the *gopīs* wonder how Viṣṇu could forcibly place his feet on the heads of those who undertook no vows, but refrain from blessing them, who have observed the *pāvai* vow so scrupulously. As if to assert the commentators' point, the last line of the verse begins with the word *iṉṟu* (now/today) to impress two things upon an apparently indifferent god. First, Viṣṇu is once again faced with devotees who expect and need his protection, compassion, and guidance, and second that their appeal is an urgent one and cannot be deferred.

This verse takes the form of a panegyric, or a *maṅgalāṣāsanam*, with every line save the final two, ending with the word *pōṟṟi* (praise, hail). Much like Periyāḻvār's *Tiruppallāṇṭu* that also extols Viṣṇu, here the omnipotent deity is offered both praise and protection. Like the *Tiruppallāṇṭu*, this *Tiruppāvai* verse falls into a category of poem that acts like a protective amulet (*kāppu*) for the deity. The *Tiruppallāṇṭu* is mentioned by name only once—in *Tiruppāvai* 26—but here, the commentators suggest it is imitated in form and content.

The verse may also be read as reflecting the almost familial intimacy shared by the *gopīs* and Kṛṣṇa. But this does not necessarily explain why the girls (or Āṇṭāḷ) feel the need to sing a praise-poem, a protection for an omnipotent, all-powerful god. The commentators present an interesting answer to this question. They suggest that Rāma, as the son of kings, was tutored by priests like Vasiṣṭha and warrior sages like Viśvāmitra, and was therefore capable of protecting himself. Kṛṣṇa, on the other hand, is the son of simple cowherding folk. It is for this reason that he is far more in need of protection and blessings than the heroic Rāma.

There are six aspects of god praised in the verse, which are likened to the *aṟucuvai* (six essential flavors) of food: bitter (*kaippu*), sweet (*iṉippu*), sour (*puḷippu*), salty (*uvarppu*), acidic (*tuvarppu*), and pungent (*kārppu*). The six attributes are Viṣṇu's feet, his valor, his fame, his anklets, his virtue, and finally, his spear.

In the opening verse of the *Tiruppāvai,* Nandagopa and Yaśodā are portrayed as their beloved son's fierce guardians. In *Tiruppāvai* 1, Nanda is described as carrying a spear, and here, Kṛṣṇa wields that very spear, a weapon appropriate to a cowherd. Ironically, the *gopī* girls choose to protect Kṛṣṇa by praising deeds that display his extraordinary valor. Such an approach illustrates the intimacy of their bond with Kṛṣṇa while also highlighting his character—while he is ruthless with his enemies, he protects those dear to him. An apt example of Kṛṣṇa's compassion is alluded to in line 5 of this verse: when Kṛṣṇa lifted the Govardhana mountain as an umbrella to shield the entire population of Āyarpāṭi from a devastating rainstorm.

Tiruppāvai 25 (Orutti Makaṉāy Piṟantu)

The opening lines of this verse summarize the myth of Kṛṣṇa's birth. Both his mothers are nameless but are described as *orutti* (one, singular, or unique). The literal translation of the line is "born as the son of one, you were raised as the son of another." But for the commentators, the subtext is clear: both these women are deeply fortunate. In this interpretation, *orutti* is taken to mean singular or unique. As the commentators point out, one woman (Devakī) had the blessing of giving birth to Kṛṣṇa (*avatāra rasa*) and the other (Yaśodā) had the blessing of witnessing his play (*līlā*). Spirited away into hiding from Mathurā to Āyarpāṭi, one would expect Kṛṣṇa to live freely in his new home on the opposite back of the Yamunā. However, the ever-present threat of his wicked uncle, Kaṁsa looms over the child Kṛṣṇa. Thus, Kṛṣṇa, the one who abides in all things and is omnipresent, is born and reared in hiding. All the while, Kaṁsa dreams up ways to destroy the young child. The *gopīs* are unable to articulate Kaṁsa's many atrocities, and simply say, *tīṅku niṉanaita* (he thought evil things). Characterizing Kaṁsa in this way is similar to *Tiruppāvai* 13, where Rāvaṇa is simply referred to as *pollā arakkaṉ*—his deeds are so terrible that they do not bear mentioning.

In the sixth line of this verse, the girls ask Kṛṣṇa directly for the *paṟai*-drum, citing it as the central purpose of their quest. Winning the drum from Kṛṣṇa will assure them wealth, good fortune, and the end to all their sorrows. Nonetheless, there appears to be some confusion about the purpose of their visit. In *Tiruppāvai* 24 the *gopīs* seem to insist that all they want from Kṛṣṇa is the *paṟai*-drum (*paṟai koḷvāṉ yām vandōm*: lit. we came to secure the *paṟai*-drum). In this verse the girls insist that they not only need the *paṟai*, but also desire to serve him. The commentators resolve this tension by suggesting that both the vow and the *paṟai* are simply pretexts (*vyājya*) that have allowed the *gopīs* access to Kṛṣṇa. It is for this reason that the girls insist that if Kṛṣṇa grants them the *paṟai*, they will sing his praise always, thus enacting their eventual goal—eternal service to him.

In their commentaries on the previous verse, the commentators point out that the *gopīs* were overwhelmed by Kṛṣṇa's presence and offered their praise as a protection (*kāppu*). This verse articulates the precise reasons that Kṛṣṇa requires such protection. In the commentators' readings, this verse is a play of paradox. On the one hand, the girls are here to request the drum from Kṛṣṇa in order to assure themselves of their eternal service to him. Yet, they also need to protect him from the evil designs of Kaṁsa. Thus the god who is everywhere and transcends the material world, is born into it in the dead of night and in secret.

In this verse Kṛṣṇa is described as *neṭumāl*, literally "tall lord," which picks up on the allusion to the Trivikrama *avatāra* (where he spanned the worlds) in the previous verse. It is a particularly apt characterization, for it reiterates the aforementioned tension—the lord who contains the world, and encompasses it, is nevertheless born into it as an apparently defenseless child. *Neṭumāl* is also interpreted to mean the lord who is filled with love (*aṉpu*), but also as the lord who is great (*periyavaṉ*).

Neṭumāl is further qualified with the phrase *kañcaṉ vayiṟṟil nerupeṉṉa niṉṟa neṭumāl(ē)*—literally, the tall lord who stood like a fire in Kaṁsa's belly. The most obvious meaning of this colorful phrase is that Kṛṣṇa was a profound and persistent irritant to Kaṁsa. The commentators explicate the phrase further to say that when Kṛṣṇa vanquished his evil uncle he inflicted upon him the suffering that his devotees had endured on his behalf.

Tiruppāvai 26 (Mālē Maṇivaṇṇā)

The verse begins by addressing Kṛṣṇa with two vocatives: *mālē* (great one) and *maṇivaṇṇā* (one who is the color of a dark gem). The first of these descriptives captures the twin attributes of Viṣṇu: his transcendence (*paratva*) and his accessibility (*saulabhya*). The lord who is great and beyond comprehension is manifest and embodied before these *gopīs*. It is from this latter meaning that the word *māl* is also glossed in the commentaries as the one who is filled with love, because it is his boundless love for his devotees that causes him to be born into this world. In the opening verses of the *Tiruppāvai*, the girls refer to Viṣṇu in ways that emphasize his transcendence. He is Nārāyaṇaṉ (*Tiruppāvai* 1), Paramaṉ (*Tiruppāvai* 2), and Tēvāti Tēvaṉ (*Tiruppāvai* 8). Each of these epithets—Nārāyaṇa, Supreme Lord, Lord of Gods—underscore his *nārāyaṇatvam* (the quality of being Nārāyaṇa) and his *paratva* (transcendence). However, here for the first time in the *Tiruppāvai*, the girls address him simply as Māl. Note that even in the previous verse he is referred to as *neṭumāl* (Tall Lord). This shift indicates a renewed intimacy between the girls and Kṛṣṇa. The *gopīs* come to understand that it is Viṣṇu's *saulabhya* (accessibility) and *vātsalya* (maternal love) that are his defining characteristics rather than his *paratva* (transcendence). To the *gopīs* he is the very embodiment of love.

The second vocative, *maṇivaṇṇā* (lit. the color of a [dark] gem), is meant to evoke his unparalleled beauty. It is a beauty that beguiles even his enemies. Periyavāccāṉ Piḷḷai turns to the *Rāmāyaṇa* to provide the example of the demoness Śūrpaṇakhā, who was unable to resist Rāma even after she was mutilated. Like an immaculate gem (*maṇi*), Viṣṇu's beauty is radiant, multifaceted, and mesmerizing. These are the qualities that draw both devotee and enemy alike toward him.

In *Tiruppāvai* 20 the girls request two ritual items from Nappiṉṉai and Kṛṣṇa that are necessary for the completion of their vow. Here, too, they petition Kṛṣṇa for additional ritual necessities—conches like the *pāñcajanya*, the ubiquitous *paṟai*, lovely banners, lamps, and a group of singers reciting the *pallāṇṭu*. The commentators identify that these five objects (although there are six objects mentioned in the verse) signify the *artha pañcaka*, which according to Śrīvaiṣṇava theology are the five doctrines that one needs to understand in order to achieve *mokṣa*. The five doctrines laid out in a work of the same name by Piḷḷai Lokācārya (1205–1311 C.E.) are as follows: 1. *sva svarūpa* (the nature of one's self), 2. *para svarūpa* (the nature of god), 3. *puruṣārtha svarūpa* (the nature of the goal), 4. *upāya svarūpa* (the nature of the means), and 5. *virodhi svarūpa* (the nature of an antagonist).

One can safely conclude that the *pallāṇṭu* mentioned in this verse is a reference to Viṣṇucittaṉ's *Tiruppallāṇṭu*, where he sings Viṣṇu's praise as a blessing and a protection (*kāppu*). The subtle allusion establishes a relationship, however ambiguous, between Āṇṭāḷ and Viṣṇucittaṉ. It also connects her version of this kind of protective song (*Tiruppāvai* 24) with Viṣṇucittaṉ's, indicating the impact that his short poem had already achieved. Both songs seek to establish an intimate relationship with god, pointing to his transcendence and inaccessibility as well as his immanence, which allows the devotee to reverse the hierarchical relationship.

The *Tiruppāvai* repeatedly highlights the significance of communal worship, whether it is in the rousing of sleeping girls or in gesturing to exemplary groups of worshipers. This central idea is evoked once again and cast as one of the elements crucial to the successful completion of the *gopīs*' vow. The girls further bolster their argument by citing the vow's antiquity as something performed even by their ancestors (*mēlaiyār*). However, it is unclear as to precisely what shape the ancestral ritual observance took. The *pāvai* vow dates back to the Caṅkam period, and as discussed in the introduction, Āṇṭāḷ makes a number of alterations to the form of the vow. Whether the girls here refer to the *pāvai* vow as described in the Caṅkam poems and in the *Bhāgavata Purāṇa*, the *tai nīrāṭal*, or its adaptations to Kṛṣṇa worship is ambiguous.

This particular verse is of special ritual and liturgical significance during the ten-day *Mārkaḻi Nīrāṭṭa Utsavam* (Festival of Ceremonial Bathing in Mārkaḻi) celebrated for Āṇṭāḷ at Śrīvilliputtūr. During this festival, Āṇṭāḷ is imagined to be undertaking the *pāvai* vow and every morning, her image, adorned in various costumes, appears at the gateway of the adjoining Viṣṇu temple. The Araiyar (a member of a special category of ritual performers) assumes Āṇṭāḷ's identity and recites this particular verse, calling out to the god slumbering inside to hear her plea. The verse is chosen only because it mentions Kṛṣṇa as the "lord who floats upon a banyan leaf." In an interpretation specific to Śrīvilliputtūr, it is taken as a direct reference to the deity enshrined as Vaṭapatraśāyi (lit. the lord who reclines on a banyan leaf) at their local Viṣṇu temple, the very temple at which, in local lore, Āṇṭāḷ is said to have worshipped.

pāñcajanya: the name of Visnu's conch.

Tiruppāvai 27 (Kūṭārai Vellum)

This verse is one of the most important in the cycle of thirty that make up the *Tiruppāvai*. It depicts the conclusion of the vow and is parallel to verse 4, where the *gopīs* enumerate the goals of and their gains from observing the vow. As in its earlier counterpart, their successes are measured in terms of material gains—agrarian and material abundance—and symbolic ones—in the acquisition of the *paṟai*-drum. In the second verse of the poem, the girls are unadorned and abstaining from rich foods. Here, to celebrate their success, they are fully adorned and partaking of a rich and delicious meal. The girls, having won Kṛṣṇa, can once again beautify themselves, unlike Sītā who when separated from Rāma shed all her jewels.

In *Tiruppāvai* 26 the *gopīs* enumerated the various ritual objects they required in order to complete their vow successfully. But in the commentaries, Kṛṣṇa is imagined to add to their requests, for he is unable to provide them with anything that equals either Nappiṉṉai (*kōla viḷakku*: beautiful lamp), or the Garuḍa banner, both of which the girls requested in *Tiruppāvai* 26. In interpreting verse 26, commentators offer a metaphorical explanation for each of the ritual objects that the girls request on that occasion. To make this point, the commentators compare the singing of the *pallāṇṭu* to the great *āḻvār* poet Nammāḻvār, who in his *Tiruvāymoḻi*, sang *polika, polika, polika* (May you shine) in praise of Viṣṇu. The phrase *polika* occurs in *Tiruvāymoḻi* 5.2.1, which rejoices in the accessibility of the ocean-hued lord (*kaṭal vaṇṇaṉ*) who has descended on earth in his many forms.

Tiruppāvai 27 ends with the assertion of togetherness. The quest was communal, and fittingly its culmination in the joy of union with Kṛṣṇa is also celebrated with friends. The girls are neither separated from each other, nor from Kṛṣṇa. Their enjoyment of Kṛṣṇa is a joint one, and the fever of longing is cooled once they experience the joy of their union with him. In verse 5, the girls beseech Kṛṣṇa to accept their vow and to turn their transgressions into ash. Now, because of the success of their vow, those violations have indeed turned to ash and the girls are cooled.

The commentaries for this verse return to a familiar theme: that of a god who charms even his enemies. The opening phrase of this verse signals the possibility of such an interpretation. Kṛṣṇa is described as *kūṭārai vellum cīr govindā*—(lit. he splendid Govinda who defeats enemies) because his victories are achieved through his valor and his beauty.

In the commentaries Kṛṣṇa is imagined to tell the *gopīs* that they triumphed over him by declaring that they simply wanted to praise his feet

(*Tiruppāvai* 21, 24). The *gopīs* respond by saying that it is his nature (*svabhāva*) to defeat his enemies who refuse to come together (*kūṭōm*), but is defeated by those who wish to be with him (*kūṭuvōm*). To illustrate this difference, the commentators offer several examples. Here I offer two such citations—one from Periyavāccāṉ Piḷḷai's dear *Rāmāyaṇa* and one from the *Mahābhārata*. While Rāma punished the demoness Śūrpaṇakhā, who attempted to separate him from Sītā, he suffered from love for Sītā, who was forcibly taken from him. In the great *Mahābhārata* war, Kṛṣṇa punished Duryodhana and the Kauravas, but acted as Arjuna's charioteer and guide.

In a move similar to the previous verse, the commentaries place an emphasis on the beguiling beauty of god. Viṣṇu conquers his enemies with his irresistible beauty and wins them over because of his accessibility (*saulabhya*), his graciousness (*sauśīlya*) and his *kalyāṇa guṇa* (auspicious qualities). Sometimes his beauty overcomes all resistance, as in the case of the *gopīs*, who abandon their virtue and their modesty in order to be with Kṛṣṇa.

In the opening line of this verse, Kṛṣṇa is addressed in the vocative as "O Splendid Govinda who defeats your enemies" (*kūṭārai vellum cīr govindā*). According to the commentators, the name Govinda exemplifies Kṛṣṇa's compassion, because he undertakes the tasks of those who are weak (*śakti aṟṟavar*). It is for this reason that he leaves behind his heavenly abode of Vaikuṇṭha to become a humble cowherd. Though he protects all his cows, he is gentler with the young calves that are incapable of even grazing.

One of the most striking images of extravagant abundance in the *Tiruppāvai* occurs in this verse. In describing their feast, Āṇṭāḷ says that the *gopīs* "sit down for the rice steeped in milk/ smothered in so much butter/that it drips down [their] elbows." Periyavāccāṉ Piḷḷai narrates an interesting anecdote with regard to this line. When listening to Parāśara Bhaṭṭar's exposition of *Tiruppāvai* 27, one Tiruvaḻuti Valanādu Dāsa queried if the abundance of butter in the rice would not have overwhelmed one's taste and have been unpleasant to eat. To this, Bhaṭṭar replied that the *gopīs* were so ecstatic at being in the presence of the god, they would not have tasted their food. After all, god is everything for them. In keeping with this, Jagannathachariar notes that the finite verb "we will eat" (*uṇpōm*) does not occur in the verse, although every other action carries its finite verb—that is: we will wear clothes, we will adorn ourselves, and so on. The transition between the last action of eating and the final line of the verse, "And in this way we come together/and we are cooled," is abrupt. In trying to mirror this in my translation, I have not included the verb "to eat" and left the action of partaking of the food unfinished.

Tiruppāvai 28 and Tiruppāvai 29 (Kaṟavaikaḷ Piṉ Ceṉṟu and Ciṟṟañciṟukālē)

In *Tiruppāvai* 26 and 27 the *gopīs* receive ritual items such as conches and banners from Kṛṣṇa to mark the successful completion of their vow. The commentaries in contextualizing *Tiruppāvai* 28 insist that these rewards were won on behalf of the larger community of cowherds. It is only in the last two verses that the girls request something for themselves—and in *Tiruppāvai* 28 it is symbolized by the *paṟai*. In response to their request Kṛṣṇa is believed to ask the girls "what practices and austerities have you undertaken that you merit such a gift." Rather than reply directly to his rather redundant question, the *gopīs* offer a clever retort. They ask Kṛṣṇa what causes him to doubt their actions, when he has already seen evidence of their *aṟivu* (knowledge/wisdom) and their ritual observance. Furthermore, they insist that they only have the ability to perform rituals, but the granting of grace is completely in his hands. In pursuing this line of interpretation, the commentators seek to assert that the essence of *Tiruppāvai* 28 (and indeed, the entire *Tiruppāvai*) is that the true nature of the goal (*prāpya*) is Viṣṇu and not the *paṟai*. Despite being born amongst simple cowherding folk, the girls require no other path or aids (*upāya*) when Kṛṣṇa, by being born among them, himself acts as such.

The last two verses (28 and 29) of the *Tiruppāvai* are its climax, because they culminate in the dramatic rejection of the *paṟai*-drum. In the previous verse, the vow has been completed, the drum won, and union with Kṛṣṇa achieved. The two verses that end the poem cement the last of these ideas, with the girls insisting that the only goal they desired was Kṛṣṇa. If verse 2 and verse 3 of the poem were concerned with the path of the vow and its expected rewards, these final two verses reframe those early claims and insist that the way and the goal are both realized in and through Kṛṣṇa. Ultimately, the vow is inefficient and its material rewards transitory. It is Kṛṣṇa/Viṣṇu who acts as the way and the goal, and the means and the ends of their efforts. The rejection of the *paṟai* in verse 29 is therefore understood as a declaration of this fundamental truth.

These last verses of the *Tiruppāvai* constantly reiterate the simplicity of the cowherding community. Nandagopa guards him fiercely, yet the girls sing a song of protection for him (*Tiruppāvai* 25). Though he is the primordial one, he is born in the dead of night and is raised in secret (*Tiruppāvai* 24). His accessibility and their naïveté have bred an easy familiarity that lulls them into forgetting his omnipotence. Suddenly, like Arjuna in the *Gītā*, the *gopīs* are awakened to the realization of Kṛṣṇa's vastness and his transcendence. They appeal to him to forgive their chiding, their intimacy and informality, understanding that they achieve greatness (like the moon shining with reflected light) because he chose to be raised among them.

In *Tiruppāvai* 28, the *gopīs'* simplicity is expressed through their apparent desire for material comforts. They only seek to eat, to sleep, to survive and therefore need—no, require—god's intervention to orient them to a higher goal, which is Kṛṣṇa. This is of course ironic for the girls have expressed both overtly and subtly that their ultimate goal is union with Kṛṣṇa. For instance, in *Tiruppāvai* 20 the metaphor of bathing is used to evoke their desire for sexual union with Kṛṣṇa, where sexual union is itself a metaphor for a metaphysical joining. Nonetheless, nowhere prior to verse 29 do the *gopīs* explicitly *reject* the desire for the *paṟai*-drum or material comforts, eschewing these in favor of an eternal bond with Kṛṣṇa.

Tiruppāvai 28 is understood as equivalent to *Bhagavad Gītā* 18.66, which is known as the *carama śloka*. In that verse, Kṛṣṇa tells his friend, the warrior Arjuna:

> Relinquishing all sacred duties to me,
> make me your only refuge;
> do not grieve,
> for I shall free you from all evils.[3]

Āṇṭāḷ's version is interpreted as expressing this central tenet of Śrīvaiṣṇavism, with a particular emphasis on the fundamental character of *śaraṇāgati* (surrender), which is likened in Śrīvaiṣṇava theology to a rope that binds the devotee to god. The reality of the nature of *śaraṇāgati* is encapsulated in the phrase *aṟivu oṉṟum illāta āyakkula* (lit.we are cowherds with no wisdom). They are incapable of doing much more than follow their cows around. They are only fortunate that Kṛṣṇa was born among them.

The commentators further unpack the *gopīs*' assertion that they are without knowledge, by saying that the usual paths to *mokṣu*—the paths of desireless action (*karma mārga*), discerning wisdom (*jñāna mārga*), and exclusive devotion (*bhakti mārga*) are beyond their abilities. If they could adhere to these paths, they would never be separated from Kṛṣṇa. However, being as they are simple folk, Kṛṣṇa's advice that they should reach him by their own effort is useless. Kṛṣṇa therefore has no choice but to accede to their requests.

The commentators make the above argument through a striking poetic contrast in the verse. The *gopīs* characterize themselves as *aṟivu oṉṟum illāta āyakkula* (lit.cowherds with no wisdom). In contrast, Kṛṣṇa is praised as *kuṟaivoṉṟum illāta Govindā* (lit.O faultless Govinda). It is of some significance that Kṛṣṇa is addressed in the vocative, almost exclusively as Govinda, not just in this verse, but also in *Tiruppāvai* 27 and 29. In order to fully apprehend the significance that this epithet has in the commentaries for the *Tiruppāvai*, one must examine two rhetorical moments in the verse. The first is the phrase that qualifies the epithet Govinda—he who is without fault. The second is the phrase that occurs later in the poem, when the *gopīs* implore Kṛṣṇa to forgive them for calling him *ciṟu pēr* (lit.small names).

As pointed out above, the epithet Govinda is preceded by the phrase *kuṟaivoṉṟum illāta*, which generates the meaning that he (Govinda) is without fault. However, the phrase may be split in two ways: *kuṟaivu oṉṟum illāta govindā* (Govinda who has no lack) or *kuṟai oṉṟum illāta govindā* (faultless Govinda). These two derivations are interpreted to produce a plethora of meanings. Because Kṛṣṇa fulfills all their wishes, the *gopīs* feel no lack (*kuṟaivu*) with respect to their merit (*puṇya*). As he gets rids of all of their transgressions (*pāpa*) they have no lack (*kuṟaivu*) in this respect either. He is without lack (*kuṟaivu*) as he always aids all struggling sentient beings (*cetana*). When Viṣṇu felt that there was something lacking in Vaikuṇṭha, he took birth among the cowherds to fulfill this lack (*kuṟaivu*). He is without fault (*kuṟai*) and is therefore the *upāya* (way) and one can abandon all other useless *sādhana* (practices). However, as there is such a vast difference between the humble and ignorant cowherds and the immaculate god, Kṛṣṇa wonders if anything actually binds him to complete the task the girls have placed before him. For the commentators, this question is answered partially in *Tiruppāvai* 28, but merits a full exposition in the *Tiruppāvai*'s penultimate verse.

Apartial answer to this question comes with the exegesis of the phrase *ciṟu pēr*, which literally means "small names," implying an easy familiarity between the *gopīs* and Kṛṣṇa, which allowed them to assume all kinds of liberties with him. In the commentaries this idea achieves a full-fledged explication, where *ciṟu pēr* is understood as actually implying its opposite. That is, the girls ask Kṛṣṇa's forgiveness for addressing him as Nārāyaṇa, Padmanābha, and so on. These names are apt only for the lord who resides in Vaikuṇṭha. It is a name that distances him from his devotees and is indicative of his *paratva* (transcendence). For this reason, it is the *ciṟu pēr* or the lesser name. Govinda is the more suitable address, because it gestures to his accessibility (*saulabhya*). But how does one reconcile this reasoning to girls' exclamation *iṟaivā* (lord) at the end of the verse? Commentators suggest that *iṟaivā* denotes Kṛṣṇa's lordship over the *gopīs* as the king of cowherds and does not indicate his over-lordship over the gods.

The phrase *ciṟu pēr* is interpreted in still one more way. Since it is not qualified with a pronoun (*uṉṉai*, you) it is also interpreted to refer to the *gopīs*. In waking each other (*Tiruppāvai* 6–15), they chastised, mocked, and teased one another. In doing so, they called out to one girl as *pēy peṇṇē* (ghost girl), *ūmai* (mute), *ceviṭu* (deaf), and so on, which are characterized, in this context as diminutive speech (*ciṟu pēr*). They beg forgiveness for their harsh speech, but defend it by protesting that they were overtaken by the zeal of their quest.

Tiruppāvai 29 is arguably the most significant verse of the text because it distills later Śrīvaiṣṇava notions of interdependence between god and his devotees as well as the manner in which *śaraṇāgati* (surrender) must be undertaken. Therefore lay Śrīvaiṣṇava devotees are often exhorted to recite just this one verse in order to accrue the benefit of reciting the poem in its entirety.

It is in this verse that the longed for *paṟai*-drum is explicitly rejected—a gift requested or alluded to a total of eight times over the course of the poem (*Tiruppāvai* 1, 8, 10, 16, 24, 25, 26, 28). In the commentaries, the *paṟai*, just like the Mārkaḻi *nōṉpu* itself, is but a pretext (*vyājya*) that allows the *gopīs* access to Kṛṣṇa. Their true goal is to be of eternal loving service (*nitya kaiṅkarya*) to Kṛṣṇa, a goal already obliquely established as their true goal in *Tiruppāvai* 6–15, where various girls were urged to join the quest. Having faithfully observed all the ritual injunctions necessary for the completion of their vow—bathing before the break of dawn, abstaining from particular foods, participating in a community of like-minded devotees—the *gopīs* argue that Kṛṣṇa is their just reward.

In the commentaries, anticipating an unfair argument that ritual alone may be an insufficient cause for Kṛṣṇa's grace, the girls revert to evoking their naïveté and simple-minded nature. While someone may mistake them as *karma yogis*, because they attempt to do their duty (*Tiruppāvai* 28), they do so only because they are motivated by the desire to eat, thereby nullifying the very concept of desireless action. If one were to say that they undertake a kind of pilgrimage every time they enter the forest while following their cows, they respond by saying that these are but ordinary forests, not one like Daṇḍaka, made sacred by Rāma's presence. Ultimately, the girls' approach is to impress upon Kṛṣṇa that they are incapable of deep philosophical thinking and are only capable of acts of loving worship. Kṛṣṇa is clearly one of them, having been raised as a cowherd (*Tiruppāvai* 1 and 25), and therefore is beholden to them and cannot deny them their request. Not only *must* he allow the *gopīs* to perform their acts of loving service, but he must accept them as well. If he refuses them, then his birth among them as a cowherd would be for naught.

In the commentaries, the final lines are interpreted as representing one side of a dialogue, namely that of the *gopīs*. The commentators supply Kṛṣṇa's questions and responses to the questing girls. Thus, Kṛṣṇa is imagined to have replied to the *gopīs*' arguments highlighted above that he would indeed gift them the *paṟai*. It is in response to Kṛṣṇa's deliberate misapprehension of their request that the girls explicitly reject the symbol of their vow—the *paṟai*.

To them the *paṟai* is simply *puruṣārtha kaiṅkarya* (the goal of life as loving service to god). They claim that even if Kṛṣṇa resides in Vaikuṇṭha, they would follow him there intending to fulfill their desire. However they express this desire by saying *iṟṟai-p-paṟai koḷvāṉ govindā*—"Govinda/We have not come here/for the *paṟai*-drum" "." Hearing this Kṛṣṇa teasingly responds that the *gopīs* desire to serve him today, for they appear to reject the *paṟai* explicitly only for today. It is in response to this perceived criticism that the commentators suggest that *gopīs* immediately demand to be attached to Kṛṣṇa for eternity (lit. seven times seven births), implying that they wish to be inseparable from him—like Lakṣmī, Sītā, Rukmiṇī, and Nappiṉṉai.

It is important to note that a virtually identical phrase (seven times seven births) makes it appearance in the sixth section of the *Nācciyār Tirumoḻi*, where Āṇṭāḷ dreams of her wedding to Kṛṣṇa. The verse is as follows:

> Nārāyaṇa is my lord for this birth
> and every birth that follows.
> He clasped my foot in his perfect lustrous hand
> and placed it upon the *ammi*.
>
> Such a vision I dreamed, my friend.
>
> *Nācciyār Tirumoḻi* 6.8

Like so many of the verses between *Tiruppāvai* 6–15, *Tiruppāvai* 29 also begins by invoking the very early morning, a time that precedes actual daybreak. In those earlier verses, the sleeping girls are admonished for sleeping too long and are impelled to join the ritual journey because the rest of their group is already awake and alert. Here, the *gopīs* suggest that for a similar reason Kṛṣṇa should grant them their desires. After all, they are young girls unused to waking up so early and observing so difficult a vow. Moreover, it is really Kṛṣṇa who should have come to them, but their love for him is so great, their need to serve him so profound, they have abandoned their modesty to attend him in this way.

If in the opening verse of the *Tiruppāvai*, Kṛṣṇa's face is characterized as that which dispels suffering, in this penultimate verse, the focus is entirely on his feet. His feet (*poṟṟāmarai aṭi*: lit. golden lotus feet) are as special as gold, and as beautiful and fragrant as the lotus. The commentators point out that the girls emphatically state that even if they were asked to sing the praise of his crown or the head upon which it rests, they would not do so, for as they declare in *Tiruppāvai* 25, there is glory only in his feet. Not only are his feet the place of refuge, i they also describe the community of devotees who serve at his feet (*aṭiyār*). Viṣṇucittaṉ makes precisely this point in his *Tiruppallāṇṭu* 2, saying that he praises Viṣṇu along with his fellow devotees (*aṭiyōmōṭum*). Alluding to the second verse of the *Tiruppallāṇṭu* is particularly apt, because Periyāḻvār contends that there is an unbreakable and inseparable bond between god and his many devotees (*aṭiyōmōṭum niṉōtum piriviṉṟi āyiram pallāṇṭu*: lit. we [*aṭiyōm*] and [*ōṭum*] you [*niṉ*] are inseparable [*piriviṉṟi*] for many thousand years [*āyiram pallāṇṭu*]).

In *Tiruppāvai* 5 the girls suggest the following:

> . . . let all our past misdeeds
> and even those still to come
> burn
> and turn to ash.

At the conclusion of *Tiruppāvai* 29, the *gopīs'* request is altered. They do not ask Kṛṣṇa (Govinda) to destroy their other desires (*maṟṟai nam kāmam*), but rather that these very desires are sublimated (*māṟṟu*: lit. transform/change) into the transcendent desire of serving him.

Tiruppāvai 30 (Vaṅkakkaṭal)

The final verse of the *Tiruppāvai* is the *phala śruti* and summarizes the benefits that one achieves from reciting these thirty verses. A *phala śruti* ends a poem or occurs at the end of a section (usually a decad) of a longer *bhakti* poem. So, for instance, a *phala śruti* concludes almost each of the fourteen sections of the *Nācciyār Tirumoḻi*.

The *phala śruti* is a kind of meta-poem and is often composed in the third person. This shift in poetic voice is of particular interest for the tension it creates between a first-person voice *within* the poem and the third-person point of view in the *phala śruti*. While this does not become an issue in the *Tiruppāvai*, for it concerns a community of devotees rather an individual voice, the conflict becomes marked in the verses that conclude the *Nācciyār Tirumoḻi* decads. This tension is further heightened in the *Nācciyār Tirumoḻi* where the decads concern loss, separation, and unrequited love, while the *phala śruti*'s optimistic tone assures the fulfillment of desires of the poem's readers and listeners.

The *phala śruti* is significant also for the limited biographical information it provides about the author, and the poem In addition to recounting the merits of reciting or listening to the poems, these verses also divulge precious tidbits, revealing the name of the author, a place of birth or patronage, the name of an important fellow devotee and often lavish descriptions of their favored cities.

As discussed in the introduction, from the *phala śrutis* of the *Tiruppāvai* and *Nācciyār Tirumoḻi* we can glean minimal information on Āṇṭāḷ's life. We can infer that she was closely associated with another important Vaiṣṇava who lived in the city of Villiputuvai (Viṣṇucittaṉ Kōtai: lit. Kōtai of Viṣṇucittaṉ). Hagiographic tradition has interpreted the several references to Viṣṇucittaṉ in her poetry to establish that Āṇṭāḷ was his daughter. However there is nothing in these concluding meta-poems to indicate that this is in fact the case. In the *phala śruti* verses, Āṇṭāḷ (who refers to herself in the third person as Kōtai) compresses the relationship with Viṣṇucittaṉ to an ambivalent possessive case. She simply says, without qualification that—as in the *phala śruti* of the *Tiruppāvai*—she is *paṭṭar pirāṉ kōtai* (the chief-priest's Kōtai) or elsewhere that she is *viṣṇucittaṉiṉ viyaṉ kōtai*: "Viṣṇucittaṉ's beautiful Kōtai." Contrary to his hagiography that paints him as a humble garland maker, in Āṇṭāḷ's *phala śrutis*, Viṣṇucittaṉ is the head of the Brahmins, the chief priest of Putuvai, a great devotee with a special bond with Viṣṇu that even the great god dare not break. But nowhere does she establish, in any clear way, a kinship relationship with him. Please refer to the introduction for further discussion of the relationship between Āṇṭāḷ and Viṣṇucittaṉ.

From the sparse information contained in these verses, we can speculate that Āṇṭāḷ most likely lived in the city of Villiputuvai (modern-day Śrīvilliputtūr) because she describes it in loving and extravagant terms. From her account, the city emerges as a cultural and devotional center, filled with virtuous priests, glorious mansions, and good people. In her imagination, Putuvai *was* Āyarpāṭi. In the *phala śruti* verses, she describes herself as beautiful and more specifically refers to herself variously as Kōtai of curly tresses, Kōtai whose brow surpasses Viṣṇu's bow, Kōtai of slender waist, much in the vein of a young girl admiring her own youth. In the *Nācciyār Tirumoḻi*, these extravagant verbal self-portraits become all the more heartbreaking for they simultaneously lament its loss, because of her unending separation from her chosen beloved.

There has been considerable discussion on the authenticity of these verses—if in fact they were sung by the "original" authors, in this case, Āṇṭāḷ. As Norman Cutler observed in *Songs of Experience*, in some instances it is impossible to omit the *phala śruti* as in the case of Nammāḻvār's *Tiruvāymoḻi*, which is written in the style of *antāti*, where every last word of a verse becomes the first word of the following verse. Removing the *phala śruti* would disrupt the organic order of the text. Though the *Nācciyār Tirumoḻi* does not follow this particular prosody, there is an inherent structure to these verses that functions much like the garland she calls them. Most *phala śruti* are the tenth verse of the section and often refer back to the previous verses. Having adopted the rhetoric structure of a decad of verses for each section, the omission of the *phala śruti* would disrupt the structure of the poem. In three cases, the *phala śruti* is the eleventh verse (sections 4, 5, and 6) and in some cases, the *phala śruti* is not really a *phala śruti*, because it does not mention the merit of recitation, though it mentions Kōtai and has all the other distinctive features of a *phala śruti*.

The argument that the *phala śrutis* represent later anonymous additions to the text to praise the poet (in this case, Āṇṭāḷ) is an important but problematic assertion. Medieval *bhakti* literature and the later Śrīvaiṣṇava commentarial tradition have created a special genre called *taṉiyaṉ* or laudatory poem that serve precisely this need. These *taṉiyaṉs* are often appended to the beginning of the poem for which they are composed and included in liturgical recitation. Not only do these poems highlight the significance of the text, but they also praise the poet, the great merit of the poem, and sometimes allude to the benefits of reciting the poem. For the Śrīvaiṣṇava *sampradāya*, the *taṉiyaṉ* has become inseparable from the poem to which it is appended. Uyyakoṇṭār (10th century C.E.) composed a Tamiḻ *taṉiyaṉ* in two verses for the *Tiruppāvai*, and Parāśara Bhaṭṭar (11th century C.E.) composed one in Sanskrit, also for the *Tiruppāvai*. Two Tamiḻ *taṉiyaṉs* of a later date (12th or 13th century C.E.) for the

Nācciyār Tirumoḻi have also been composed. See appendix 1 for a translation of the *taṉiyaṉ* verses to the *Tiruppāvai* and *Nācciyār Tirumoḻi*.

Aside from this debate of authenticity, there is a facet of particular interest in Āṇṭāḷ's *phala śruti* verses. The dynamic established between the preceding text of longing and anguish ends always on a note of fulfillment—even if that fulfillment is for the audience reciting/hearing the text. Somehow, the narrative of Āṇṭāḷ's longing will bring the devotee closer to Nārāyaṇa. This is not a suggestion or even a speculation on the part of Āṇṭāḷ. As far as the poet herself is considered, her verses (even if they are despairing as in the *Nācciyār Tirumoḻi*) have the power to pave the path for the eager and diligent devotee.

In the *Tiruppāvai*, verses 28 and 29 explicitly state the reward for steadfast devotion. This is reiterated in the *phala śrutis*, except the devotee now does not need to undertake a similar vow. Rather, she can vicariously practice it by reciting the *Tiruppāvai*, which, according to the poet, is sufficient to win Viṣṇu's grace. Unlike the beginning of the poem, where the rewards are listed in material terms, the poem ends by simply asserting its efficacy in achieving the grace of god, as if to emphasize the message of the final two verses (28 and 29).

As mentioned above, the *phala śruti* is written in the third person and is the only hint that the *Tiruppāvai* is a frame narrative. That is, the poet Kōtai imagined a poetic situation where young *gopī* girls undertook such a vow and won the *paṟai* from Kṛṣṇa. It is of course unclear if she imagined herself to be one of these *gopī* girls. Certainly, the commentarial tradition is ambiguous on this point, though the hagiographic tradition, at various points, collapses the plural *gopī* voices with the singular voice of Āṇṭāḷ.

In the *phala śruti*, the poet Kōtai characterizes her *Tiruppāvai* in the following manner: *kōtai coṉṉa caṅka-t-tamiḻ mālai*. Quite literally, this phrase would mean "the garland (*mālai*) of Caṅka Tamiḻ that Kōtai spoke." The commentarial gloss on the word Caṅkam indicates that it refers to the legendary Tamiḻ literary academies (Caṅkam), and her use of the word in the poem indicates that she believes in its devotional *and* literary merit. In fact, its literary excellence is of utmost importance to its success as an efficacious religious tool. It is clear from allusions in several verses in the *Nācciyār Tirumoḻi* that Āṇṭāḷ was aware of her Tamiḻ literary past, and that as an accomplished poet took pride in extolling the poem's high literary quality. In what are certainly poetic conventions, in *Nācciyār Tirumoḻi* 9.10 she refers to her poem as *cen tamiḻ* (pure Tamiḻ), in 12.3 as *ceñcol mālai* (garland of pure words), and in several instances to it as *tūya tamiḻ* (pure Tamiḻ).

Though the most obvious meaning of the phrase Caṅkam Tamiḻ is "Tamiḻ of literary merit or strong Tamiḻ," the actual commentary takes its exposition of the word Caṅkam, and specifically the phrase, *caṅka-t-tamiḻ mālai* in a different direction. The aforementioned line is thus interpreted as "a garland of songs meant to be recited, enjoyed, and practiced together." Here the word *caṅkam* is taken in its literal meaning—that of coming together, a gathering, a joining, an association, or society. If one takes this interpretation seriously, then the *phala śruti* ends with an emphatic assertion of one of the central themes of the *Tiruppāvai*—that it is best and most efficacious to love god with like-minded companions.

vaṅka-k katal: "the ocean with its many waves." The word *vaṅka* presents some problems for the translator. The word can mean wave (from the Sanskrit *bhaṅga*) or a bend in the river. It can also refer to Bengal (*vaṅga*), and thus to the Bay of Bengal. In the commentaries, it is taken as referring to the ocean of milk, or the ocean upon which ships sail. I have interpreted it in the most obvious meaning, as waves.

Notes

1. Miller, Barbara Stoler. *The Bhagavad Gita: Krishna's Counsel in Time of War.* New York: Bantam Dell, 1986.

2. Jagannathachariar, C. *Tiruppāvai: Textual, Literary and Critical Study.* Madras: Tiruvallikeni Devasthanam, 1982. p. 32.

3. Miller, Barbara Stoler. *The Bhagavad Gita: Krishna's Counsel in Time of War.* New York: Bantam Classic, 1986.

Nācciyār Tirumoḻi

Fourteen Songs for the Love of Māl

The Song to Kāmadeva
Tai Oru Tiṅkaḷ
In the Month of Tai

1.1

In the month of Tai
I swept the ground and drew sacred *maṇḍalas.*
In the beginning of Māci
I decorated the street with fine sand.

After all this adornment for beauty's sake, O Anaṅga
I asked you and your brother:
"Is it still possible to live?"
Unite me
    with the lord of Vēṅkaṭam
    the one who holds in his hand
    the discus tipped with fire.

1.2

I adorned the street with fine white sand.
I bathed at the crack of dawn.
I fed the fire with tender thornless twigs.
I have completed my vow to you, O Kāmadeva.

Now take up your bow.
String up a honey-drenched flower
write the name of the only one
    dark as the ocean
    who ripped open the beak of the bird
aim it at him and unite me.

1.3

Three times a day I worship your feet
with fragrant blossoms of *dātura* and *marukai.*
My heart is on fire and
if I must refrain from saying:
    "You are without honor"

then ready your arrows woven with flowers
write the name of my beloved
    the matchless Govinda
    the essence of all knowing
    the master of Vēṅkaṭam
Aim it at him, pierce him
and let me enter that glorious light.

1.4

O ancient Kāmadeva,
I painted the walls with your names,
your banner bearing the shark,
horses, attendants waving their fly-whisks, your black bow.
Have you even noticed?

From childhood,
I pledged my broad, swelling breasts
to the lord of Dvārakā
Quickly, unite me with him.

1.5

O Manmatha! My voluptuous breasts swell
for that lord alone
    who holds aloft the flaming discus and conch.
If there is even talk of offering my body
to mortal men, then I cannot live.

It is equal in violence to a forest jackal
stealthily entering and sniffing at the sacrificial food

the learned Brahmins, the holders of the Vedas,
offer the gods in heaven.

1.6

Even through the month of Paṅkuṉi
I kept my vow to you, O Kāmadeva.
I follow the beautiful, young people
who excel in the arts of love.

All day, I watch the streets for my lord
  dark as the rain clouds,
  lustrous as the dusky *kāyā* blossoms,
  resplendent as the black *karuvilai* blooms.

Coax his glance toward me.
Persuade his face tender as a lotus to consider me.
Make him shower his grace upon me.

1.7

O Manmatha!
I cooked fresh newly harvested grain.
I offered you sugarcane, sweet rice, and flattened paddy.
And learned men praise you with great words!

Coax Tiruvikrama
  who long ago measured the worlds,
to caress this delicate waist and these broad breasts
  and great will be your glory in this world.

1.8

My body is filthy, my hair unkempt
my lips are pale and I eat but once a day.
O radiant and mighty Kāmadeva,
take note of my vow!

Now there is only one thing left to say:
Grant me the pleasure
of clasping the feet of Keśava
  who claimed my womanhood.

Let such glory be mine.

1.9

O Kāmadeva
I worship you three times a day.

I offer fresh flowers at your feet.
If I cannot serve the perfect lord
    dark as the ocean
my endless tears, my unfulfilled love,
my pitiful cries—"Mother! Mother!"
will taint you:

I am like an ox laboring under a yoke
beaten and left to starve.

1.10

Kōtai of Viṣṇucittaṉ
    king of Putuvai
        city of towering mansions that rise like mountains
sang this garland of sweet Tamiḻ
to plead with Kāmadeva
    with his sugarcane bow and five-flower arrows
to unite her with the lord
    who broke the tusk of the elephant
        as it screamed in agony,
    who ripped apart the beak of the bird
    that one dark and lustrous as a gem.

Those who sing this soft song of plea
will remain forever at the feet
of the supreme king of the gods.

The Song of the Sandcastles
Nāmam Āyiram
Praised with a Thousand Names

2.1

O Nārāyaṇa! Praised with a thousand names!
O Nara! Raised as Yaśodā's son!
We are unable to escape the troubles
you inflict upon us.
The time of Paṅkuṉi is here
and we have adorned the streets for Kāmadeva.
Do not be wicked now, O Śrīdhara!
Do not break our sandcastles!

2.2

Our backs aching, we toiled
over these sandcastles all day.
Allow us to enjoy our efforts;
let us gaze upon them fully.
O lord, who is the beginning of everything!
That time, long ago
you slept as an infant upon a banyan leaf.
Can you show us no compassion?
Is this the result of our transgressions?

2.3

O fierce lion slumbering upon the boundless ocean!
You who delivered that wild elephant
from his anguish.
Merely seeing you makes our heart ache.
Do not torment us with your teasing sidelong glances.
We have toiled so hard,
sifting fine sands with our wrists
 thick with bangles.
You who recline upon the brimming ocean
Do not break our sandcastles!

2.4

Lord, dark as the rain clouds
your charming words hold us in a thrall,

your endearing ways captivate us
your face bewitches us like an incantation.
We are but innocent children
and never speak harshly to you.
O dearest one, with eyes bright and long as the lotus
Do not break our sandcastles!

2.5

We built these lovely sandcastles with fine white sand,
to decorate every threshold.
Even when you destroy them
even when our hearts break
even when we melt
we cannot be angry with you.
O Keśava! Duplicitous Mādhava
are you blind to our pain?

2.6

We are still young
our breasts have not yet ripened.
All day, you eye our sandcastles
but we do not understand your clever schemes.
O lord, who tamed the ocean
crossed it and vanquished the clan of demons.
O victorious lord, who wrecked Laṅka,
Torment us no more!

2.7

To those who understand,
your clever words are sweet.
But what use are they to simple children like us,
    who know nothing?
Lord, dark as the boundless ocean,
    lord who spanned the sea
upon your love for your many wives
Do not break our sandcastles!

2.8

We gathered sand in a broad pot,
scattered it in a winnowing fan and built our sandcastles.
What is your pleasure in ruining our play?
You touch them, you kick them,

O how you torment us!
You hold the flaming discus in your hand
    Lord, dark as the ocean
do you not know that even sweetness is bitter
to a sorrowful heart?

2.9

You enter our courtyard
show us your lovely face, your sweet smile
do you intend to break our sandcastles
and our hearts as well?
O Govinda, who leaped and stretched
    to span the earth and the sky
if you embrace us like this
what will our neighbors say?

2.10

"O lord who tasted the sweetness of Sītā's lips
do not break our sandcastles!"
pleaded the young girls of Āyarpāṭi
in their child-like words, while playing on the streets.

So sang Kōtai of Viṣṇucittaṉ,
    master of Villiputuvai,
    city resounding with learned men chanting the Vedas,
Those who master these verses of Tamiḻ,
will certainly attain Vaikuṇṭha!

The Song for the Clothes
Kōḻi Aḻaippataṉ Muṉṉam
Even Before the Rooster Crowed

3.1

Even before the rooster crowed
we set out to bathe.
Now the glorious sun has risen.
Lord, who slumbers upon the serpent
you have shamed us
and we will never return to this pond again.
My friend and I each will raise a hand
and bow to you.
Please return our clothes to us.

3.2

Why have you come here?
What path brought you to this pond?
O lord, whose lustrous curls are entwined
    with honey-drenched *tulasī*!
O elusive lord
    sweeter than nectar!
Alas, our fate binds us,
we cannot do *that*.
O clever boy, do not hurry.
You who leaped from the *kuruntai* tree
and danced upon the serpent's crest,
Please return our clothes to us.

3.3

What is this childishness?
If our mothers caught us, they would not approve.
Lord, perched upon the blossoming *kuruntai* tree
do you not think that this is cruel?
O you who destroyed Laṅka with your bow
we will give you whatever you desire,
we will even slink away unseen
Please return our clothes to us.

3.4

Look around you—this is a pond
where so many come to bathe.
See how our eyes brim with tears
that fall unheeded.
O, you are without any compassion
lord who destroyed Laṅka.
We know that you are the king of monkeys.
Now, please return our clothes to us.

3.5

The *kayal* and the *vāḻ* are biting our legs.
Will it still be any fun
if our brothers chase you away with their spears?
O beautiful dark lord
climb no higher on the *kuruntai* tree
with our lovely clothes.
Please return our clothes to us.

3.6

The thorny stems of the broad lotus blooms
clustered in this pond cut our legs
and it burns like poison from a scorpion's sting.
Our suffering is terrible,
O wily master,
skilled in the dance of the water-pots
abandon your shameful mischief.
Please return our clothes to us.

3.7

We stand in the water and suffer
your behavior is unjust.
O no! Our homes in the village are far away.
O lord who knows the world,
We are bound only to you.
If our mothers hear of this, they will not approve.
Do not climb that *kuruntai* any further.
Please return our clothes to us.

3.8

We are unmarried girls.
Moreover, everyone gathers here.

O lord with eyes lovely as fresh flowers
you sleep without a care through the ancient night.
We tell you this in no uncertain terms
this is just not right.
O perfect prince, lord of the cowherds
perched upon that *kuruntai* tree
Please return our clothes to us.

3.9

You escaped Kaṁsa's savage net
in the midst of that deep dark night
only to torture the hearts of hapless maidens
stranded here.
Yaśodā lets you stray, bold and unpunished.
O you who suckled the milk
        from the breast of the deceitful demoness
Shameless one
Please return our clothes to us.

3.10

Kōtai
        of that priest,
        chief of Putuvai,
                city of towering mansions embellished with gold
strung a garland of a sweet song,
of the dark lord and his game with the maidens.

Those who master these two sets of five
will enter Vaikuṇṭha
and forever reside beside Mādhava.

The Song of Divination
Teḷḷiyār Palar
Scholar and Gods

4.1
Scholars and gods bow before you
noble bridegroom, lord of Tirumāliruñcōlai.
If I should remain forever in that place where he reclines
to press and caress his holy feet,
Fall together, O *kūṭal*!

4.2
My lord, who came as a dwarf
lives happily and without concern
in the forests of Vēṅkaṭam and the city of Kaṇṇapuram.
If he should come quickly and clasp my hand,
Fall together, O *kūṭal*!

4.3
Lord extolled by Brahmā and praised by the gods
peerless son of Devakī, she of the radiant brow
incomparable son of virtuous Vasudeva.
If that one, my prince should come to me,
Fall together, O *kūṭal*!

4.4
When Āyarpāṭi's men and women trembled in fear
he climbed the tall flowering *katampa* tree,
leapt down and danced upon the crest of the conquered Kāliya
If that dancer should come to me,
Fall together, O *kūṭal*!

4.5
The lord of Mathurā, city of lofty mansions
the one who killed the wild elephant with a single kick
If he should walk through these streets
and make me his,
Fall together, O *kūṭal*!

4.6

Desireless lord, who crawled between the twin *maruta* trees
O clever one, who surpassed Kaṁsa in cunning
Great master of flourishing Mathurā
If he should come here,
Fall together, O *kūṭal*!

4.7

At that time, my valiant lord vanquished
depraved Śiśupāla, the tall *maruta* trees, the seven bulls,
the bird, and Kaṁsa who wields a terrible spear.
If that lord should come to me,
Fall together, O *kūṭal*!

4.8

Elusive lord, who abides in the hearts of those who love him,
protector of Dvārakā, city surrounded by fragrant groves,
playful prince, who gently tends his cows
If he should come here,
Fall together, O *kūṭal*!

4.9

Long ago, as a beautiful dwarf at Mahābali's great sacrifice
he spanned the earth and the sky
in a single great stride.
If only that lord should come here,
Fall together, O *kūṭal*!

4.10

The lord who is the essence of the four Vedas
the beautiful lord who saved the wild elephant
lord who abides in the hearts of the lovely women of Āyarpāṭi
If he should come here,
Fall together, O *kūṭal*!

4.11

Kōtai of Viṣṇucittaṉ
sang a song about the lovely maidens of Āyarpāṭi
of their quarrels and friendships, their intimacy and bickering
of long waits and a *kūṭal* game.

Those who master this song of ten
will be released from all their transgressions.

The Song to the Kuyil
Maṉṉu Perum Pukaḻ Mātavaṉ
The Greatly Famed Mādhava

5.1

Is it fair that my love
for the eternal Mādhava
dark as the sapphire
greatly famed and beautiful
adorned with his jeweled crown
should cause me to lose my bangles of conch?

O you *kuyil* that resides in the hollows
of the grove abounding
in *puṉṉai*, *kurukai*, *ñāḻal* and *cerunti*
sing a litany of his name
so my lord with lips red as coral
will return quickly to me.

5.2

My perfect lord
who holds the spotless white conch in his left hand
refuses to reveal himself to me.
Instead he enters me, tortures me all day,
toys with my life,
and leads me on a merry dance:

O *kuyil* singing drunkenly
having sipped the honey
of the bursting *campaka* blossoms
don't evade me.
Murmur a summons
to the Lord of Vēṅkaṭam
and make him come to me.

5.3

Charioted by Mātali
my lord of mystery
showered his arrows upon Rāvaṇa
and again and again severed his many heads
Why cannot I see that lord anywhere?
O *kuyil* you live with your beloved

in this grove
fragrant with blossoming flowers
and murmuring bees, small and beautiful
Sing and summon my lord
dark as a blue sapphire.
Make him return to me.

5.4

My bones melt and my eyes
long as spears
resist even blinking.
For days now, I am plunged into a sea of distress
and I ache to attain
that great boat, Vaikuṇṭha
but I cannot see it.

O *kuyil,* you too know
the anguish of separation
from a beloved.
Summon the immaculate lord
whose body is like gold
whose banner bears Garuḍa
to me.

5.5

Because I ache
to gaze upon the golden feet
of the lord of Villiputtūr,
where graceful swans flit about and play,
my eyes fight sleep
like two sparring *kayal* fish.

O *kuyil,* I will make my pretty parrot
pampered with sweet treats,
your companion,
if only you will sing and summon
the lord who measured the worlds
to me.

5.6

Tormented by that Hṛṣikeśa
who is exalted by the gods of every direction
I lost the luster of my pearly white smile

the redness of my full lips,
and my young breasts surrendered their beauty.

O tender *kuyil* who sleeps
in the flower groves bursting with blossoms
If you sing to summon my lord,
    who is the sole reason for this life
I will forever bow to you.

5.7

Because I yearn to unite with the lord
who reclines upon the surging ocean of milk.
my breasts swell in excitement
they rise and fall and torture my very soul.

O lovely *kuyil* why do you persist
in hiding from me?
If only you call to him
    my lord who holds the conch and discus
    and bears the mace,
and entreat him to return to me,
what great virtue will be yours!

5.8

My clever and perfect lord
    whose mighty arms easily wield the *śārṅga* bow
between him and me
a secret has passed
that only he and I know.

O delicate *kuyil* living in this grove
    amid these trees laden with sweet ripe mangoes
sing your sweet song of summons
to my beautiful lord.
Make him return to me quickly
Then you will witness what I do to him.

5.9

I am caught in the net of desire
that is Śrīdhara,
    lustrous as the green-hued parrot.

O *kuyil* that lives in the grove of flowers
buzzing with the murmurs of bees
listen to this and mark it well:
If you want to live here
you must do one of two things:
either, sing to summon the lord of discus and conch
or make him give his gold bracelet to me.

5.10

Unable to love and serve the lord
who measured the worlds,
I suffer. The hot southern breeze
and the cool bright moon heighten my anguish
Where is the justice in this?

And you too *kuyil* linger here.
Do not increase my pain further.
If you don't sing your song of summons
to Nārāyaṇa, at least today
I will have to drive you away.

5.11

Desiring the lord whose
long strides spanned the worlds,
the maiden with eyes long as spears
sang this message to the dark *kuyil*—
"bring my lord dark as the ocean to me."

Those who master
this garland of words
strung by Kōtai of Viṣṇucittaṉ
chief among priests
and king of Putuvai
city where the four Vedas are sung—
will always chant,
"Namo Nārāyaṇa"

The Song of the Wedding Dream
Vāraṇam Āyiram
Surrounded by a Thousand Elephants

6.1

Surrounded by a thousand elephants, Nāraṇa
my great lord strode through the festive streets.
Every threshold was decked
with bright banners and auspicious golden pots.

Such a vision I dreamed, my friend.

6.2

They decreed, "Tomorrow is the auspicious day of your wedding!"
The proud young lion Mādhava,
that Govinda of bull-like power entered the green canopy
decorated with palm fronds and areca nut.

Such a vision I dreamed, my friend.

6.3

Indra and the entire clan of gods arrived,
approved me as his bride and chanted sacred verses.
Antarī draped me in the bridal garment
and placed the bridal garland about my neck.

Such a vision I dreamed, my friend.

6.4

A host of sages and seers sprinkled water from the four directions,
chanted sacred verses, and tied a thread
smeared with turmeric around our wrists
I stood beside the purest one, adorned in garlands of fresh flowers.

Such a vision I dreamed, my friend.

6.5

Beautiful young maidens carrying bright golden pots
danced and greeted the lord of Mathurā,
who wore lovely sandals on his feet.
And as he strode, the earth trembled.

Such a vision I dreamed, my friend.

6.6

The drums throbbed and great white conches resounded
beneath a canopy heavy with strings of pearls
Madhusūdhana my beloved lord
took my hand in his.

Such a vision I dreamed, my friend.

6.7

Virtuous Brahmins sang the Vedas and chanted sacred verses
they kindled the sacrificial fire with perfect dry twigs and encircled it
  with grass
My lord of great prowess, that mighty elephant
clasped my hand and circled the fire.

Such a vision I dreamed, my friend.

6.8

Nārāyaṇa is my lord for this birth
and every birth that follows.
He clasped my foot in his perfect lustrous hand
and placed it upon the *ammi*.

Such a vision I dreamed, my friend.

6.9

My brothers with their bright faces and brows arched like bows
stoked the brilliant flames of the sacrificial fire.
They drew me forward and placed my hand over the lotus hand
of Acyuta, grand and prideful as a lion.

Such a vision I dreamed, my friend.

6.10

We were smeared with vermilion and cool sandalwood
then he and I together rode on the elephants
and circled the festive streets
They drenched us in fragrant waters.

Such a vision I dreamed, my friend.

6.11

Kōtai of the king of Villiputtūr
  city of Vaiṣṇava fame
wove this garland of pure Tamiḻ

of her dream for the lord of cowherds.

Those who perfect these two times five verses
will find joy in their noble and fine children.

The Song to the White Conch
Karuppūram Nāṟumō
Are They Fragrant as Camphor

7.1

Are they fragrant as camphor? Are they fragrant as the lotus?
Or do those coral red lips taste sweet?
I ache to know the taste, the fragrance of the lips
 of Mādhava, who broke the tusk of the elephant.
Tell me, O white conch from the deep sea.

7.2

O fine virtuous conch!
You were born in the sea and nurtured in Pāñcajanya's body.
Yet you claim as your home
 the hand of the lord, supreme in the deluge
and now your great sound stills the deeds of wicked demons.

7.3

O beautiful great conch!
Like a full autumn moon rising high above the broad mountains
you have claimed as your home the hand
 of Vāsudeva,
king of Mathurā of the North.

7.4

O Valampuri!
Glowing like the moon
you rest forever in Dāmodhara's hand
and seem to whisper secrets in his ear.
Even Indra cannot compete with your fortune.

7.5

O Pāñcajanya!
So many others lived in that ocean with you
they remain unknown and unsung.
But you revel in the sweet nectar of the lips
of the great lord, Madhusūdhana.

7.6

O Valampuri!
You don't need to travel to far away sacred streams.
You climbed into the hand
    of the one who split the twin *maruta* trees
and bathe in the unsullied nectar of the lips of the lotus-eyed one.

7.7

O king of conches!
You are like a swan sipping honey from a fresh red lotus
nestled into Vāsudeva's lovely broad hand
    that dark lord, whose eyes are like lotuses.
Your fortune is glorious indeed!

7.8

O Pāñcajanya!
Your food is the nectar from the lips of the one who measured the worlds.
Your bed is the hand of the one dark as the ocean.
Women everywhere scold you soundly
What you do is unfair.

7.9

O great and glorious conch!
Sixteen thousand women watch you
sip the nectar of Mādhava's lips.
If you do not share that which belongs to all
Why should they not quarrel with you?

7.10

Kōtai of Viṣṇucittaṉ
    lord of the priests of beautiful Putuvai
        city of renown and fame
sang these ten Tamiḻ verses
extolling the intimacy of Padmanābha and his Pāñcajanya.

All who excel in this recitation will always be near him.

The Song to the Dark Rain Clouds
Viṇ Nīla Mēlāppu
O Clouds Spread Like Blue Cloth

8.1

O clouds spread like blue cloth
across the vast sky
Has Tirumāl my beautiful lord
 of Vēṅkaṭam, where cool streams leap
come with you?
My tears gather and spill between my breasts
like waterfalls.
He has destroyed my womanhood.
How does this bring him pride?

8.2

O clouds that spill lovely pearls
What message has the dark-hued lord
 of Vēṅkaṭam
sent through you?
The fire of desire has invaded my body
I suffer.
I lie awake here in the thick of night,
a helpless target for the cool southern breeze.

8.3

So easily they left me
my luster, my bangles, thought, sleep
and I am destroyed.
O compassionate clouds!
I sing of Govinda's virtues
 lord of Vēṅkaṭam,
  where cool waterfalls leap.
How long can this alone guard my life?

8.4

O clouds bright with lightning
Tell the lord of Vēṅkaṭam
 upon whose lovely chest Śrī resides

that my supple young breasts
yearn everyday
for his resplendent body.

8.5

O great clouds, rising into the sky.
Climb high, rain hard on Vēṅkaṭam
and scatter the flowers brimming with honey.
Ask the one who tore the body of Hiraṇya
    with his long nails flecked with blood
to return the conch bangles
he has taken from me.

8.6

O cool clouds heavy with water
rise high and pour down on Vēṅkaṭam,
home of the one who took the world from Mahābali.
Tell that Nāraṇa
    he entered me, consumed me and stole my well-being
    like a worm that feasts on a wood-apple
of my terrible disease.

8.7

O cool clouds, place the plea of this servant
    at the feet of the one with the beautiful lotus eyes
    that one who churned the ocean filled with conch.
Beseech him to enter me for a single day
and wipe away the vermilion smeared upon my breasts.
Only then can I survive.

8.8

Dark clouds ready for the season of rains
chant the name of the lord of Vēṅkaṭam
    that one who is valiant in battle.
Tell him, like the lovely leaves that fall in the season of rains
I waste away through the long endless years
waiting for the day when he finally sends word.

8.9

Rain clouds rising like great war elephants over Vēṅkaṭam
What word has that one
    who sleeps upon the serpent

sent for me?
The world will say: "heedless that he was her only refuge
he killed this young girl."
What honor is there in this?

8.10

Kōtai of the king of Putuvai,
    the peerless city,
desired the one reclining upon the serpent
and sent the clouds as her messengers
to the king of Vēṅkaṭam.

Those who place in their hearts these verses of Tamiḻ
    sung by her of a lustrous forehead,
those who sing these words of Tamiḻ
will forever abide by him.

The Song in the Groves of Tirumāliruñcōlai
Cintūra Cempoṭi
Crimson Ladybirds

9.1

Crimson ladybirds flutter everywhere
in the groves of Tirumāliruñcōlai
scattering like a fine vermilion powder.
Once long ago, he used the mighty Mandara,
churned the ocean and made it yield its nectar.
Now I am caught in the net of the lord with beautiful shoulders.
Can I escape it alive?

9.2

In the lovely flower gardens of Tirumāliruñcōlai
mighty war elephants tussle in play,
creepers of jasmine display their bright white smiles,
the dark flowering creepers laugh at me mockingly.
My dear friend, to whom can I divulge the
torment his garland inflicts upon me?

9.3

O bright *karuvai* blooms and dark *kāyā* flowers,
you have assumed the brilliant form of my Tirumāl.
Show me how to endure my agony.
The master of Tirumāliruñcōlai,
  whose broad shoulders are for Śrī's pleasure
entered my home and wrested my beautiful bangles.
Is this right?

9.4

O you hosts of *kuyil* and crowds of peacocks,
clusters of bright *karuvai* blooms, fresh *kalaṅkai* fruit
and fragrant flowers
all of you that that live in this vast grove.
You are five great sinners:
Why have you assumed the splendid dark color
of my lovely dark lord who dwells in Tirumāliruñcōlai?

9.5

The bees that hover over the red lotus blooms
remind me of the one
    whose eyes are like lotuses,
    whose body is dark as the rain clouds
that one who stands amid the tall groves of Tirumāliruñcōlai.
O cool ponds dense with flowers
O red lotuses floating in those ponds
please guide me to a place of refuge.

9.6

For the lord
    of the sweet fragrant groves of Māliruñcōlai
I offered a hundred pots of butter
and yet another hundred brimming with sweet rice
Will the beautiful lord who rides on Garuḍa
not come to claim my offering?

9.7

If only he will claim my offerings
I would offer yet another hundred thousand pots.
If only the lord who abides
    in the groves of Tirumāliruñcōlai
    fragrant with the breeze from the South
would take me into his heart:
I, who have always been his slave.

9.8

With the awakening dawn
hosts of black sparrows sing sweetly
and call out the arrival of the dark lord.
Do they repeat the words
    of the lord of Tirumāliruñcōlai,
    the king of Dvārakā,
    the one who floats upon a banyan leaf.
Can it be true?

9.9

I wait in vain
    in the Māliruñcōlai groves
    bursting with ripe *koṅkai* fruit
withering like the garlands of golden *koṉrai* blooms.

When will he place the conch to his beautiful lips
and release its great sound?
When will I hear the majestic sound of his *śārṅga* bow?

9.10

Kōtai,
over whose fragrant hair bees hover
wove this garland of ten verses
and sang the praise of the lord of Māliruñcōlai,
where the Cilampu river bearing sandalwood and *akil*
rushes down washing away its banks.
Those who repeat her ten verses of perfect Tamiḻ
will be forever united with Tirumāl's feet.

The Song of Lament
Karkōṭal Pūkkāḷ
O Dark Flowers

10.1

O dark flowers
where is the lord, dark as the ocean
who has unfairly sent you to wage battle with me?
Alas, now whom can I beg?
My heart clamors after his cool *tulasī* garland.

10.2

O flowers climbing high into the sky
stretch past the high heavens
and place me beside those dear to him
    who do not scorch
    just like the blazing flame he holds aloft in his right hand
    that one, the light who is the essence of the Vedas.

10.3

O *kōvai* vine you flaunt your luscious red fruit
and remind me of the one with the beautiful lips.
Please do not drag my life from me. I fear you now.
I am a sinner, born again for all my past offenses
Still, I feel no shame.
But his tongue is forked
like the serpent he has chosen as his bed.

10.4

Fair jasmine, do not torment me
with your bright smiles.
O you who are graceful as woman
I surrender to you.
If the words of the lord
    who slashed the nose of the terrible demoness
are false,
is my birth a falsehood as well?

10.5

O singing *kuyil*, what song is this?
Sing, only if the lord of immaculate Vēṅkaṭam

gives purpose to my life.
If the one with Garuḍa on his fluttering banner
shows me compassion and unites with me,
sing your songs and we will both listen.

10.6

O you crowds of excellent peacocks
as lovely of form as Kaṇṇaṉ
you with your graceful gait and skilled dance
I fall at your feet.
See how my beloved
who for aeons has reclined
upon his serpent with its swaying hood
has brought me to such a state.

10.7

Incomparable peacocks dancing with your feathers unfurled!
Deprived and unfortunate, I have nothing left for you.
Govinda who danced with the pots
plundered me and took everything.
Is it fair that you torment me?

10.8

Rain, O rain! Rain down on Vēṅkaṭam
where my beautiful lord lives
like hot wax poured into a clay mold.
Show him how to enter my heart and melt me.
Make him caress me and hold me tight
so that my beautiful lord lodges in my heart.
Can you rain down in this way?

10.9

O oceans! He entered you, churned you
and stole your nectar from your depths.
Just so, the cunning one entered me
and deprived me of my life.
Can you go to his serpent
and convey my terrible suffering?

10.10

My dear friend, what defense do we simple mortals have
against the great and splendid lord

stretched upon the serpent?

If Villiputuvai's lord Viṣṇucittaṉ
    of immaculate virtue
prevails upon his lord to reveal himself
we will behold him then.

The Song for the Conch Bangles
Tām Ukakkum
What Is Dear to Him

11.1

The conch he holds in his hand is dear to him.
Aren't my conch bangles as dear to me?
Then O my mothers, richly adorned
why does the lord of Tiruvaraṅkam
  reclining upon the serpent spitting fire
not even glance at me?

11.2

O lovely mothers, my sweet lord of Tiruvaraṅkam
is beautiful and peerless of form.
His hair is beautiful, his mouth is beautiful.
His lotus eyes are beautiful, the lotus rising from his navel
  is beautiful.
He loosened my already loose bangles
I have lost them to him forever.

11.3

My lord faultlessly rules all that he owns
  this earth embraced by crashing oceans
  and the heavenly worlds.
How has the lord of Tiruvaraṅkam
  who reigns with a perfect scepter
added to his wealth
with my simple conch bangles?

11.4

The lord living in Tiruvaraṅkam
  city famed for its stately palaces,
  its richly ornamented mansions
perhaps still feels a lack
after he begged alms as a dwarf so long ago.
If he desires my conch bangles as well
why does he not just walk by this street?

11.5

My lord came as a cunning dwarf
stretched out his lovely hand, meekly plead for alms
and then measured the worlds.
My lord who is stretched upon the serpent
and reclines in Tiruvaraṅkam,
    that sacred city where only the virtuous live
has deprived me of my bangles.
He has stolen my smallest wealth.

11.6

Long ago he usurped the petty wealth of my hands
the splendid lord of Tiruvaraṅkam
    where the lovely Kāviri waters fertile fields
the one palpable everywhere yet still intangible
he who is the embodiment of the four Vedas.
Now he claims my very life.

11.7

Forgoing both food and sleep,
he ripped apart the crashing ocean
all for the love of his woman.
Now ensconced within the strong walls of Tiruvaraṅkam,
the lord, wealthy and magnificent
has forgotten his long-ago madness and instead
revels only in his virtues.

11.8

A long time ago for the maiden of the earth
    covered in moss,
he took the shameful form of a boar
    dripping water from its filthy body.
The lord of Tiruvaraṅkam, that lustrous one
beguiled me with his words.
Now they can never be dislodged from my heart.

11.9

Śiśupāla was certain
that he would grasp the maiden's hand and make her his.
He grew pale, when at that very moment
that enchanter of women
clasped the maiden's hand.

Now that lord resides in Tiruvaraṅkam,
his chosen abode.

11.10

Viṣṇucittaṉ has heard
these words of truth spoken
by the mighty and righteous king
of Tiruvaraṅkam:
    "Those who love me
    I will love in return."
If even his words are proved false
what is there left to believe?

The Song of Sacred Places
Maṟṟu Iruntīr
All of You Do Not Understand

12.1

All of you do not understand
my love for Mādhava.
You say meaningless things
    like the deaf speaking to the mute.
My lord left the mother who bore him
to be nurtured in the home of another.
He reached Mathurā before the wrestlers
and vanquished them.
I implore you to take me to that city.

12.2

There is no need for shame
since everyone knows.
If I am to return to what I once was,
do not delay.
I must see that lord of mystery,
    who long ago spanned the worlds
    in the guise of a youthful dwarf.
If you truly desire to protect me
take me to Āyarpāṭi.

12.3

When word gets out that I abandoned
my father, my mother, my relatives
to seek my own path,
it will be impossible to protect me from censure.
That lord of mystery has come
and revealed his form to me.
In the dead of night,
take me to the doorstep of Nandagopāla
    whose mischievous son
    delights in scandal and blame.

12.4

My breasts seek the gaze of the one
    whose beautiful hand lifts the discus.
Bound tightly in a red cloth, their eyes
shy away from the gaze of mere mortals
desiring none other than Govinda.
I cannot live here a moment longer.
Please take me to the shores of the Yamunā.

12.5

O dear mothers no one understands
this disease. But do not fret.
The one dark as the deep blue ocean
can soothe away my sickness
with a simple caress of his hand.
He is that very one,
    who climbed the *katampa* tree on the river bank
    leapt and danced upon the crest of Kāliya
    and created such a battle scene.
Please take me to the shores of that river.

12.6

The dark cool clouds, the *karuvilai* blossoms
the *kāyā* blooms, the lotus flowers urge me
"Go to him! Go to him!"
    to that Hṛṣikeśa
    who sweating, hungry and fatigued
    asked for his share of sacrificial rice
    and waited for a long time
    at Bhaktilocana.
Please take me there.

12.7

I am ashen, my heart is despondent.
I have lost all shame. My lips are pale
I cannot eat, my mind is weak
I have grown frail.
There is only one, dark and beautiful
    as the deep blue ocean,
bring his garland of cool beautiful *tulasī*,
drape it around me and cool me.

Please take me to the banyan tree in Bāṇḍīram
where his brother Balarāma
broke the bones of Pralamba
and destroyed him.

12.8

O you delinquents, who whisper and gossip
"He is that simple cowherd, who herds his host of cows!"
"He was born into a clan that roams the forests!"
"He was bound to the mortar!"
do not repeat all that you have simply heard.
and make me condemn you.
Triumphant, he held aloft the mountain as an umbrella
shielded his herd of cows from the relentless rains.
Now, take me there to that Govardhana.

12.9

The parrot in its cage ceaselessly screeches
"Govinda! Govinda!"
If I punish it and withhold its food
"He measured the worlds!" it shrieks.
O friends, do not earn the city's disregard,
lose your fair reputations and hang your heads in shame.
Take me to Dvārakā
that city surrounded by tall mansions.

12.10

The maiden of long and curly tresses
Kōtai of Viṣṇucittaṉ
king of Putuvai,
city of glittering mansions
entreated her relatives, boldly demanded
to be taken everywhere
from Mathurā to Dvārakā
the lands of her lord.

Those who master her sweet words
will reach Vaikuṇṭha, where he abides.

The Song of Desire
Kaṇṇaṉ Eṉṉum
Kaṇṇaṉ, My Dark Lord

13.1
I lie here yearning for the familiar sight
of Kaṇṇaṉ, my dark lord.
Do not just stand there, mocking me
It is like pouring sour juice upon a raw and open wound.
Instead, bring the golden silk
wrapped around the waist of my great lord
who does not know
the agony of a woman's heart.
Fan me with it and cool my burning fever.

13.2
I am snared in the nets of the supreme lord
who sleeps on the banyan leaf
its stem seeping milk.
Do not speak reckless words
they pierce me like spears.
The Yādhava, lord of the cowherds,
staff in hand tenderly grazed his cows.
That very one also danced with the pots in Kuṭantai.
Bring me his beautiful blue *tulasī*
and place it in my soft, tangled curls.

13.3
The lord who destroyed Kaṁsa,
the one with dark brows and
a treacherous sidelong glance
his gaze enters me like an arrow
My heart burns. My sanity slips.
I suffer, but he says nothing,
not even "Fear not!"
If he should relinquish it
bring me the garland adorning his chest
and gently rub it on my chest.

13.4

In this world who can console me?
After all, he has enchanted all Āyarpāṭi.
That black bull harasses me, tortures me
and I lie here weak and broken.
His sweet lips are soaked in the nectar
that never sates. Let me not wilt.
Bring that sweetness to me.
feed it to me and end my fatigue.

13.5

I weep for him. I worship him.
Yet he does not show himself.
He does not say, "Do not fear."
He does not consume me with his caress,
nor does he envelop me in his embrace.
The lofty lord follows his cows
    into the groves thick with tender leaves
and plays his flute.
Bring me the nectar from the lips of that flute
spread it over my face and cool me.

13.6

In this unscrupulous world
Tirumāl
    the harsh and cruel son of Nandagopāla
inflicts such agony that I cannot move
or even turn on my side.
Quickly bring me the dust from his footsteps
smear it on me and prevent my life from fleeing.

13.7

The world exalts the one
who hoists the banner of victory imprinted with Garuḍa.
His mother raised him to bow to no one
and he is as bitter to me as the margosa tree.
Press my flawless breasts
to the youthful one's beautiful shoulders
    broad as palm trees
bind them tightly to him
and end the sorrow of my separation.

13.8

I melt. I fray. But he does not care
if I live or die.
If that stealthy thief, that duplicitous Govardhana
should even glance at me
I shall pluck these useless breasts of mine
from their roots
I will fling them at his chest
and staunch the fire scorching me.

13.9

What is the purpose of future penance
if in this life, I cannot serve my Govinda
in small familiar ways and end the anguish
of my swollen and tender breasts?
Let him enfold me to his perfect chest
or let him stand before me,
face me and bid me farewell.
I will accept even that.

13.10

Proud Kōtai of Viṣṇucittaṉ,
    master of Villiputuvai
maiden with dark arching brows
    that surpass the curve of his bow,
sang of her intense yearning and love
for the radiant beacon of Āyarpāṭi,
the great lord who made her suffer.

Those who expertly sing these words of praise
will never flail in the ocean of sorrows.

The Song of Questions and Answers
Paṭṭi Mēyntu
Have You Seen Him Here?

14.1

Have you seen him here
that mischievous lord, the dark bull
younger to Baladeva
that one who roams at will, causing mischief?

We glimpsed him playing in Vṛndāvana
grazing his dear cows,
calling them by name and
tending them carefully.

14.2

Have you seen him
stinking of butter, enchanting all in Āyarpāṭi,
that Govardhana, the young bull
who has made me suffer in separation?

We glimpsed him playing in Vṛndāvana
with his friends,
his *vanamālā* sparkling
like lightning around a dark cloud.

14.3

Have you seen him here
that lord who is love
love itself born as a bridegroom
that one who speaks intolerable lies?

We glimpsed him coming to Vṛndāvana
flying high above
shaded from the sun by noble Vinatā's son
whose wings were spread like a canopy.

14.4

Have you seen him
my lord who caught me
in the unbreakable leash of his cool lotus eyes,
drags me everywhere, and toys with me?

We glimpsed him playing in Vṛndāvana
    a mighty elephant calf
    beaded with sweat
    as if draped in a garment of pearls.

14.5

Have you seen him
    that Mādhava, my dark jewel
    who has escaped from a net like a pig,
    the lord who relents nothing?

We glimpsed him in Vṛndāvana
    trailing his yellow silk
    like a great dark cloud, like a calf frolicking
    he overwhelmed the streets.

14.6

Have you seen him
    that deceitful wretch without virtue
    whose beautiful brows arch
    like the *śārṅga* he bears in his cool hand.

We glimpsed him in Vṛndāvana
    dark bodied and bright faced
    like the sun spreading dawn
    above the mountains.

14.7

Have you seen him
    that great intangible dark cloud,
    the lord whose blackness of skin
    equals the darkness of his soul?

We glimpsed him around Vṛndāvana
    with his great group of friends
    like the night sky thick
    with clusters of glittering stars.

14.8

Have you seen him
the one who owns the white conch,
the one draped in yellow silk, that Tirumāl,
lord of boundless compassion, who holds the fiery discus?

We glimpsed him playing in Vṛndāvana.
he whose fragrant hair, entwined with flowers
brushes his broad shoulders
like intoxicated bees.

14.9

Have you seen him
that immaculate lord who created
from his lovely navel, a grand lotus as home for Ayaṉ
and commanded him in play, to make the worlds?

We glimpsed him in Vṛndāvana.
going toward the forest
to hunt and slay
Dhenuka, the elephant and the bird.

14.10

Those who live considering
the words of Kōtai of Viṣṇucittaṉ
as balm for the pains of the world,
will never be separated
from the splendid feet of the lord
who graced the great elephant.
that supreme lord
who is glimpsed on this earth in Vṛndāvana.

Commentary and Notes to the *Nācciyār Tirumoḻi*

The notes to the *Nācciyār Tirumoḻi* are based on Periyavāccāṉ Piḷḷai's Maṇipravāḷa commentary and summarize his most significant interpretations for each decad (*Tirumoḻi*). Although there are several contemporary commentaries on the *Nācciyār Tirumoḻi*, they rely on Periyavāccāṉ Piḷḷai's authoritative exposition of Āṇṭāḷ's longer poem. It is for this reason that I have based these notes solely on Piḷḷai's commentary. However, there are moments when a contemporary commentator, such as Uttamur Veeraraghavachariar, veers away from Piḷḷai's interpretation. In the notes below, I discuss where these differences occur, and why.

Periyavāccāṉ Piḷḷai reads the *Nācciyār Tirumoḻi* as a linear narrative, contiguous with the *Tiruppāvai*, despite the differences of voice, points of view, and content in the two poems. Though the commentator often acknowledges these very same differences, he quickly sets them aside in favor of a reading where the heroine in the *Nācciyār Tirumoḻi* is Āṇṭāḷ herself, just as all the *gopī* voices in the *Tiruppāvai* coalesce into a single female identity.

His commentary for each decad—referred to as a *Tirumoḻi*—opens with a succinct synopsis of the previous ten verses to provide both context and continuity, and then articulates relevant theological points. One of the key issues that Periyavāccāṉ Piḷḷai grapples with is Āṇṭāḷ's appeal to various sentient and insentient beings such as Kāmadeva (the god of desire), the clouds, or the *kuyil* bird. He keeps returning to this fundamental question: "If Āṇṭāḷ has already surrendered to Viṣṇu in the *Tiruppāvai*, and has accepted him as her sole refuge, how can one explain her entreaty to these various entities?" The answer to this query varies little—it is unfailingly attributed to a loss of discriminatory capabilities caused by Āṇṭāḷ's despair at having to suffer the terrible effects of unrequited love. In Periyavāccāṉ Piḷḷai's eyes, the perfect parallel for Āṇṭāḷ's sorry plight is that of the abducted Sītā, who too yearned to be united with her beloved. Piḷḷai does not assert that Sītā and Āṇṭāḷ's experience is exactly the same, but rather that their situations are similar—a case Āṇṭāḷ herself makes in the *Nācciyār Tirumoḻi*. This nuanced position on the parallels between Āṇṭāḷ and Sītā comes through most clearly in the messenger *Tirumoḻis* such as 5 or 8, where the heroine's association with clouds and various birds is compared to Sītā's relationship with Hanumān. This is not to say that Piḷḷai is unaware of Āṇṭāḷ's divine status—he makes the assertion on several occasions that she is the embodiment of Bhū Devī. Such a position enables the commentator to identify Sītā's iconic struggle in the *Rāmāyaṇa* with that of Āṇṭāḷ's without actually making them the same.

Periyavāccāṉ Piḷḷai is imaginative and his commentary is quite beautiful in parts, but his commitment to a fairly conservative reading of the *Nācciyār Tirumoḻi* means that it is often repetitive and constrained by the self-imposed boundaries of Rāmānuja's qualified nondualist theology (*viśiṣṭādvaita*). This is reflected in the shorter explications for the later decads of the poem. As a result, while the commentary for the opening verses are quite long and detailed, his comments for the later decads become both abbreviated and repetitive.

The notes below offer a summary of Periyavāccāṉ Piḷḷai's commentary for each decad rather than for each individual verse. I have indicated where the ideas are Piḷḷai's and where they are mine. Where applicable, I have highlighted myths, unfamiliar vocabulary, and relevant literary allusions for individual verses. In the notes, I follow Piḷḷai's lead and refer to the heroine of the poem as Āṇṭāḷ. These notes are meant as a supplement to the translations, rather than a comprehensive translation or paraphrase of the Periyavāccāṉ Piḷḷai commentary.

Nācciyār Tirumoḻi 1. The Song to Kāmadeva

Like most Tamiḻ literary texts, the *Nācciyār Tirumoḻi* opens with an invocation to a deity (*kaṭavuḷ vāḻttu*), except here it is addressed not to Viṣṇu, but to Kāmadeva (the god of desire). It is a particularly significant choice, because the goal is not so much the invocation of a poetic muse, as is the case in other literary works, but an appeal for a mediatory presence in Āṇṭāḷ's quest of love. Such a position inevitably raises the question of why Āṇṭāḷ would seek a different *upāya* (means/path), when according to Periyavāccāṉ Piḷḷai, it is clear in the *Tiruppāvai* that she has already fully surrendered to and accepted Viṣṇu as her only refuge. If at the conclusion at the *Tiruppāvai* it is understood that she fulfilled her quest and that it was successful, how does one explain Āṇṭāḷ's choosing to fall at Kāma's feet? Piḷḷai posits several different answers to her puzzling actions. He first suggests that *ajñāna* (ignorance) might have led her down this unfortunate path. But this is not a viable response and is not one that the commentator actively pursues. After all, Āṇṭāḷ is a divine being, and as will become clear in his expositions of the later decads, is an emanation of Bhū Devī. He therefore softens his harsh charge, and instead suggests that Āṇṭāḷ's momentary ignorance is caused by a single-minded focus on Viṣṇu that has led her to experience the terrible pain of unrequited love, which in turn causes her to lose sleep. Piḷḷai compares her actions to the citizens of Ayodhyā, who, mad with grief, appealed to various gods when their beloved Rāma left for his fourteen years of exile. He also alludes to the fact that Kāma is really Viṣṇu's son, so in the larger scheme of things Āṇṭāḷ's propitiation does not violate her surrender to Viṣṇu (see appendix 2 for a synopsis of the myth that recounts the relationship between Kṛṣṇa and Kāma). It must be noted here that Āṇṭāḷ does not allude to Kāma's filial relationship to Viṣṇu. The contemporary commentator Uttamur Veeraraghavachariar takes an alternate position. He suggests that Āṇṭāḷ did not in fact indulge in the worship of a deity other than Viṣṇu. That is, the vow to Kāma is simply an instance of Āṇṭāḷ following a prescribed ritual duty (*naimittika karma*). And when she performed this duty, worship was offered either to Viṣṇu, who resides *in* Kāma (as he resides in all things and in all beings), or that she worshipped Kāma as Viṣṇu.

Catherine Benton points out in her book *God of Desire* that in textual descriptions of a ritual known as the *Damanakotsava* (Festival of the Damanaka Flower), Viṣṇu was often substituted for Kāma. As described in the *Padma Purāṇa*, this ritual is one observed by Vaiṣṇavas during the months of March–April, and in it Kāma becomes a "multiform of Viṣṇu, receiving prayers of supplication while granting his devotees' petitions, behaving much like the great god [Viṣṇu]."[1] There is no contemporary evidence of festivals and rituals to Kāma, and it is impossible to know if Āṇṭāḷ's vow to Kāmadeva is imagined or if it depicts a ritual that was in circulation during her time. Āṇṭāḷ does provide a fair amount of detail on the elements of her ritual vow to Kāma—she talks of drawing sacred diagrams on the earth, making paintings on the wall, and she mentions all of Kāma's symbolic accoutrements, including his sugarcane bow and flower arrows. Āṇṭāḷ's description of the vow makes no mention of Kāma's wife, Ratī, who, Benton points out, is often evoked in these rituals alongside the god of desire.[2]

Periyavāccāṉ Piḷḷai reads the *Nācciyār Tirumoḻi* as beginning where the *Tiruppāvai* ends. The *Nācciyār Tirumoḻi* does create both a chronological and thematic continuity with the former poem, beginning as it does in the month of Tai (January–February), and with another vow. The *Tiruppāvai* is an enactment of a ritual prayer (the *pāvai nōṉpu*) undertaken by young unmarried girls for the attainment of a virtuous husband. In the *Nācciyār Tirumoḻi*, the desire is unaltered, and the virtuous husband remains Viṣṇu.

The first verse of the *Nācciyār Tirumoḻi* quickly moves from the Tamiḻ solar months of Tai (mid-January to mid-February) to Māci (mid-February to mid-March), and we greet the following month Paṅkuṉi (mid-March to mid-April) in *Nācciyār Tirumoḻi* 2. So in a span of three lines Āṇṭāḷ invokes the *pāvai nōṉpu* that she describes in exquisite detail in *Tiruppāvai*, while also indicating the length, arduousness, and her commitment to securing her desire. The connection to the *Tiruppāvai*, especially verses 2 and 8, is also asserted when she details the ritual requirements for her vow to Kāma. She wakes up early in the morning and takes a bath in cold water, purifying herself, following, as Piḷḷai points out, Bharata's example in the *Rāmāyaṇa*, when he bathed in the Sarayū before approaching Rāma. But the purpose of the bath is also to cool the fire of separation ravaging her.

Like the *pāvai nōṉpu* of the *Tiruppāvai*, this vow too requires special dedication and commitment. Piḷḷai says that she draws beautiful magical diagrams (*maṇḍala*) only with soft, fine white sand, because it is bright as the *sattva guṇa* (the virtue of luminosity) that Viṣṇu embodies. The sand is soft, Piḷḷai goes on to explicate, so that it will not hurt Viṣṇu's feet when he finally comes for her. She chooses perfect thorn-less twigs, picking off any ants, so that her fire sacrifices are untarnished by the blemish of killing a living being.

One of the curious moments in this first decad occurs in the opening verse (*Nācciyār Tirumoḻi* 1.1), where Āṇṭāḷ invokes Kāma and his brother. While there is no mythological basis for it, Periyavāccāṉ Piḷḷai identifies him as Sāma and adds that it is common practice to invoke a brother in addition to the main figure of propitiation or at the beginning of any arduous quest. To make his point, he offers a comparison from the *Rāmāyaṇa*, when

Hanumān bowed down to both Rāma and Lakṣmaṇa before he undertook his ventures to Laṅka. It is possible that Piḷḷai in identifying Kāma's brother (Sāma) is referring to one of Kṛṣṇa's son Pradyumna's siblings. (Kāma was born as Kṛṣṇa's son Pradyumna). In the *Bhāgavata Purāṇa* 10.61, a list of Kṛṣṇa's sons is provided. While there is no son by the name Sāma—although there is a Samba—this might be the source that Piḷḷai is invoking his commentary.

1.1

Tai: The month the Tamiḻ solar calendar that roughly parallels the months of mid-January to mid- February of the western calendar.

maṇḍalas: Intricate designs with specific symbolic meanings that are drawn/created and used to guide ritual practice.

Māci: The month of the Tamiḻ calendar corresponding to the months of mid-February to mid-March.

Anaṅga: Aname of Kāmadeva, the god of love. This specific epithet means the "formless one." The gods appeal to Kāma to awaken desire for the goddess Pārvatī in Śiva's heart. Kāma shoots his arrow of flowers at Śiva and is successful. Śiva is furious at Kāma's intervention in his austerities, and turns him to ash with his fiery gaze. It is in this episode that earns Kāma the name, Anaṅga—the formless/limbless one. Periyavāccāṉ Piḷḷai does not explicate either the relevance of the myth or the name to the *Nācciyār Tirumoḻi,* though he offers a gloss of this particular epithet.

1.10

This is the traditional *phala śruti,* the concluding verse of a verse or decad that recounts the rewards accrued from reciting or hearing the poem. A *phala śruti* ends either a section (usually a decad) of the poem or the poem itself. I have discussed the *phala śruti* in detail in the notes to *Tiruppāvai* 30.

A curious feature of the *phala śruti,* dramatically in evidence in the *Nācciyār Tirumoḻi,* is the tension between the text of longing and the meta–*phala śruti* that closes the decad on a note of fulfillment, even if that fulfillment is reserved solely for the audience reciting/hearing the text. Somehow the narrative of Āṇṭāḷ's longing will bring the devotee closer to Nārāyaṇa, though this is not a feature unique to Āṇṭāḷ. There is a suggestion on the part of the poet that verses (even if they are so despairing), will prove just as efficacious for the eager and diligent devotee as her various vows were.

Nācciyār Tirumoḻi 2. The Song of the Sandcastles

This Tirumoḻi describes the youthful Kṛṣṇa's mischief in the mythic world of Āyarpāṭi. Of course, we never "see" Kṛṣṇa; we only hear the pleas of the young gopī (cowherd) girls pleading with him not to break their sandcastles (*ciṟṟil*).

In the *Tiruppāvai*, Caṅkam topologies of *akam* (interior) and *puṟam* (exterior) are literally realized through a careful use of spatial relationships. The *Nācciyār Tirumoḻi* does not exploit the possibilities of *akam* and *puṟam* in the same ways that we see in the shorter poem. But this *Tirumoḻi* provides a unique window into Āṇṭāḷ's deft realignment of these antecedent literary traditions. The narrative situation of this decad is that of young *gopī* girls building sandcastles (*ciṟṟil*) that the mischievous Kṛṣṇa insists on destroying. The making of the *ciṟṟil* is a game featured in the Caṅkam poems, where like in this instance, it is a metonymy for the interior world of the heroine.

In *Nācciyār Tirumoḻi* 2, the *gopīs* describe their *ciṟṟil* in elaborate detail, with a focus on how they have carefully constructed the interiors of their sandcastles. A heedless Kṛṣṇa then destroys these very interiors by touching and kicking them. The paradox is further developed as the young girls repeatedly insist through the ten verses of the poem that they are innocent, naïve, and incapable of indulging the mischievous Kṛṣṇa in his whims. What these whims are we can only speculate—though we are given an insight in 2.9, where he is described as entering their homes just for the perverse pleasure of destroying their beautiful worlds. The girls end the verse (2.9) with the query, "what will our neighbors say?" Furthermore, the motif of the sandcastle-home, physical-home, and the female body as home is fully realized in the penultimate verse of the second section of the second *Tirumoḻi*, where the girls say:

> You enter our courtyard
> show us your lovely face, your sweet smile
> do you intend to break our sandcastles
> and our hearts as well?
> O Govinda, who leaped and stretched
>   to span the earth and the sky
> if you embrace us like this
> what will our neighbors say? (2.9)

The second *Tirumoḻi* begins on the threshold of the *gopīs*' homes, where they claim they have just adorned the streets for Kāmadeva (2.1). In 2.5, they say that they have built their castles on the threshold of their homes. In 2.9, Kṛṣṇa moves from the courtyard of the girls' homes, to embracing their bodies, and enters their minds. Āṇṭāḷ plays off the broken *ciṟṟil* and the sorrowful hearts of the young girls, leaving no ambiguity of the correlation. Kṛṣṇa's invasion of the interior space of the home, seen as contiguous with that of the heroine's (Āṇṭāḷ's) own body, is developed further in the later decads of the *Nācciyār Tirumoḻi*, where he is accused of entering her and/or her house without her permission to make love to her, to wrest her bangles, or as in this case, to break her/their sandcastles.

Periyavāccāṉ Piḷḷai does not explore the above angle in his commentary, as he is little interested in the poem's literary dimensions. Instead he focuses on the relationship of Kṛṣṇa's apparently callous behavior and the previous decad in praise of Kāma. He does not find the shift from first person point of view to the plural voice jarring. Rather, he reads both as the voice of Āṇṭāḷ, except in *Nācciyār Tirumoḻi* 2 the voice is a plural one, like in the *Tiruppāvai*. The central question in *Tirumoḻi* 1 was "why would Āṇṭāḷ, who had surrendered to Viṣṇu, propitiate Kāma?" Here the question is "what could prompt the usually benevolent and gentle Viṣṇu to torment his devotees in this manner?" Piḷḷai begins by asserting that having witnessed their (her) surrender to Kāma, Viṣṇu was upset, but also saddened that his disregard for the *gopīs* had prompted them to worship another deity. Piḷḷai suggests that the *gopīs'* (Āṇṭāḷ's) prayers to Kāma were much like the errant cowherds who worshipped Indra and the Govardhana mountain (see appendix 2 for a synopsis of the relevant myth). Not wanting the girls to suffer, Kṛṣṇa decided that he wanted to protect them just as he had rescued the elephant Gajendra from the clutches of the crocodile. But the girls paid him no heed and instead continued to focus all their attention on their sandcastles. This is why, Piḷḷai explains, Kṛṣṇa began to destroy the *ciṟṟil*, resulting in a mighty battle between them that was akin to the great *Mahābhārata* war. The girls accuse Kṛṣṇa that he used the *ciṟṟil* as an excuse for something else, and their suspicions are confirmed when their verbal sparring ends in union (*saṁśleṣa*). But all union inevitably also ends in separation, and so it is for these young girls/Āṇṭāḷ.

This *Tirumoḻi* begins with the line "O Nārāyaṇa! Praised with a thousand names! /O Nara!" which is of great significance to Piḷḷai. He offers two major interpretations for the phrase Nara-Nārāyaṇa. The first is that Viṣṇu descended from heaven (Nārāyaṇa) to take the form of a man (Nara) like Rāma, in order that those embroiled in the coils of *saṁsāra* could experience him in an embodied form in this world. He goes on to say that Viṣṇu is after all the eyes of the world, the one bright as the sun. Rāma captivated everyone with his purity and loveliness, but Kṛṣṇa did so by tormenting all the women. In Piḷḷai's second explanation, Nara-Nārāyaṇa points to the importance of the *ācārya* (teacher) in guiding devotees to Viṣṇu, where Nara is the teacher and Nārāyaṇa the supreme deity. When the student questions how one may attain the feet of Viṣṇu, Piḷḷai responds that it is through the recitation of the thousand names of Viṣṇu (*nāmam āyiram*), thus emphasizing a central theme of the *Tiruppāvai*—the recitation of the names of god (*nāma saṅkīrtana*).

Nācciyār Tirumoḻi 3. The Song for the Clothes

Piḷḷai reads verses 2.8 and 2.9, the final two verses of the previous *Tirumoḻi*, as signaling Kṛṣṇa's union with the *gopī* girls (and Āṇṭāḷ), where their two bodies become one, like a pot in two pieces that is seamlessly joined when dry. But according to Piḷḷai, a union is useless if it only occurs when desired. It is appreciated only when it occurs after a lengthy separation. Piḷḷai declares that union prefigures an inevitable separation and creates a beautifully imagined scenario described below that provides the context for the series of ten verses.

The relatives of the *gopīs*, recognizing the signs of their union with Kṛṣṇa, decide that the joy of union might prove too overwhelming for the girls and intervene by separating them from Kṛṣṇa. Piḷḷai draws a parallel here to Sītā and Rāma who suffered terribly, forgoing food and water during their lengthy separation. Similarly, Kṛṣṇa and the *gopī* girls are tormented by their imposed separation. Faced with their daughters' growing emaciation, their parents consider the options and realize that to continue to keep the lovers apart would result in losing their daughters. But if they allow the union, they would lose their parental authority over their girls. Therefore they devise a plan. They dispatch all their daughters to the riverbank to observe a ritual vow to obtain a suitable husband. They correctly surmise that Kṛṣṇa would follow them, and the desired union would materialize, apparently unbeknown to the parents.

However the young girls had a different plan in mind and are adamant to resist Kṛṣṇa's seduction. They know that the clever boy would follow them, and so decide to make their way to a different pond one at a time, rather than as a group. But Piḷḷai ends this scenario by saying that one cannot escape Kṛṣṇa so easily and like the shadow that creeps ahead of the sun, he arrives at the riverbank before the *gopīs*, hides himself, and steals their clothes whilst the girls are occupied with their bath. It is only then that they spy him atop the *kuruntai* tree, and so proceed to chastise, cajole, and beg for the return of their clothes. To the inevitable question, "how could the *gopīs* be so bold as to chastise Kṛṣṇa?" Piḷḷai provides a simple answer. He says that Viṣṇu has two attributes. He protects those like the elephant Gajendra who surrender to him. But he also protects those, like the wayward Śiśupāla, who wish to do him ill. Thus when worship fails to appease him, the *gopīs* scold him.

The episode described here is included in the *Bhāgavata Purāṇa* (Book 10, Chapter 22) and is considered emblematic for the need to abandon all shame and sense of self when one approaches Kṛṣṇa. While Piḷḷai does bring up this interpretation in his commentary, it is not the central thrust of his exegesis.

3.2

The reference "our fate bind us/we cannot do *that*."(*viti iṉmaiyāl atu māṭōm*) is ambiguous. The *atu* (literally "that") is unqualified in the verse, though Periyavāccāṉ Piḷḷai categorically interprets the ambiguous *atu* as referring to sexual union (*saṁśleṣa*). While this is the most obvious interpretation, I would suggest that there are other possibilities. For instance, it could refer to the girls' refusing to come out of the water, or raising their hands above their heads. We are to imagine the voice of Kṛṣṇa as a subtext of the poem. The "that" in this verse would naturally be a response to Kṛṣṇa's interjection at the cleverness of the girls: each raising one hand while the other covers their nakedness, 3.1.

3.4

You are the king of the monkeys: The girls mock Kṛṣṇa hoping that at least this will make him forget his cruelty toward them. Āṇṭāḷ once again alludes to Kṛṣṇa's preceding *avatāra* as Rāma. In the *Rāmāyaṇa* Rāma had an army of monkeys and was their leader. The *gopīs* mention this disparagingly as Kṛṣṇa has climbed up the tree much like a monkey and refuses to return their clothes.

3.9

Kaṁsa's savage net: refers to the imprisonment of Kṛṣṇa's natural parents, Devakī and Vasudeva.

For this perversity alone have you found your way here: refers to the story of Kṛṣṇa's birth, when he was brought from Mathurā to Gokula to protect him from the wrath of Kaṁsa. Also see Tiruppāvai 25 for a reference to this particular story.

Nācciyār Tirumoḻi 4. The Song of Divination

This *Tirumoḻi* describes a game of *kūṭal*, a divination game that was popular among young girls in South India. There are several ways the game can be played. One involves circumscribing a circle while closing one's eyes—a closed circle signifies imminent union. One can also cast tiny seashells and divine the union based on the patterns in which they fall. Periyavāccāṉ Piḷḷai describes the *kūṭal* as drawing concentric circles within a larger circle, with an even number signifying union, and an odd number signaling separation. The word *kūṭal* means "to come together," but is also an old name for the city of Maturai.

The verses of the fourth *Tirumoḻi* function on two levels. Since the verses are in the first person singular, we can assume that each verse represents the wishes of one particular girl. But superimposed upon this is a picture of Āṇṭāḷ playing the *kūṭal* game desiring her exclusive union with Viṣṇu. Unlike the previous two *Tirumoḻi*, section 4 returns to the first person singular and it is easy to read Āṇṭāḷ into the poem. But the *phala śruti* (4.11) disrupts such a reading, establishing that the *kūṭal* game is an imagined situation involving the *gopī*s, and that the action of the preceding ten verses is located, like in the *Tiruppāvai*, in the mythic world of Āyarpāṭi.

The *kūṭal* itself is asked to predict the union of the girls with their beloved dark lord. The meter of the poem reflects the urgency and the eagerness of the desire for this union. Unlike detailed descriptions in the first section of the prayer to Kāmadeva and the descriptions of the construction of the *ciṟṟil*, Āṇṭāḷ does not give us any details of the *kūṭal* game. Instead, we gather the sensation of it from the rhythm and the desire that each verse of this decad explicates. She uses the *kali viruttam* meter, which consists of four lines of four metrical feet each. The same prosody is also used in *Tirumoḻis* 2, 4, 6, 7, 8, and 9.

Periyavāccāṉ Piḷḷai does not ignore the dual voices of this *Tirumoḻi*, and expertly links them to the narrative set up in the previous two *Tirumoḻi* (2 and 3), as well as to Āṇṭāḷ's own quest. In *Tirumoḻi* 3 Kṛṣṇa stole the *gopī*s' clothes, and they tried different tactics by which to ensure their return. Eventually the girls agreed to do whatever it is Kṛṣṇa wanted (the ambiguous *atu* in 3.2) and subsequently enjoyed the desired union (*saṁśleṣa*). As Piḷḷai repeatedly declares, union inescapably ends in separation and that is the state that the *gopī* girls find themselves in *Tirumoḻi* 4. Kṛṣṇa abandons them because he knows that no experience (*bhoga*) in this world is permanent. But caught in the pangs of separation, the girls who enjoyed union with Kṛṣṇa are even willing to undergo the torment of having their clothes stolen again, if it would bring Kṛṣṇa back to them. Piḷḷai suggests that it is for this reason that the girls play the game of divination.

Though Piḷḷai provides these answers to the act of divination, he poses the same question again—why does Āṇṭāḷ ask insentient things such as a *kūṭal* for aid, when she has already surrendered to Viṣṇu, and has accepted him as both the way (*upāya*) and the goal (*upeya*). The answer is the expected one. He attributes it to the terrible confusion brought on by love-sickness. Still, in 4.1 Āṇṭāḷ/*gopīs* compares her sorry fate to the *nityasūri* (divine beings), who are lucky enough to be eternally beside Viṣṇu, even without resorting to things like the *kūṭal*.

4.1

The girls' first wish is to caress the lord's feet—an act of absolute surrender and a service that Lakṣmī, consort of Viṣṇu, specifically performs. They desire to attain him and be united with him in this intimate and inseparable manner of wifely service.

Māliruñcōlai: the dark grove of Māl—Māl referring to the old Caṅkam name of Viṣṇu, meaning great god. Māliruñcōlai is the old name of the town that is today called Aḻakar Kōyil, and is approximately fifty miles from Śrīvilliputtūr.

4.3-4.10

In the next eight verses, the young Āyarpāṭi girls do not make a special request. They urge the *kūṭal* to fall together so that their beloved will simply come to them. The verses are used to sing the glories and the exploits of the god. Among the many stories alluded to are Kṛṣṇa's conquest of the serpent Kāliya, (4.4), his slaying of the elephant Kuvalayāpīḍa that Kaṁsa sends to kill him (4.5), the breaking of the *maruta* trees, which is a reference to the time that Yaśodā tied him to a mortar (4.6), the destruction of Śiśupāla, the conquering of the seven bulls in order to win the hand of Nappiṉṉai, the slaying of the stork-demon Bakāsura and finally the killing of Kaṁsa (4.7). The four verses effectively encapsulate all of Kṛṣṇa's early exploits that are detailed in the later(?) *Bhāgavata Purāṇa*. The killing of Kāliya is referred to only once more in the *Nācciyār Tirumoḻi* (12.5), while this is the sole reference of Kṛṣṇa's defeat of the seven bulls for the hand of Nappiṉṉai.

The fourth section of the *Nācciyār Tirumoḻi* is the centerpiece of a ritual performance tradition known as the *muttukkuṟi* (divination with pearls), performed by a community of hereditary performers known as Araiyars. The *muttukkuṟi* is performed at the temples in Śrīraṅgam, Śrīvilliputtūr, and Āḻvār Tirunakari during the Annual December Festival of Recitation. In Śrīraṅgam and Āḻvār Tirunakari, the divination is imagined as being performed by a generic in girl in love (*talaivi*). In Śrīvilliputtūr, where it is also performed during the festivals celebrating Āṇṭāḷ's birth (August) and her marriage to Viṣṇu (April), the heroine of the *muttukkuṟi* is Āṇṭāḷ. See the introduction (Divining with Pearls: *Nācciyār Tirumoḻi* and *Araiyar Cēvai at* Śrīvilliputtūr) for a detailed discussion of the *muttukkuṟi*.

Nācciyār Tirumoḻi 5. The Song to the Kuyil

This set of ten verses follows the sequence of ten verses on divination (*kūṭiṭu kūṭalē*) and precedes the famous "dream-wedding" section. In his introductory comments on this section, Periyavāccāṉ Piḷḷai points out that frustrated with the vacillation of the insentient (*acetana*) divinatory tool, Āṇṭāḷ decides to uses a sentient being (*cetana*) to deliver her message to Viṣṇu and thus determine her fate. He posits that she chooses the *kuyil* bird for two reasons. First, it can both hear and speak. Therefore it can take the message to the lord of Vēṅkaṭam as well as bring his message back. Second, as a bird it has the endurance to navigate treacherous paths and fly great distances.

So, in the fifth decad of the *Nācciyār Tirumoḻi* Āṇṭāḷ calls her first messenger—the little *kuyil* bird—and uses a number of rhetorical devices to convince it to indulge her wishes. She contrasts her own separation from her beloved with the blissful life of the *kuyil* and its mate and declares this disparity unfair (5.3). She bribes it with a new friendship with her pet parrot (5.5), promises to bow down before it (5.6), and finally threatens to chase it away (5.9). Periyavāccāṉ Piḷḷai imagines Āṇṭāḷ's entreaties to the *kuyil*, and her indirect arguments with Viṣṇu in several ways. In his mind, Āṇṭāḷ is neither diminished nor misguided in seeking her beloved lord, who is faultless and compassionate. According to Piḷḷai, Āṇṭāḷ is confident that Viṣṇu's compassion will ensure that he answer her summons and appear before her, his weapons blazing, accompanied by Śrī and Nīlā, if for nothing else than to prevent her from growing thin from her separation. Periyavāccāṉ Piḷḷai (as Āṇṭāḷ) asks: did not the lord rescue Gajendra when he cried out to him? Just so, he certainly will respond when the *kuyil* cries out its song of on her behalf. However, she also says that she *knows* that the god penetrates all things, that he is everywhere, including inside her. But she wishes to see his embodied form and to enjoy him physically. Piḷḷai wonders (again, as Āṇṭāḷ), how she can embrace her beloved to her chest when he resides (hides) inside her.

It is also important to note that in this decad the world of Āyarpāṭi and its *gopīs* has been left behind and this begins the motif of *tūtu/sandeśa* (messenger) poems. In section 8 of the *Nācciyār Tirumoḻi*, Āṇṭāḷ sends the cloud as her messenger and in the later sections her human companions are bid to carry her woes to Viṣṇu. However, in a twist to this motif in *Nācciyār Tirumoḻi* 12 Āṇṭāḷ insists on being taken to the *places* that the lord resides—Dvārakā, Vṛndāvana, Vēṅkaṭam—arguing that if the lord remains unresponsive despite her pleas and messages, she will go to him, embodying the message of unrequited love herself. Each of these messenger poems is separated by the intervention of other significant themes and motifs—conches and conch bangles being one of the most prominent. So when the motif of message and the messenger is evoked again after such narrative gap, it literally replicates the lapsed time and space between messages, as well as elongates the time and space of Āṇṭāḷ's separation itself.

The fifth decad is significant for several reasons and can be understood as one of many narrative turning points in the *Nācciyār Tirumoḻi*. It introduces a new voice (perhaps Āṇṭāḷ's unmediated voice?) after the intervening sections describing the young *gopīs* of Āyarpāṭi. The effect of such a return starkly exaggerates the heroine's despair. In contrast to the Āyarpāṭi girls, she is neither the beguiled innocent of the "sandcastle" song (*Nācciyār Tirumoḻi* 2) nor the recalcitrant women of the song of the stolen clothes (*Nācciyār Tirumoḻi* 3). She has exceeded the eager hope of the *kūṭal* (*Nācciyār Tirumoḻi* 4) and represents herself as a woman who is in the full throes of unrequited love.

The *kuyil* section also adapts several motifs common to Tamiḻ Caṅkam poetry to mark the extent of her separation from her beloved. This in itself is not unusual, as the *Nācciyār Tirumoḻi* is replete with delicate allusions to Caṅkam poetry. However, particular symbols that become important in the rest of the *Nācciyār Tirumoḻi* are introduced here, the two most immediate being the bird and the conch/conch bangles. In this section, there are two kinds of birds—the *kuyil* (and its mate) and Āṇṭāḷ's pet parrot. The parrot recurs in several places in the poem, most significantly in *Nācciyār Tirumoḻi* (12.9) where it tortures her by repeating "Govinda! Govinda!" Birds and parrots are infamous in both Sanskrit and Tamiḻ poetry for tormenting or embarrassing the heroine in various ways, especially by speaking of lovemaking or of the hero's name at inopportune moments. In verse 5.8, she hints that a secret has passed between her and her beloved. Yet it is left to conjecture what that secret might be. The verse (5.8) leads us to believe that the *kuyil*, having been witness to the intimacy shared by Āṇṭāḷ and her dark lord, has been chosen as her messenger. The bird therefore is invested with the authority to call the beautiful lord to her. When he arrives, Āṇṭāḷ promises to allow the bird to remain as a witness to what she proposes to do to the beloved because of the suffering she has been forced to endure. The wording of this line is also ambiguous and can be interpreted as "what I will do with him" or "to him." Periyavāccāṉ Piḷḷai does not retain this ambiguity but says that what Āṇṭāḷ proposes is to tempt the lord and then to deny him, in retaliation for his delay. The analogy that he offers is that it is akin to putting food before a starving person, only to remove it without warning.

Like the conch (discussed at length in the introduction), the parrot is polyvalent. It signifies the sweetness of speech as well as the silly prattle of girls. Later in *Tirumoḻi* 5, Āṇṭāḷ describes the beloved as "lustrous as the green-hued parrot" (5.9), and while Āṇṭāḷ does not make mention of it, the parrot is the vehicle (*vāhana*) of Kāmadeva. Of course, no discussion of parrots and Āṇṭāḷ would be complete without mentioning that one of her iconographic markers is a parrot, held either in her right or left hand. In her temple of Śrīvilliputtūr, a family of hereditary flower sellers makes a parrot of tender leaves and fresh flowers to be offered to Āṇṭāḷ every morning.

5.3

Mātali: Indra's charioteer. He guided Rāma's chariot during his epic battle against Rāvaṇa.

5.5

The reference to the parrot is significant because Āṇṭāḷ is depicted in iconography and painting with a parrot perched on her left or right hand.

Nācciyār Tirumoḻi 6. The Song of the Wedding Dream

This decad is the most popular and well-known section of the *Nācciyār Tirumoḻi*. It describes Āṇṭāḷ's dream of her wedding to Viṣṇu and comprehensively details every rite associated with the wedding. This decad is sung in contemporary Brahmin Śrīvaiṣṇava weddings, and for that day, the bride and groom are considered embodiments of Āṇṭāḷ and Viṣṇu. The sixth *Tirumoḻi* enacts all the marriage rites, beginning with the entry of the groom to the town of the wedding and ending with their tour around the city with on elephants. Missing from the rituals described is the tying of the *tāli* or sacred thread around the bride's neck, which is the central ritual event in contemporary South Indian Hindu marriages.

Periyavāccāṉ Piḷḷai locates the sixth *Tirumoḻi* within the cycle of separation and union that he imposes on the first quarter of the poem. He begins by stating that in the previous *Tirumoḻi*, Āṇṭāḷ addressed the lovely *kuyil* bird and asked it to bring Kṛṣṇa to her. But because Kṛṣṇa has yet to oblige her request, she assumes that the bird failed to do as she instructed. However, according to Piḷḷai, Viṣṇu did hear her plea, but thought that she should suffer the pangs of separation for a while longer, simply because such a desire should not be realized immediately. Piḷḷai supports his claim by alluding to the opening verse of Nammāḻvār's *Tiruvāymoḻi* (1.1.1), where Nammāḻvār asks his heart to reside at the feet of the lord who dispels doubt. Nammāḻvār's verse is as follows:

> Who is he possessing the highest good?
> Who is he, who slashes ignorance,
>   by graciously bestowing wisdom and love?
> Who is he, the commander of the never-tiring immortals?
> O my mind!
>   Worship his radiant feet
>   that destroy all sorrow,
> and rise.
>   (Trans. John Carman and Vasudha Narayanan, p. 195)

Piḷḷai goes on to say that the journey from *ajñāna* (ignorance) to union with Viṣṇu requires *jñāna bhakti*, which in itself must go through the stages of *para bhakti* (great devotion) characterized by a mental image of deity, *para jñāna* (discerning knowledge), where one has intermittent but complete vision of deity, and *parama bhakti* (supreme/exclusive devotion), where the devotee achieves complete union with the divine. To drive home his position, he offers the analogy of the dyeing process, in which a garment is not dyed all at once, but only bit by bit. Just so, the journey to Viṣṇu unfolds slowly and the experience must soak into the heart of the devotee. Despite taking this position, Piḷḷai also acknowledges that there is a difference in the case of Āṇṭāḷ, because she is the emanation of Bhū Devī and was born with *parama bhakti* (supreme devotion), unlike the other *āḻvār*, who had to wait their entire lives to reach that stage. Piḷḷai is quick to point out that even Sītā, who is Śrī herself, had to be separated from Rāma for a while, and so such a separation should be no different for Āṇṭāḷ.

Having made this point, Piḷḷai immediately states that Āṇṭāḷ *is* different from Sītā, and that she is unable to bear the separation and the wait for reunion. Her suffering was so great that Viṣṇu realized that she would be incapable of withstanding the experience, and so resolved to reveal himself to Āṇṭāḷ in a dream. In this regard, Āṇṭāḷ is even greater than Sītā, who desperately wanted to be united with her beloved Rāma at least in a dream and was not blessed with that experience. If one were to ask why there is such a differentiation, Piḷḷai answers that Āṇṭāḷ was utterly alone, while Sītā at least had the company of demonesses like Trijāṭā and others.

6.3

Antarī : Durgā, who is considered to be Viṣṇu's sister. The sister usually drapes the bridal garment around the bride and ushers her to the wedding canopy.

6.8

ammi: a flat black solid pockmarked grinding stone upon which the groom places the bride's foot. This is regarded as the culmination of the Tamiḻ marriage ceremony.

6.9

Āṇṭāḷ makes mention of her brothers, but her hagiography does not attribute any other filial relations to her, aside from her father Viṣṇucittaṉ. Although he is mentioned in the *phala śruti* verses, Viṣṇucittaṉ does not make an appearance in her elaborately imagined wedding scene. At the conclusion of this particular decad (6.11), Āṇṭāḷ indicates that the dream is hers and not an imagined poetic reality.

Nācciyār Tirumoḻi 7. The Song to the White Conch

The topic of this decad—the praise of Viṣṇu's conch—is unique in *āḻvār* literature. Although there are instances in *āḻvār* verses in praise of Viṣṇu's various accoutrements, this is the only series of songs devoted entirely to the conch. In the *Nācciyār Tirumoḻi*, the conch, both as Viṣṇu's attribute and as Āṇṭāḷ's ornament, is constantly evoked as a symbol of union (the conch) and separation (her bangles). See the section on Conches and Conch Bangles in the introduction for a detailed discussion of Āṇṭāḷ's use of the conch as a polyvalent symbol.

Periyavāccāṉ Piḷḷai builds his commentary by understanding Viṣṇu's conch as an intermediary (*puruṣakāra*), a position it achieves because of its special closeness to him. In the previous decad, Āṇṭāḷ dreamed that she married her beloved, and now is imagined to awaken and find the dream to be false. Thus, she boldly addresses the conch: "Are they fragrant as camphor? Are they fragrant as the lotus?/Or do those coral red lips taste sweet?" (7.1). If one wonders at the audacity of Āṇṭāḷ's demand, Piḷḷai is quick to assure his audience that it is perfectly legitimate, for she had at least dreamed that she had married Viṣṇu. Nevertheless, a dream is still a dream and like lightning in the sky, such an experience cannot be permanent.

But the intimacy that the conch shares with Viṣṇu is insufficient to explain why Āṇṭāḷ singles out the conch for such extravagant praise, when the other divine beings (*nityasūri*), Garuḍa, and Viśvaksena also surround Viṣṇu at all times. Piḷḷai provides several responses to this imagined query from his audience, which are as follows. First, the heroine once enjoyed the sweetness of Viṣṇu's lips just as the Pāñcajanya (Viṣṇu's conch) does always. Next, when a heroine (*nāyikā*) and the king are alone in bedchamber they are surrounded by certain indispensable figures. Similarly, the Pāñcajanya is inseparable from Viṣṇu. Unlike Āṇṭāḷ whose union is always intermittent, the conch's relationship is inseparable and unbreakable. If one says that the solar disc (*cakra*) is also essential to Viṣṇu, one must remember that it actually is separated from him when he dispenses it on some important mission. The conch, on the other hand, never leaves Viṣṇu's side. Moreover, when Viṣṇu needs the conch, he does not send it away, like he does his discus; instead he brings it closer, by placing it on his lips! What greater place of intimacy could there be?

7.1

Conch from the deep sea: this refers to the story of the Pāñcajanya, Viṣṇu's conch. The demon Pañcācana turned himself into a conch and hid in the deep sea. Kṛṣṇa found him there, killed him, and claimed the conch as his own. It is therefore known as Pāñcajanya—that which is born from Pañcācana.

7.2

Your resonance stirs fear: the conch born of Pañcācana is used by Viṣṇu to warn other demons from pursuing their wicked deeds.

7.4

Valampuri: a proper name of Viṣṇu's conch. A conch that has spirals turning toward the right, unlike most conches that spiral to the left.

Nācciyār Tirumoḻi 8. The Song to the Dark Rain Clouds

The *Tirumoḻi* continues the messenger theme introduced in *Tirumoḻi* 5: The Song to the *Kuyil*. Messenger poems are a common genre of early Indic love poetry, possibly made most famous by Kālidāsa's (c. 4th cent. C.E.) *Meghadūta*. Here Āṇṭāḷ recruits the dark rain clouds as messengers to the lord of Vēṅkaṭam to inform him of her terrible plight of her loneliness and suffering.

Periyavāccāṉ Piḷḷai establishes the narrative context for this decad by describing Āṇṭāḷ's appeal to the conch as a failed mission. He goes on to elaborate the idea, arguing that the conch did not deign to answer Āṇṭāḷ entreaties, and Viṣṇu's continued absence is evidence of its apathy. He suggests that the dark rain clouds resembling Āṇṭāḷ's beloved have arrived, but Viṣṇu has not. In *Tiruppāvai* 4 Āṇṭāḷ draws a similar comparison, playing on the word *kaṇṇa*, to refer to both Kṛṣṇa and the clouds. In that situation, the clouds are harbingers of abundance and prosperity, but here they are the bearers of loss.

In Indic literature, the season of rains is always the time for union and an absent hero invariably promises to return before the coming of the monsoons. Piḷḷai further contextualizes Āṇṭāḷ's song to the dark rain clouds by implying that Viṣṇu had assured her that he would return before the first rains fell. So when Āṇṭāḷ sees the dark rain clouds so close in hue to her beloved, she is confused and thinks that Viṣṇu has come to her as promised. But she soon realizes that it is not so, although she takes some small comfort that they thunder like his conch—another comparison that she draws in *Tiruppāvai* 4.

Piḷḷai makes the further observation that the word *megha* (cloud) also refers to a class of servants, *mēkar* (Tamiḻ), who precede a king in procession. Āṇṭāḷ sees the clouds and mistakenly assumes that they had appeared to announce the arrival of her beloved. Here Piḷḷai offers a comparison from the *Rāmāyaṇa*, that Āṇṭāḷ erroneously thinks that like Rāma who followed the abducted Sītā to Laṅka, he would follow the clouds in order to hurry to her. It does not take Āṇṭāḷ long to realize that she is wrong, and overcome by her great sorrow, she weeps. Once again turning to his cherished *Rāmāyaṇa*, Piḷḷai draws a parallel between Āṇṭāḷ's lonely state in this *Tirumoḻi* and Sītā's imprisonment in Laṅka. He observes that when Hanumān witnessed Sītā crying—her tears were like dewdrops on a fresh lotus petal—he was there to assuage her fears and worries. Āṇṭāḷ, unfortunately, has no one to turn to, except these insentient beings (the clouds). The implication, then, is that in some ways Āṇṭāḷ's suffering is greater, and her need for Viṣṇu's grace more urgent.

In seeking to explain Āṇṭāḷ's insistent queries to the insentient clouds, Piḷḷai says that she thinks that they will be amenable to her plight, and so she interrogates them about Viṣṇu's whereabouts, but they too do not respond. She insists then that since they arise from the same place (Vēṅkaṭam) as her beloved, they must have a special connection with him that can aid her cause. To Piḷḷai, Āṇṭāḷ is like Sītā who sent Hanumān as her messenger to Rāma. Āṇṭāḷ dispatches the clouds, convincing herself that they are fully sentient and embodied Although Piḷḷai does not draw the parallel, one cannot help but recall the lover in Kālidāsa's *Meghadūta*, who distraught and alone, is unable to distinguish between sentient and insentient things, Āṇṭāḷ thus entreats the clouds without realizing that they can do nothing in return.

In considering the role of messengers in the *Rāmāyaṇa*, Piḷḷai makes an interesting observation and nicely draws a comparison to Āṇṭāḷ's situation. Sītā sent just Hanumān as her messenger, but Āṇṭāḷ has to send several clouds to Viṣṇu. Rāma, on the other hand, sent thousands of monkeys to search for Sītā, and only one—Hanumān—was fortunate enough to see her. The thousands of clouds moving toward Vēṅkaṭam suffer no such lack, as they will all have the opportunity to gaze upon Viṣṇu's face.

The Song to the Dark Rain Clouds is one of the most sexually explicit decads in the *Nācciyār Tirumoḻi*. In these ten verses, Āṇṭāḷ asks to be touched, caressed, and entered. Piḷḷai is not so much uncomfortable with such frank expression of sexual yearning, as much as he is concerned for how it reflects on Āṇṭāḷ. That is to say, he does not shy away from the fact that Āṇṭāḷ is speaking of a real physical desire. However, he feels that such explicit yearning could easily be misconstrued as a banal, mortal kind of lust. He asserts that people like Āṇṭāḷ, who are steeped in *bhakti yoga* (the discipline of devotion) and who regard Viṣṇu as their lover, blossom when united with him and fade when disunited. They choose *śṛṅgāra* (desire/love) to express their longing. He concludes by saying that like water finds its own level, it is only natural for a woman to desire a man in this manner.

8.1

The verse alludes to *Kuṟuntokai* 325: the heroine's tears gather in the space between her breasts where she imagines a heron feeding on fish.

When he said
"I'll go, I'll go,"
I mistook it
for all his former
mock departures
and I said "Fine,

leave my side
and go away forever."

O Mother
our master who supports us—
where is he now
I wonder?

The place between my breasts
has filled up with tears,
has become a deep pond
where a black-legged
white heron feeds.[3]

Kuṟuntokai 325

Even though Periyavāccāṉ Piḷḷai does not allude to, or quote, the above Caṅkam poem, he is obviously well aware of the Caṅkam poetics of landscape. He makes the observation that her longing for the beloved transformed Āṇṭāḷ's body into Tiruvēṅkaṭam, replete with mountains (breasts) and waterfalls (her tears).

8.9

The clouds are described here as "war elephants" and the question posed in 8.1—"Has he sent word for me?"—is posed once again. We should imagine the events that have occurred in the interim, at least in Āṇṭāḷ's consciousness. The clouds that have gone as messengers have rained in torrents and scattered the flowers and created havoc in Vēṅkaṭam—they have acted as her emissaries and placed her plea before him and yet, the beloved has not responded. He remains silent, and Āṇṭāḷ's angered response is that this warrior-king, who has taken possession of her, does not protect her as a good king should (she uses the word refuge [*gati*] here) and instead slays her. She implies that in ignoring her pleas he has failed in his duty as both beloved and protector. So she ends saying, "The world will say: 'heedless that he was her only refuge'/he killed this young girl.'/ What honor is there in this?"

Nācciyār Tirumoḻi 9. The Song in the Groves of Tirumāliruñcōlai

In the previous decad, Āṇṭāḷ asked the clouds to take her message of love to the lord of Vēṅkaṭam. According to Piḷḷai, Āṇṭāḷ had begun to wonder if she would survive until Viṣṇu came for her, and in this regard is like Sītā who told Hanumān that she did not know how long she would be able to sustain her life. Piḷḷai repeats the point he made in the previous decad, that while Sītā had an able messenger like Hanumān. Āṇṭāḷ has no one. The useless clouds failed to leave for Vēṅkaṭam, and instead just rained on the spot. So, all the flowers begin to bloom and they seem to Āṇṭāḷ as beautiful as the body of her beloved lord.

Piḷḷai muses that this *Tirumoḻi* reflects how difficult it has become for Āṇṭāḷ to survive, especially surrounded by this environment of abundance, fertility, and beauty. Āṇṭāḷ sees her Viṣṇu's face everywhere, and everything that surrounds her reminds her of some aspect of his beauty.

Āṇṭāḷ situates herself aptly in a grove (and that too, the Tirumāliruñcōlai, lit. the dark grove of Māl), presumably in springtime when the ladybirds are scattered about the grass after the rains and the trees burst with blossoms. The spring and the burgeoning of life it brings are in contrast to Āṇṭāḷ's slow withering away. It is apt to recall here that in 8.8 she compares herself to a dried-up leaf.

Periyavāccāṉ Piḷḷai suggests that *Tirumoḻi* 8 and *Tirumoḻi* 9 are read together. He points out the similarity of both these decads to Nammāḻvār's *Tiruvāymoḻi* 9.5. In this latter poem, Nammāḻvār in his female persona upbraids the creatures that abide in a grove for tormenting him/her. In it, he/she scolds several kinds of birds for refusing to call to her beloved, and for happily sporting with their mates. And she chastises the rain clouds for assuming the form of her beloved.

9.1

kastūri: deer musk.

9.3

karuvai: Babul tree, *Acacia arabica.*

kāyā: a hardy tree that produces purple flowers, *Memecylon malabarcium.*
He entered my home: this is the only explicit reference in the *Nācciyār Tirumoḻi* to Viṣṇu entering Āṇṭāḷ's home, although there are several verses that describe his willful entry into her body. In *Tirumoḻi* 2.9 Kṛṣṇa is described as entering the courtyard to embrace the *gopī* girls.

9.6-9.7

Commentaries attached to this verse present an apocryphal narrative involving Rāmānuja, one of the most important teachers of the Śrīvaiṣṇavas. He is said to have arrived in Śrīvilliputtūr to offer worship to Āṇṭāḷ. But before reaching his final destination, he stopped at the Tirumāliruñcōlai temple of Sundararāja Perumāḷ to fulfill Āṇṭāḷ's promise of a hundred pots brimming with sweet rice. After all, Viṣṇu had eventually claimed her as his own. When Rāmānuja arrived in Śrīvilliputtūr and entered the sanctum of the temple, Āṇṭāḷ is said to have emerged out of the main icon in the *garbha gṛha* and come running toward Rāmānuja, addressing him as "Aṇṇā"—brother. From that day on, to honor the relationship Āṇṭāḷ acknowledged, Rāmānuja was known as Kōyil Aṇṇaṉ (lit. Brother of the Temple). The temple in Śrīvilliputtūr marks the incident by placing the image of Rāmānuja beside Āṇṭāḷ on the day after the conclusion of the Annual December Festival.

9.9

In this verse, Āṇṭāḷ compares herself to a garland of blooming *koṉṟai* flowers. Piḷḷai points out that the significance of the comparison is that *koṉṟai* flowers are sacred to Śiva, because he wears them entwined in his hair. The flowers are therefore of little use in a garden of Viṣṇu. The implication then is that Āṇṭāḷ feels just as useless and wasted as a garland of cassia flowers.

koṉṟai: Golden Shower Tree, *Cassia fistula*.

Nācciyār Tirumoḻi 10. The Song of Lament

In the previous two *Tirumoḻis*, Āṇṭāḷ addressed the clouds, the bees, and flowers in the hope that they would respond to her plea, and act as her messengers. Moreover, she hoped that her desire for union would eventually be realized and so she desperately held on to her waning life. But Piḷḷai observes the time for union, the rainy season, has come and gone, and Āṇṭāḷ's beloved has yet to reveal himself to her. Under these circumstances, he surmises that it would be well-nigh impossible for Āṇṭāḷ to survive much longer.

Periyavāccāṉ Piḷḷai says that Āṇṭāḷ sees only two paths that can assure her survival. One path is the one adopted by Vibhīṣaṇa, who surrendered to Rāma as a friend and in turn Rāma promised never to let him go. Piḷḷai (as Āṇṭāḷ) asks the rhetorical question: did he not do the same for Draupadī, who took him as her sole refuge? Did he not say in the *Rāmāyaṇa* that he would always be beholden to those who have surrendered to him, and that he would never let go of such a devotee? Piḷḷai says that despite all the evidence to the contrary, Āṇṭāḷ managed to survive by simply contemplating these words of assurance that Viṣṇu had given to his devotees in the past, and this is the second path, and the one Āṇṭāḷ chooses.

If one were to ask why Viṣṇu, whose nature is infinite compassion, would torment a devotee such as Āṇṭāḷ, Piḷḷai answers that Viṣṇu is also possessed of the quality of independence (*svātantriya*) and thus one cannot necessarily hold him to his words and promises. So if this is the case, what hope does Āṇṭāḷ have? How will she survive? Piḷḷai finds the answer in the final verse of this decad (10.10), where Āṇṭāḷ alludes to the close relationship between Viṣṇu and Viṣṇucittaṉ (Periyāḻvār). Thus, even if Viṣṇu's word to her should falter, his relationship with his great devotee Viṣṇucittaṉ would ensure that her desire achieves fruition. To illustrate this point, Piḷḷai reminds his audience of the time that Rāma blessed even his enemy Rāvaṇa on account of his close relationship to Vibhīṣaṇa. So too will Viṣṇu's relationship with her father eventually rescue Āṇṭāḷ from the pit of despair.

10.1

kāntal: castor-oil plant. It has red flowers. *Ricinus communis.*

10.3

kovvai: scarlet gourd, *Coccinia indica.*

10.8

Pour down like hot melted wax: this refers to a procedure of bronze casting called *vārppaṭam*, where a wax image is enclosed in clay and fired in a kiln to make a mold into which molten metal is poured to yield the image. Here the rain clouds featured in *Tirumoḻi* 8 are implored to rain down as a demonstration of the lord as to how to mold him to her. She visualizes the clouds as dark clay bearing hot wax within them; she sees the dark lord as clay and she as the wax that will melt when enclosed in the lord. Periyavāccāṉ Piḷḷai is aware of the origin of the analogy, and refers to in his commentary to this verse.

10.10

This decad does not have the traditional *phala śruti* (see *Tiruppāvai* 30 and 1.1 for a discussion on the *phala śruti*). Instead Viṣṇucittaṉ, also in a position of intimacy with the lord, is entrusted with the duty of making Viṣṇu reveal himself. Also, the verse speaks in the personal plural—suggesting that Viṣṇu will be prevailed upon to reveal himself to all and not just Āṇṭāḷ.

Nācciyār Tirumoḻi 11. The Song for the Conch Bangles

In *Nācciyār Tirumoḻi* 7, Āṇṭāḷ addressed Viṣṇu's conch and asked it to speak to Viṣṇu on her behalf. She lauded it for its special intimacy and its close relationship with her beloved. In his interpretation of that *Tirumoḻi*, Piḷḷai suggests that the conch acts as an intermediary (*puruṣakāra*). In this *Tirumoḻi* Āṇṭāḷ focuses on her conch bangles and draws a parallel between her bangles and Viṣṇu's conch.

Piḷḷai elaborates on this theme, and the parallel between Āṇṭāḷ's bangles of conch and Viṣṇu's conch, in the latter sections of his commentary to *Tirumoḻi* 11. However, his most immediate concern is to explain how Viṣṇu could appear to violate his word to his devotee Viṣṇucittaṉ, and by extension Āṇṭāḷ. In the previous decad, Āṇṭāḷ held on to her life on the basis of verses 10.4 and 10.10, in which she speaks of the unshakable bond between Viṣṇucittaṉ and Viṣṇu, and believes that the latter's promise to protect his devotees would apply to her as well. According to Piḷḷai, Āṇṭāḷ was convinced that because she was Periyāḻvār's (Viṣṇucittaṉ's) daughter, his relationship with his lord could not fail her. Yet the evidence is to the contrary, as Viṣṇu continues to remain absent. Piḷḷai compares Āṇṭāḷ to Bhīṣma, the great hero of the *Mahābhārata*, who lay on a bed of arrows through the duration of the great *Mahābhārata* war. Just so, to Āṇṭāḷ everything is a torment and neither friends nor relatives can comprehend the cause of her suffering. Piḷḷai pictures Āṇṭāḷ's concerned relatives gathered around, questioning her. At last she says that "he has stolen my bangles." But he does not choose to rescue her like he did Sītā—forgoing food and sleep, no less—or Rukmiṇī, or Bhū Devī. In Piḷḷai's fertile imagination, Āṇṭāḷ laments, "Why does he not protect me?" and wonders if it is because she does not love him enough or because he loves her less. Or perhaps it is because he is incapable of protection, or that she appeared not to need rescue! Finally, Piḷḷai imagines Āṇṭāḷ angrily insisting that Viṣṇu declaring himself independent (*svātantriya*) is an insufficient excuse for his indifference. In this way, Piḷḷai envisions Āṇṭāḷ's musings on the fairness of Viṣṇu's behavior. In *Tirumoḻi* 7 she asked for but one conch, and in response Viṣṇu has stolen all of hers. Piḷḷai interjects here an imagined dialogue, where when someone asked Āṇṭāḷ, "why did you desire his conch, which is a weapon?" she replied, "I did not know it was so. To me it appeared as a beautiful ornament."

The bangle has long been used in Indic literature to signal a woman's loss and separation. Periyavāccāṉ Piḷḷai elaborates on this idea and draws attention to the fact that Āṇṭāḷ describes her female companions as *ēntiḻaiyīr*—richly adorned women. She contrasts herself to the women decked out in their finery, implying that they are fortunate to be united with their lovers. She herself is unadorned to signify her abandoned and lonely state.

The entire decad is in praise of the lord of Śrīraṅgam. Piḷḷai unpacks the significance of Śrīraṅgam, which by his time is a ritual and theological center for the Śrīvaiṣṇava community. Piḷḷai says that it is unbecoming of the lord of Śrīraṅgam to make women suffer (even if it is his nature), because it is the place that virtuous people come to live. Finally, it is Vaikuṇṭha on earth (*bhūloka vaikuṇṭha*), and those who live there are fortunate to enjoy Viṣṇu eternally.

11.2

Loosened my already loose bangles: Āṇṭāḷ puns on the word *kaḻal* and uses it to mean both "to lose" as well as "loosened." *Kaḻal* also refers to a warrior's victory anklets. In this latter sense (and this is the meaning that Piḷḷai offers as his gloss), Āṇṭāḷ says that Viṣṇu has taken her loose lost bangles and turned them into his victory-anklets.

11.4-11.6

In 11.5, Āṇṭāḷ ascribes the adjective *pollā* to Viṣṇu, a word that means deceptive, wicked, evil, vicious. However, Periyavāccāṉ Piḷḷai, not liking such negative attributes, assigns the word to Viṣṇu in general, and in his *avatāra* as Vamana in particular, and suggests two implied meanings. He asks how it is that Āṇṭāḷ can refer to Viṣṇu as deceptive and offers that in this case it is to be taken as a *dṛṣṭi parikāram*—a willful blemish on the lord to mask his astounding beauty and to protect him from any ill influence. The second meaning he offers is not so much interpretation as a creative solution, suggesting that that in this instance alone, the word *pollā* ought to be taken to connote beautiful.

11.10

This *Tirumoḻi* does not have a *phala śruti* verse. Instead, Viṣṇucittaṉ is once again urged to intercede on Āṇṭāḷ's behalf. Piḷḷai points out that this final verse alludes to *Bhagavad Gītā* 2.17, where Kṛṣṇa tells Arjuna that he will accept anyone who comes to him in steadfast devotion.

Nācciyār Tirumoḻi 12. The Song of Sacred Places

In the verses that follow, Āṇṭāḷ maps out Kṛṣṇa's life through a landscape of his escapades. She begins with Mathurā and ends in Dvārakā, and within this context, alludes to various other myths that highlight her anxiety at her prolonged separation. The verses are structured as a conversation between Āṇṭāḷ and her "mothers." The conversation fluctuates between trying to calm the fears of these mothers (12.5) and pushing them away because they do not understand her love, or her disease. Once again, this Song marks a turning point—so far, Āṇṭāḷ has passively waited for the lord to come to her, having sent various messengers with her messages of love. In the previous *Tirumoḻi*, she had accepted that the bond between Viṣṇucittaṉ and Viṣṇu would ensure that her beloved would come for her. But in this *Tirumoḻi*, Piḷḷai says that she once again returns to a direct address, claiming that Viṣṇu's essential quality of independence (*svātantriya*) gives him no choice *but* to protect those who have taken refuge under him.

In this *Tirumoḻi*, Āṇṭāḷ takes a much more active role, imploring her dear mothers to take her to the places sacred to Kṛṣṇa and there by to unite her with him. She alone understands that this is the only cure for the disease that consumes her, while her mothers continue to remain ignorant. Here Piḷḷai compares Āṇṭāḷ's disease of separation to that experienced by Bharata in the *Rāmāyaṇa*. When Bharata heard of Rama's exile, he fell into a faint and suffered terribly. However no one else, including Rama's mother Kausalyā, could discern the reason for his illness, and assumed that it was simply an ordinary affliction.

Āṇṭāḷ begins 12.1 in Mathurā, the place of Kṛṣṇa's birth. The next verse (12.2) situates Kṛṣṇa in Āyarpāṭi, while. 12.3 occurs in the actual home of Nandagopāla. The next two verses, 12.4 and 12.5, refer to sites of Kṛṣṇa's play and his conquests on the banks of the river Yamunā. Verses 12.6-12.8 refer to stories associated with Kṛṣṇa and 12.9 ends in Dvārakā. In a sense, these verses encapsulate Kṛṣṇa's early childhood life, and conclude with his reign as a great and noble king.

According to Piḷḷai, Āṇṭāḷ is impatient that all of her efforts have yielded no results. Although she is is ready for him, Viṣṇu has yet to come for her. Therefore, she resolves that it is time for *her* to go to him. But her great suffering has robbed her of all her strength, and Āṇṭāḷ cannot make the long, arduous journey to his beloved sacred places. It is for this reason that Piḷḷai opines that she begs her mothers to take her to these places so she can see him in his embodied form. But these mothers ask her to be patient. To this, Piḷḷai imagines Āṇṭāḷ replying "No, you do not understand my pain. Was it not Yaśodā's responsibility to raise him properly?" She argues that Kṛṣṇa's callousness is on account of Yaśodā and Nandagopa's lax rearing. Her plight is therefore their responsibility and she demands to be taken and left at their doorstep.

It is unclear who the mothers in the poem are. Piḷḷai is content to see them as well-meaning but misguided relatives, who fail to grasp the true nature of Āṇṭāḷ's illness. Caṅkam poems feature different kinds of mothers (for instance, a natural mother and a foster mother), who are often cast in a similar role. Very often in these Caṅkam poems, the mother will mistake her daughter's illness for possession by the god, and summon an exorcist (*vēlaṉ*) to cure her daughter. In *bhakti* poems of course, the illness *is* both love-sickness *and* possession by the god.

12.1

The language used in this verse is similar to that used in *Tiruppāvai* 25, which also describes Kṛṣṇa's midnight journey from Mathurā to Āyarpāṭi.

12.6

Bhaktilocana: refers to a myth where Kṛṣṇa, tired and hungry with his friends, asked for food at a Brahmins' sacrifice. They were refused food but upon requesting the Brahmins' wives, were fed amply.

12.7

Take me to Bāṇḍīram: this refers to the episode of Balarāma's defeat of the demon Pralamba, who took the guise of a cowherd and joined in on the games of Kṛṣṇa, Balarāma, and their friends. Kṛṣṇa recognized him for who he was, and suggested the game of a member of the losing team carrying a member of the victor's on their shoulders. Pralamba had to carry Balarāma on his shoulders. Balarāma grew heavier and heavier, at which point the demon assumed his true identity. Balarāma then smote him, and the demon fell dead.

Nācciyār Tirumoḻi 13. The Song of Desire

In the previous *Tirumoḻi*, Āṇṭāḷ asked to be taken to all of the places associated with, and favored by, Kṛṣṇa—from Mathurā of the North to Dvārakā. Periyavāccāṉ Piḷḷai provides the following context for this very important *Tirumoḻi*. The relatives (her mothers) witness Āṇṭāḷ's plight and consider their options. It is clear to them that Āṇṭāḷ does not possess the strength to walk and is incapable of making the journey on her own. Piḷḷai envisions them discussing their various options—perhaps they would have to build a comfortable bed and carry Āṇṭāḷ to these various destinations. But even if they were able to do so, would her life last that that long? Would she have the strength to survive this long journey? So they hesitate to oblige her requests. To their indecisiveness, Piḷḷai imagines Āṇṭāḷ replying: "Then at least bring things associated with him to me and help me sustain this life." In this manner, Āṇṭāḷ requests them to help her foster a relationship with Viṣṇu.

The culmination of Āṇṭāḷ's misery and fury is reached in 13.8, when she threatens to rip out her breasts and fling them at Viṣṇu's chest. It is a moment clearly reminiscent of the heroine Kaṇṇaki's pivotal and furious action at the conclusion of the Tamiḻ epic poem, *Cilappatikāram*. In that poem, Kaṇṇaki, angry at the king of Maturai for unjustly executing her husband Kōvalaṉ, enacts her revenge on the city by tearing out her breast, flinging it into the city, and consigning it to flames. In his commentary to this verse, Periyavāccāṉ Piḷḷai makes no mention of the *Cilappatikāram* or to this episode. While it is likely that the Jain subtext of the poem made it irrelevant to his commentary, it must also be noted that rarely does Piḷḷai venture a literary analysis of the *Nācciyār Tirumoḻi*. Even where allusions to antecedent literary forms are evident, he sidesteps the issue. He is little interested in the aesthetic and literary influences inherent in the poem. His take on this crucial episode is nonetheless interesting. He says that breasts are the site of *parama bhogyam* and *bhakti* (great intoxication and devotion). Āṇṭāḷ threatens to rip out her breasts so that Viṣṇu can experience her suffering as well. Furthermore, he notes that Āṇṭāḷ specifies that her intention is to throw them at his chest and not just on the ground and provides the explanation that in her mind, relief from her anguish can come only with his embrace. Therefore, according to Piḷḷai, Āṇṭāḷ seems to say, "at least let my breasts enjoy the embrace of his chest as they are useless to me. This way they will prove useful to assuage my sorrow."

Nācciyār Tirumoḻi 14. The Song of Questions and Answers

The dialogic format of the concluding decad marks it as unique in the *Nācciyār Tirumoḻi*. The prosody is light and folksy, and the conversation occurs between the two prominent personae evident in the poem—the questioner (identified with Āṇṭāḷ) is represented by the first person singular and her interlocutors provide the answer in a first person plural. Āṇṭāḷ adopts a question-and-answer format for what we regard as the last decad of the poem.

In his comments on this *Tirumoḻi*, Periyavāccāṉ Piḷḷai recapitulates the journey that has finally brought Āṇṭāḷ to this point. Āṇṭāḷ's quest began in the *Tiruppāvai*, where she declared that Nārāyaṇa alone could give her/them the *paṟai* drum. Eventually, she abandoned the drum in favor of eternal service to him. Clearly that desire was not fulfilled, and in the previous *Tirumoḻi* we witness her suffering on account of her unrequited love. Piḷḷai observes that the *Nācciyār Tirumoḻi* documents Āṇṭāḷ's ripening *bhakti*, and here in this final *Tirumoḻi* it has matured into *parama bhakti* (exclusive, supreme devotion), and it is therefore here in these ten verses that she finally attains Kṛṣṇa.

As this is the final decad of the *Nācciyār Tirumoḻi*, Piḷḷai finds it imperative to offer a synopsis of each of the previous thirteen sections, to reinforce the journey that led Āṇṭāḷ to this point. His summary is as follows. The *Nācciyār Tirumoḻi* begins with Āṇṭāḷ's entreaty to Kāma and her observance of a vow to win his favor and assistance. Next, she describes the destruction of the sand-castles (*Tirumoḻi* 2), followed by the adventures of the girls, who go for an early morning bath and are tormented by Kṛṣṇa (*Tirumoḻi* 3). In *Tirumoḻi* 4 she describes their divination and in *Tirumoḻi* 5 she begs the *kuyil* to bring Viṣṇu to her, because he had awakened in her the unquenchable desire see him face to face. But when she is unable to see him, she experiences her union in a dream (*Tirumoḻi* 6). The dream proves so real that when she awakens and finds it to be a fiction, she sings to his conch, when she heard its report of its enjoyment of Kṛṣṇa (*Tirumoḻi* 7). Like Sītā sending Hanumān as her messenger, Āṇṭāḷ sends the clouds that resemble her beloved with a message of love for him (*Tirumoḻi* 8). When he does not appear even after the season of the rain, she is distraught and questions all the things around her (*Tirumoḻi* 9 and 10). In the tenth *Tirumoḻi* she hopes that Viṣṇu's special relationship with Viṣṇucittaṉ would ensure that her mission would be realized. In *Tirumoḻi* 11 she continues this theme and says that if the words of Viṣṇu to Viṣṇucittaṉ prove false, then there is very little in this world left to believe. It is her belief in the unshakeable relationship between Viṣṇu and his devotee that helps her survive, and she begins to undertake a journey to the places favored by her beloved. However, her strength fails her and she appeals to her companions and mothers to take her to Kṛṣṇa's sacred sites (*Tirumoḻi* 12). They do not heed her urgent request and so she asks them to bring various items associated with Kṛṣṇa to her and to cool the fire of her longing (*Tirumoḻi* 13).

It is this Āṇṭāḷ, Piḷḷai continues, who was born into a lineage that surrendered to Viṣṇu fully. In the *Tiruppāvai*, Āṇṭāḷ decided that Viṣṇu is both the way and the goal. But when her great love was not realized, despite her complete reliance on Viṣṇu, she could not sustain her life and the *Nācciyār Tirumoḻi* was the result. Viṣṇu knew of her great love, but decided that her desire for him could ripen further and therefore did not grant her dearest wishes. But when she continued to insist on union, and her love for him matured into *parama bhakti*, he finally accepted her, just as he did Nammāḻvār, who speaks of that union in the penultimate verse of *Tiruvāymoḻi* 10.10.10:

O supreme cosmic matter
  that surrounds, spreads wide,
  Dives deep, and soars high!
O supreme transcendent, flaming flower
  that encompasses [creation]!
O incomparable blazing fire of wisdom and bliss
  that pervades [the universe]!
Greater than these was my desire
  that was quenched
  when you filled and embraced me.

(Trans. John Carman and
Vasudha Narayanan, p. 256)

Notes

1. Benton, Catherine. *God of Desire: Tales of Kāmadeva in Sanskrit Story Literature.* Albany: State University of New York Press, 2006. p. 94–95.
2. Benton, Catherine. *God of Desire: Tales of Kāmadeva in Sanskrit Story Literature.* Albany: State University of New York Press, 2006. p. 94.
3. Selby, Martha. *Grow Long, Blessed Night: Love Poems from Classical India.* New York: Oxford University Press, 2000. p. 127.

Appendix 1

Taṉiyaṉs to the Tiruppāvai *and* Nācciyār Tirumoḻi

A *taṉiyaṉ* (lit. a single one) is a laudatory verse, composed in either Tamiḻ or Sanskrit, that is appended to the main text. A poem may have more than one taṉiyaṉ. It may offer a brief synopsis of the life of the āḻvār poet, a summary of the main points of the poem, and invariably emphasizes the merit earned from reading, reciting, or listening to the relevant text. The taṉiyaṉ is as much a praise of the poem it is appended to, as it is of the poet who composed it. Liturgical recitations of any āḻvār poem always begin with a recitation of the relevant taṉiyaṉs.

The *Tiruppāvai* has two *taṉiyaṉs*, one in Sanskrit and one in Tamiḻ. The *Nācciyār Tirumoḻi* also has two *taṉiyaṉs*, both composed in Tamiḻ, one of which is anonymous.

TIRUPPĀVAI TAṈIYAṈS

The earliest *taṉiyaṉ* to the *Tiruppāvai* is in Tamiḻ and is attributed to Uyyakoṇṭār (ca. mid-10th century). Uyyakoṇṭār is believed to have been a disciple of Nāthamuni, the first preceptor of the Śrīvaiṣṇava community. Uyyakoṇṭār's *taṉiyaṉ* (*aṉṉa vayal putuvai*) is in two verses, and goes like this:

Praise
    Āṇṭāḷ of Putuvai,
        with its swans and fields
    the woman who gave the lord of Araṅkam
        the many verses of the *Tiruppāvai*
        that lovely and melodious garland of songs
    her who gave the lord
        the garland of flowers
        she had worn.

Radiant creeper
    who gave what you had worn
You whose wrists are stacked with bangles
    expertly sang of the ancient *pāvai* vow
You quested for the lord of Vēṅkaṭam
knowing him to be your fate
and sang of it:

We pray that we never forget these poems.

The first verse of the *taṉiyaṉ* begins by reiterating Āṇṭāḷ's lush descriptions of her native Putuvai as a grand and beautiful city. It concludes with a reference to the central event of Āṇṭāḷ's hagiographic narrative, namely her transgressive act of wearing the garland meant for the deity, and praises her as *cūṭikoṭuttavaḷ* (lit. she who gave what she had worn). The second verse of Uyyakoṇṭār's *taṉiyaṉ* alludes to the opening section of the *Nācciyār Tirumoḻi*, in which Āṇṭāḷ prays to Kāmadeva to unite her with the Lord of Vēṅkaṭam.

Although the Tamiḻ *taṉiyaṉ* is the older of the two *taṉiyaṉs*, liturgical recitations of the *Tiruppāvai* always begin with the Sanskrit composition of Parāśara Bhaṭṭar. Parāśara Bhaṭṭar (late 12th century) was the chief priest of the Viṣṇu temple at Śrīraṅgam. The story attached to the composition of this *taṉiyaṉ* goes as follows. When he was banished from Śrīraṅgam by the local Cōḻa king, and living in the town of Tirukkōṭṭiyūr, he was saddened by his separation from the god of Śrīraṅgam. At that time, one of his disciples urged him to compose a verse in praise of Āṇṭāḷ. This *taṉiyaṉ* in Sanskrit is believed to be the result.

She awakened Kṛṣṇa
    who slept on Nīlā's breasts that rise like twin hills
She bound him
    with the garland of flowers that she had worn
She reminded him
    of his duties revealed in a hundred *śrutis*
to that Godā
    we bow again and again.

The Sanskrit *taṉiyaṉ* begins with a reference to *Tiruppāvai* 19, where Kṛṣṇa is depicted resting on Nappiṉṉai's (Skt. Nīlā) breasts, thereby reminding the audience of one of the central ideas of the *Tiruppāvai*, and the philosophy of Rāmānuja: the inseparability of Kṛṣṇa and his consort. The *taṉiyaṉ* also makes mention of the transgressive garland episode, and refers to her as Godā, the Sanskritized form of Kōtai, the name she uses in the poems. One can argue that the ideas that Bhaṭṭar articulates in his four-line verse acts as the introduction to the *Tiruppāvai* and establishes the context for the devotee's experience (*anubhava*) of both Āṇṭāḷ and her poem.

NĀCCIYĀR TIRUMOḺI TAṈIYAṈS

The two Tamiḻ *taṉiyaṉs* appended to the *Nācciyār Tirumoḻi* are probably of a later date than those composed for the *Tiruppāvai*. The first *taṉiyaṉ* was composed by

Tirukaṇṇamaṅkai Āṇṭāṉ (ca. 12–13th century). In his *taṉiyaṉ*, Āṇṭāṉ visualizes Āṇṭāḷ as an incarnation of Bhū Devī, something that is absent from the two *Tiruppāvai taṉiyaṉs*. It provides a compelling reason to date these *taṉiyaṉs* as later in date, as the apotheosis of Āṇṭāḷ into Bhū Devī began around the late twelfth century.

> O, sweet companion to the goddess seated on a fresh-bloomed lotus!
> Innocent peacock, who ruled over Malli Nāṭu! O gentle one!
> Perfect consort of the king of the cowherds
> O glorious light of the Brahmins of Southern Putuvai.

In this *taṉiyaṉ*, Āṇṭāṉ does not refer to Āṇṭāḷ directly as Bhū Devī. Instead, he does so obliquely by referring to her as the "sweet companion" to Lakṣmī (the goddess seated on a fresh-bloomed lotus). Malli Nāṭu here refers to the region around Śrīvilliputtūr. The reference to Āṇṭāḷ as the light of the Brahmins (*vēyar*) is understood in the commentaries as a reference to Viṣṇucittaṉ.

The second anonymous *taṉiyaṉ* begins with a direct reference to Āṇṭāḷ's song to the conch, and again praises her as the queen of Malli Nāṭu. This *taṉiyaṉ* mentions the garland episode, and ends by declaring as Āṇṭāḷ's feet are the devotees' refuge. The *taṉiyaṉ* makes no claims about Āṇṭāḷ's divine status, and seems to assert her distinction as an exemplary devotee. For this reason, it is possible that this *taṉiyaṉ* is earlier than Āṇṭāṉ's, which does not refer to Āṇṭāḷ's story, or allude to any significant sections of the *Nācciyār Tirumoḻi*.

This anonymous *taṉiyaṉ* is often not included in printed editions of the *Nācciyār Tirumoḻi*. It is also omitted during liturgical recitations of the *Nācciyār Tirumoḻi* in several Śrīvaiṣṇava temples.

> She is the one
>   who asked the lovely conch with its spirals about Māyaṉ's red lips.
> She is the queen of the Malli Nāṭu.
> She is the wild parrot
>   who adorned her lovely hair with a garland
>   meant for the lord of Araṅkam
> We find refuge in her pure and virtuous feet.

For a detailed discussion of the *taṉiyaṉ* and its relationship to the apotheosis of Āṇṭāḷ see Venkatesan, Archana. "Āṇṭāḷ and Her Magic Mirror," 47–59.

Appendix 2

Major Myths

EPIC SOURCES

The *Rāmāyaṇa* is one of the most important sources for the commentators who write on the poems of the *āḻvār*. Periyavāccāṉ Piḷḷai, in particular, does not pass up an opportunity to cite from the *Vālmīki Rāmāyaṇa*. The *Vālmīki Rāmāyaṇa* consists of seven books in total. I summarize the major plot elements of each book below. The number and the name of the relevant book are given within parenthesis at the conclusion.

Rāmāyaṇa

King Daśaratha of Ayodhyā has three principal wives—Kausalyā, Sumitrā, and Kaikeyī. After being childless for a number of years, he performs a grand sacrifice and is blessed with four sons, who are all emanations of Viṣṇu. Rāma is the eldest and is born to Kausalyā. Sumitrā gives birth to two sons, Lakṣmaṇa and Śatrughna, while Kaikeyī is mother to Bharata. The boys grow up into handsome and noble princes, with Rāma beloved by all, for he embodies every virtue.

When they are but mere youth, Rāma and Lakṣmaṇa accompany the great sage Viśvāmitra into the forest to aid him in vanquishing demons, who seek to disrupt his great sacrifice. During their sojourn they defeat the demoness Tāṭakā, release the beautiful Ahalyā from a curse, and acquire various magical weapons. Viśvāmitra then takes the boys to the city of Mithilā, ruled by King Janaka. Rāma wins a contest and marries the king's lovely daughter, Sītā. Rāma and Lakṣmaṇa and their wives return to Ayodhyā triumphant, and thus spend many blissful years (Book 1: *Bālakāṇḍa*).

One day, Daśaratha, aware of his old age, decides to anoint Rāma as his successor. He makes the announcement immediately, even though Bharata is away. Everyone is delighted by the news, except a loyal maid to Queen Kaikeyī. She convinces the noble Kaikeyī that it is not in her best interests for Rāma to become king, and urges her to redeem two promised boons from Daśaratha. Kaikeyī does so, requesting that Bharata be made king in Rāma's place, and that Rāma be exiled to the forest for fourteen years. Daśaratha is heartbroken, but accedes to her wishes, because he cannot go back on his word. Rāma accepts his father's decree without comment or protest, and prepares for his exile. Both Lakṣmaṇa and Rāma's wife Sītā insist on accompanying him to exile, and the three of them leave. Daśaratha, separated from his beloved Rāma, dies of a broken heart.

Bharata returns to hear the news of Rāma's exile. He is thunderstruck and falls into a swoon. He disowns his mother and prepares to follow Rāma into the forest, and to beg him to return. Bharata implores Rāma to forgo his exile, but Rāma, steadfast in upholding his father's vow, refuses. Bharata eventually accepts Rāma's decision, and agrees to rule in his place for the duration of his exile. He takes Rāma's sandals as a symbol, installs them on the throne of Ayodhyā, and vows not to enter the city until Rāma returns. He swears that should Rāma not return in exactly fourteen years, he, Bharata, would leap into the fire and kill himself. (Book 2: *Ayodhyākāṇḍa*)

Rāma and Sītā have many adventures in the forest. Toward the end of their exile, Śūrpaṇakhā, the demon sister of Rāvaṇa, the king of Laṅka, falls in love with Rāma and attempts to seduce him. Śūrpaṇakhā sees the beautiful Sītā, decides to kill her rival, and attacks her. Lakṣmaṇa intervenes and mutilates her. When a local band of demon relatives are unable to defeat the two princes, Śūrpaṇakhā turns to her brother Rāvaṇa and secures his aid by inciting his lust for Sītā.

Rāvaṇa decides to abduct Sītā and enlists the help of Mārīca, whom he commands to assume the form of a magical deer. Mārīca prances in front of Sītā and beguiles her with his false beauty. Sītā requests Rāma to capture the deer for her, and Rāma agrees to do so, despite Lakṣmaṇa's warnings. Rāma chases the deer, corners it, and kills it. But Sītā urges Lakṣmaṇa to follow Rāma. Lakṣmaṇa refuses, but eventually agrees, defying Rāma's orders. Rāvaṇa seizes the opportunity and abducts Sītā. The great vulture king Jaṭāyus gives chase, but is killed. Rāvaṇa imprisons Sītā in his island city of Laṅka. (Book 3: *Araṇyakāṇḍa*)

Rāma and Lakṣmaṇa return to find Sītā gone. Rāma is distraught, but urged by Lakṣmaṇa he begins the search. Finally, the two brothers find themselves in Kiṣkindhā, the land of the monkeys, where they meet Hanumān and his friend Sugrīva. Sugrīva is an exiled monkey prince, and Rāma aids him to regain his throne, after securing his promise of aid in return. Rāma secretly kills Vālin, Sugrīva's brother, and installs Sugrīva on the throne of Kiṣkindhā. As the monsoon arrives, Sugrīva forgets his promise and the monkeys are immersed in having a good time. Rāma sends Lakṣmaṇa as an emissary to Sugrīva and once again secures his help. All of the monkeys, including Sugrīva, Vālin's son, Aṅgada, and Hanumān rally to support Rāma. (Book 4: *Kiṣkindhākāṇḍa*).

Sugrīva dispatches his monkey army to search for Sītā. Hanumān and a small contingent of monkeys are sent south, where they learn that Sītā is in Laṅka. Hanumān, who is the son of the wind, and is blessed with great strength and wisdom, leaps across the ocean to Laṅka. He searches far and wide for Sītā, until he finds her imprisoned in a grove of *aśoka* trees. He introduces himself as Rāma's messenger and gifts her with Rāma's ring. Hanumān offers to rescue her, but Sītā refuses, not willing to be touched by any man other than her husband. She requests Hanumān to urge Rāma to hurry to Laṅka and avenge the insult to her (and his) honor. Hanumān causes havoc in Laṅka and allows himself to be captured by Rāvaṇa's guards. Rāvaṇa punishes him by setting fire to his tail. Hanumān, in turn, escapes and burns down Laṅka. Hanumān returns to Rāma and gives him Sītā's message. (Book 5: *Sundarakāṇḍa*)

Rāma and his monkey army ready for battle. Rāvaṇa's advisors warn him of Rāma's might and valor, but he ignores them. Chief among his detractors is his brother, Vibhīṣaṇa, who is virtuous and noble. Unable to support Rāvaṇa's misguided actions, Vibhīṣaṇa defects and surrenders to Rāma. Rāma accepts him into the fold, despite the warnings of his allies, saying that he would give refuge to even an enemy if he came in the guise of a friend. Vibhīṣaṇa proves an invaluable asset. Rāma and his army of monkeys build a bridge across the ocean to Laṅka. A terrible battle rages between the forces of Rāma and Rāvaṇa, and finally, Rāma kills Rāvaṇa.

Sītā is freed, and she returns to Rāma. Rāma however rejects her, and demands that she enter the fire to prove her chastity. She does so and emerges from the flames, unscathed. Rāma and Sītā are reunited. They return to Ayodhyā, where a jubilant Bharata and the entire citizenry of Ayodhyā greet them. Rāma is crowned, and rules over a happy and peaceful Ayodhyā for a number of years (Book 6: *Yuddhakāṇḍa*).

Rāma and Sītā rule for several years, until rumors surface among the population of Ayodhyā of Sītā's infidelity with Rāvaṇa. Rāma, cleaving to the role of a good king, banishes the pregnant Sītā, although he knows the rumors to be false. Many years later, Rāma performs a sacrifice, at which the twin boys Lava and Kuśa, students of Vālmīki, recite the story of Rāma. He discovers that they are his sons, and Rāma is ready to reclaim Sītā. Sītā, however, has suffered too much, refuses, and disappears into the bosom of the Earth from which she was born. Rāma, unable to bear this final separation from Sītā, divides the kingdom between his two sons, enters the Sarayū river, accompanied by the citizens of Ayodhyā, and returns to Viṣṇu's abode. (Book 7: *Uttarakāṇḍa*).

Mahābhārata

The *Mahābhārata* is not as significant a text for the commentators as the *Rāmāyaṇa*. In their commentaries to the *Tiruppāvai* and *Nācciyār Tirumoḻi*, they rarely quote directly from it.

The one episode that is of immense importance concerns Draupadī, the heroine of the *Mahābhārata*. When the oldest of the five Pāṇḍava brothers, Yudhiṣṭhira, loses everything in a game of dice against his Kaurava cousins, who are his archenemies, the oldest brother Duryodhana orders Draupadī to be brought before the assembly. Draupadī is menstruating and refuses to do as he bids. She is finally dragged by her hair and then disrobed in public. At this time of dishonor, Draupadī appeals to Kṛṣṇa to protect her. He does so by supplying endless length of cloth to cover Draupadī, thus protecting her honor.

However, the *Bhagavad Gītā*, which is a part of the *Mahābhārata*, is of enormous significance to the Śrīvaiṣṇava commentators.

The *Bhagavad Gītā* (Song of God) is Kṛṣṇa's discourse to Arjuna, the hero of the *Mahābhārata*. It takes place on the battlefield of Kurukṣetra, on the eve of the great battle between the two sets of cousins, the Pāṇḍavas and Kauravas. The *Bhagavad Gītā* is divided into eighteen chapters, and it deals with a variety of issues, including the nature of desireless action (*niśkāma karma*), the relation between sacrifice and action, and the discipline of devotion (*bhakti yoga*).

Śrīvaiṣṇava theologians see verse 18.66 as the crux of the *Gītā*. In this verse, Kṛṣṇa tells Arjuna to practice an exclusive devotion to him. Verse 29 of the *Tiruppāvai* is understood in Śrīvaiṣṇava commentaries as reiterating the central ideas of this verse, which is known as the *carama śloka*.

The verse is as follows:

> [Kṛṣṇa says]
> Relinquishing all sacred duties to me,
> make me your only refuge;
> do not grieve,
> for I shall free you from all evils.
> (Trans. Barbara Stoler Miller, p. 144)

Bhāgavata Purāṇa

The Kṛṣṇa legend is a rich source of material for the Śrīvaiṣṇava commentators. While they do quote from the *Bhāgavata Purāṇa* and the *Viṣṇu Purāṇa*, these instances are frequent as the quotations from the *Rāmāyaṇa*. Instead, they often retell favorite stories to illustrate a point about Kṛṣṇa's compassionate nature, his accessibility, or his valor. Therefore, it is not possible to determine if the commentators are relying solely on the *Bhāgavata Purāṇa*, or if they are working from a set of circulating narratives that include oral and multiple written versions. However, it must be noted that by the period of the commentaries (mid-twelfth to thirteenth centuries), the *Bhāgavata Purāṇa* is a well-known text, and the Śrīvaiṣṇava commentators are no doubt aware of it.

Although the *Bhāgavata Purāṇa* is not the earliest compilation of Kṛṣṇa stories–the *Hari Vaṁśa* and *Viṣṇu Purāṇa* are probably older—it is, without a doubt, the most well known and popular among Vaiṣṇavas. It is for this reason that I refer to the *Bhāgavata Purāṇa* version of the Kṛṣṇa stories in the synopses below.

I give below a summary of the stories that occur most frequently in the commentaries to the *Tiruppāvai* and *Nācciyār Tirumoḻi*. These are based on Edwin Bryant's translation of the *Bhāgavata Purāṇa*, book 10; on Swami Venkatesananda's retellings; and the references in Vettam Mani's *Purāṇic Encyclopedia*. The *Bhāgavata Purāṇa* is a voluminous work of eighteen thousand verses. The bulk of the Kṛṣṇa narrative takes place in book 10 and book 11. All citations below refer to the relevant book and chapter in the *Bhāgavata Purāṇa*. Therefore, "10.22" refers to book 10, chapter 22.

In addition to this summary of stories, I have also included a very brief synopsis of those Kṛṣṇa stories that occur frequently in the *Tiruppāvai* and *Nācciyār Tirumoḻi* in the "Index of Myths and Names in the *Tiruppāvai* and *Nācciyār Tirumoḻi*."

1. Kṛṣṇa's Birth, 10.3 and 10.4

Kṛṣṇa is born in the city of Mathurā at midnight as the eighth child of Devakī and Vasudeva. Kaṁsa, Devakī's brother, has imprisoned them because of a prophecy that their eighth child will kill him. Furthermore, he has killed all their previous seven children. Aided by the divine child, the doors to their prison fly open, and Vasudeva spirits the child away, across the swollen Yamunā, which magically recedes to grant him passage to Gokula. On the same night, Yogamāyā (divine illusion) is born as a daughter to Nandagopa and Yaśodā. Unbeknownst to the cowherds of Gokula, Vasudeva switches the babies, and brings Yogamāyā back to Mathurā. When Kaṁsa attempts to kill Yogamāyā, she escapes his grasp and announces that the one who will kill him has already been born elsewhere.

2. Kṛṣṇa Kills Pūtanā, 10.6

Kaṁsa dispatches Pūtanā, the devourer of children, to kill Kṛṣṇa. She wanders the area killing children. One day, she changes her form into that of a beautiful woman and arrives in Gokula. She enters Nanda's house and proceeds to suckle Kṛṣṇa at her poisoned breast. Kṛṣṇa sucks her life breath out of her body, reveals her true form, and kills her. When the cowherds cremate Pūtanā's body, a delightful fragrance wafts from the pyre, because all her sins have been destroyed when she suckled Kṛṣṇa.

3. Kṛṣṇa Submits to Yaśodā, 10.9

Kṛṣṇa steals butter from Yaśodā, much to her frustration and anger. She beats the child until he cries. Then she takes a rope and tries to bind him to a grinding stone. But because Kṛṣṇa is the supreme lord, she is unable to do so, as no length of rope is sufficient. Finally, Kṛṣṇa takes pity on his mother, and allows himself to be bound, demonstrating his devotion to his devotees. It is for this reason that he is known as Dāmodara—the one whose belly was bound by a rope.

4. Kṛṣṇa Kills Bakāsura, 10.11

A terrible demon assumes the form of a crane and swallows Kṛṣṇa. The watching cowherds are distressed, but the demon immediately disgorges Kṛṣṇa, who is like a fire in his belly. When the crane-demon approaches Kṛṣṇa once again, intent on killing him, Kṛṣṇa destroys him by splitting his beak.

5. Kṛṣṇa Vanquishes Kāliya, 10.16

A giant thousand-headed snake, Kāliya, takes up residence in the Yamunā and poisons it. Kṛṣṇa decides to vanquish it, and leaps into the river from the top of a katampa tree. He tussles with the snake and at one point, pretends to be inert. All the cowherds are distraught and gather on the banks of the Yamunā. Realizing their distress, Kṛṣṇa subdues the snake and begins to dance on its crest. In this way, he subdues Kāliya, who surrenders to Kṛṣṇa and offers him worship. The Yamunā once again returns to its pure state.

6. Kṛṣṇa and Balarāma Vanquish Pralamba, 10.18

A demon named Pralamba disguises himself as a cowherd, and joins Kṛṣṇa, Balarāma, and their friends in their games. He is intent on killing Kṛṣṇa and Balarāma. They play a game in which the loser has to carry the victor on his back. Thus Pralamba finds himself carrying Balarāma. He tries to kidnap the boy, but, because of Balarāma's great weight, is brought to a halt. Then Pralamba assumes his true form, but Balarāma smites him and thus kills him.

7. Kṛṣṇa Steals the Gopīs' Clothes, 10.22

The *gopīs* observe a vow in the winter months to the goddess Kātyāyanī to win Kṛṣṇa as their husband. They make images of the goddess out of sand on the banks of the river and bathe in the river. They call to each other in the morning to join in the vow. One day, Kṛṣṇa follows them to the river and steals their clothes. From high above in a *katampa* tree, he teases them, until they reveal themselves to him naked and worship him. He returns their clothes to them and promises to fulfill all their desires.

8. Kṛṣṇa Lifts Mount Govardhana, 10.24–10.25

Kṛṣṇa questions the cowherds' worship of Indra and suggests instead that they worship the Govardhana hill. Kṛṣṇa assumes the form of the hill and receives their delighted worship. Indra, angered, brings down a terrible thunderstorm on the land of the cowherds. Realizing that he is their sole refuge, Kṛṣṇa lifts the Govardhana hill with one hand and shelters all of Gokula under it for seven days. Indra realizes his foolishness, and he withdraws the rain. The cowherds come out from under the protective umbrella of the Govardhana hill, and Kṛṣṇa places it gently back on the ground.

The Story of Akrūra's Devotion, 10.36–10.39

Akrūra is a great devotee of Kṛṣṇa, but is also Kaṁsa's minister. Kaṁsa dispatches Akrūra to invite Kṛṣṇa and Balarāma to Mathurā. Akrūra is delighted, because he finally gets the opportunity to see Kṛṣṇa. He makes his way to Gokula immersed in contemplation of Kṛṣṇa. When he enters Gokula, Akrūra sees Kṛṣṇa's footprints and, overcome with devotion, prostrates on the ground and rolls in the dust of Kṛṣṇa's footprints. And when he finally sees Kṛṣṇa and Balarāma, he once again falls at their feet. Kṛṣṇa embraces him, overcome with love for the devotee who has taken refuge in him.

Balarāma and Kṛṣṇa depart for Mathurā with Akrūra. En route, they pause at the banks of the Yamunā. While the two brothers wait in the chariot, Akrūra takes a dip in the river. As he immerses himself in the water, he sees Kṛṣṇa in the water. When he breaks the surface, he sees that the boys are still seated in the chariot. Witnessing this miraculous feat, Akrūra is overcome by love and devotion for Kṛṣṇa.

10. Kṛṣṇa Kills Kuvalayāpīḍa, 10.43

When Kṛṣṇa arrives in Mathurā, Kaṁsa sends the king of the elephants, Kuvalayāpīḍa to kill him. Kṛṣṇa fights the elephant, and finally kills him by grabbing him by the trunk and hurling him to the ground.

11. Kṛṣṇa Kills Kaṁsa, 10.44

After Kṛṣṇa kills Kuvalayāpīḍa, Kaṁsa sends the two wrestlers Cāṇūra and Muṣṭika to fight against Kṛṣṇa and Balarāma respectively. They fight long and hard, but Kṛṣṇa succeeds in killing Cāṇūra, while Balarāma does the same to Muṣṭika. Kaṁsa, witnessing this, is afraid. He commands that the wealth of the cowherds be seized and Nanda imprisoned. Angered, Kṛṣṇa advances on him. Kaṁsa takes up his sword and shield, but Kṛṣṇa leaps up on the throne and overpowers Kaṁsa, flinging him into the center of the arena, thus ending his life. Since Kaṁsa spent every waking moment contemplating Kṛṣṇa, he was released from the cycle of life and death.

12. Kṛṣṇa's Marriage to Rukmiṇī, 10.52–10.53

The beautiful princess Rukmiṇī wishes to marry Kṛṣṇa, but her brother Rukmi is his sworn enemy. She dispatches a love message to Kṛṣṇa through a trustworthy Brahmin. In that message, Rukmiṇī declares her love for Kṛṣṇa and asks him to rescue her from marriage to another. She tells him to abduct her as she emerges after performing the pre-wedding rituals at the temple of the goddess. Kṛṣṇa heeds her message, steals her away, defeats all that stand in his way, and weds Rukmiṇī.

13. The Story of Kṛṣṇa's son Pradyumna, 10.55

Śiva burned Kāma, the god of desire, but also blessed him that he would regain his bodily form and be reunited with his wife, Ratī.

Rukmiṇī's son Pradyumna is none other than Kāma. A prophecy foretells that he will kill the demon Śambara. The wicked demon steals the newborn baby and flings him into the ocean. The baby Pradyumna is swallowed by a fish, which is subsequently caught and then sold to the cooks of Śambara's kitchen. The cooks find Pradyumna and are surprised. They entrust the child to Māyāvatī, who is none other than Ratī. Māyāvatī realizes that Pradyumna is her husband reborn. Pradyumna grows up into a strapping young man, Māyāvatī reveals their true identity, and Kāma and Ratī are reunited as Pradyumna and Māyāvatī. Pradyumna, now aware of Śambara's mischief, kills him in a pitched battle. Pradyumna returns with Māyāvatī to Dvarakā, where he is reunited with his mother Rukmiṇī and his father Kṛṣṇa.

14. The Story of Kṛṣṇa's Grandson Aniruddha, 10.62–63

Aniruddha is the son of Pradyumna and Rukmavatī, the daughter of Rukmi (the brother of Kṛṣṇa's wife Rukmiṇī). The demon Bāṇa's daughter Uṣā dreams of a beautiful youth, and falls in love with him. Her friend Citralekhā paints the pictures of various eligible young men, and eventually Uṣā identifies Aniruddha as the lover in her dream. Citralekhā, who possesses magical powers, spirits a sleeping Aniruddha to Bāṇa's kingdom and unites the two lovers. Aniruddha and Uṣā spend several months together. Bāṇa soon finds out about his daughter's secret lover, who has stolen her chastity. Bāṇa succeeds in imprisoning Aniruddha. In the meantime, Kṛṣṇa and Pradyumna also discover Aniruddha's whereabouts. A great battle ensues between the forces of Kṛṣṇa and those of Bāṇa. As Kṛṣṇa is about kill Bāṇa, he is rescued through the intervention of his mother. Bāṇa is a great devotee of Śiva, so Śiva also lends his aid to Bāṇa's cause.

Eventually Kṛṣṇa defeats Bāṇa, but spares his life because Śiva appeals to Kṛṣṇa on his devotee's behalf. Aniruddha is released, and Uṣā and he are married.

15. Kṛṣṇa Kills Śiśupāla, 10.74

Śiśupāla insults Kṛṣṇa in the midst of a great sacrifice. When the assembled kings, angered on his behalf, rise up to defend his honor, Kṛṣṇa lifts his sword and beheads Śiśupāla. Immediately, a light emerges from Śiśupāla's headless body and enters Kṛṣṇa. Śiśupāla was cursed to be born as a demon for three consecutive births. He had spent those three births consumed with hatred of Kṛṣṇa and had therefore spent every waking moment in contemplation of Kṛṣṇa. Therefore, in death he merged into Kṛṣṇa.

REFERENCES

The Rāmāyaṇa of Vālmīki. Vols. 1–6, trans. and ed. Robert P. Goldman et al.
The Bhagavad Gītā: Krishna's Counsel in Time of War. Trans. Barbara Stoler Miller.
Bryant, Edwin. *Krishna: The Beautiful Legend of God*.
Venkatesananda, Swami. *The Concise Srimad Bhagavatam*.
Mani, Vettem. *The Puranic Encyclopedia*.

Appendix 3

Index of Myths and Names in the Tiruppāvai *and* Nācciyār Tirumoḻi

I have catalogued below the myths alluded to in the *Tiruppāvai* and *Nācciyār Tirumoḻi* (table 3). These are organized in the order in which they appear in the *Tiruppāvai*. Where a myth or name occurs only in the *Nācciyār Tirumoḻi*, it is listed after *Tiruppāvai* 30 (table 4). Where a myth occurs more than once, I have indicated the relevant verse numbers in both texts. Included in this list are also Kṛṣṇa's names that appear in the two poems and have specific mythic connotations. But when a myth occurs only in the form of a specific name (for example, Keśava), I have marked it with an asterisk. This compilation only refers to the myths and names associated with Viṣṇu that occur in the *Tiruppāvai and Nācciyār Tirumoḻi*. For the names of other characters that occur in the two poems and in the commentaries, please refer to the glossary of terms.

Table 3. Index of Myths in the Tiruppāvai and Nācciyār Tirumoḻi

Tiruppāvai and *Nācciyār Tirumoḻi* Verse Number	Reference to Myth	Myth Narrative
Tiruppāvai 1 *Nācciyār Tirumoḻi* 2.1, 5.10, 6.1, 6.8, 8.6	Nārāyaṇa* (in *Nācciyār Tirumoḻi* also appears as Nārāṇa)	A name of Viṣṇu that references his identity as the cosmic creator and the goal of all humans (*nara*).
Tiruppāvai 3 *Nācciyār Tirumoḻi* 1.7, 2.9, 4.2, 4.9, 5.10, 5.11, 7.8, 8.6, 11.4, 11.5, 12.2, 12.9	Trivikrama (also *Tiruppāvai* 17 and 24) Also appears in *Nācciyār Tirumoḻi* as the one who took the form of a dwarf (*Vāmana*).	Viṣṇu took the form of the dwarf Vāmana in order to vanquish the prideful king Bali. When the king granted Vāmana's request for three steps of land, he immediately assumed his immeasurable cosmic form. He spanned the earth and heavens with his first two strides. Up on Bali's request, he then took his final step by placing it on the king's head and sent him to the subterranean world.
Tiruppāvai 4 *Nācciyār Tirumoḻi* 2.2, 3.7, 7.2, 9.8, 13.2	Mahāpralaya (as lord supreme in the final deluge; also *Tiruppāvai* 26) Also appears as lord sleeping on the banyan leaf	Refers to Viṣṇu floating on the banyan leaf at the end of the world. It can also refer to his *avatāra* as the fish, where he rescued the first man, Manu, from being destroyed.
Tiruppāvai 4 Nācciyār Tirumoḻi 7.10	Padmanābha*	This name, which means one whose navel is a lotus, refers to a creation myth where a lotus containing Brahmā grew out of Viṣṇu's navel while he was engaged in *yoga nidrā*. Brahmā then proceeded to create the worlds.
Tiruppāvai 5 *Nācciyār Tirumoḻi* 7.4	Dāmodara*	The epithet Dāmodara refers to an incident in Kṛṣṇa's life in Āyarpāṭi, where he bears the scar on his waist left by the rope (*dāma*) with which Yaśodā bound him to a grinding stone.
Tiruppāvai 6	Kṛṣṇa's defeat of the demon Śakaṭāsura (also *Tiruppāvai* 24)	Kaṁsa sent the demon Śakaṭa to kill the infant Kṛṣṇa. Taking the form of cart, the demon approached the sleeping child and began to make a racket. Kṛṣṇa awakened and kicked apart the cart, thus killing him.
Tiruppāvai 6 *Nācciyār Tirumoḻi* 3.9	Kṛṣṇa's defeat of the demoness Pūtanā	Kaṁsa sent the demoness Pūtanā to kill Kṛṣṇa. She disguised herself as a cowherdess and attempted to suckle him. The infant sucked her life out of her along with her milk. Giving up her false form, Pūtanā died.
Tiruppāvai 7 Nācciyār Tirumoḻi 1.7, 2.5	Keśava	Kṛṣṇa is said to have received the name Keśava because he defeated the demon Keśi, who had been sent by Kaṁsa. Keśi came in the guise of a horse. Kṛṣṇa killed him by thrusting his hand into the horse's mouth until it vomited blood and thus died.

Tiruppāvai and *Nācciyār Tirumoḻi* Verse Number	Reference to Myth	Myth Narrative
Tiruppāvai 8	Kṛṣṇa's defeat of Keśi (*Tiruppāvai* 7)	*Tiruppāvai* 7; note to Keśava
Tiruppāvai 8	Kṛṣṇa's defeat of Kaṁsa's wrestlers	Kaṁsa invited Kṛṣṇa and Balarāma to a wrestling match. Kṛṣṇa fought and killed a wrestler named Cāṇūra, while Balarāma did the same to the wrestler Muṣṭika.
Tiruppāvai 9 *Nācciyār Tirumoḻi* 2.5, 3.10, 5.1, 6.2, 7.1, 7.9, 12.1, 14.5	Mādhava*	Lit. One who is of the clan of Madhu. A name of Kṛṣṇa. Mādhava is derived from Madhu, a king of the Yadu dynasty.
Tiruppāvai 10	Reference to Kumbhakarṇa's sleep	*Tiruppāvai* 8, Rāvaṇa's brother, through a trick on the part of the gods, gained the boon of continuous sleep from Brahma.
Tiruppāvai 12 *Nācciyār Tirumoḻi* 2.6, 3.3, 3.4, 5.3,	Rāma's defeat of Rāvaṇa (also *Tiruppāvai* 13)	Rāma killed Rāvaṇa in a pitched battle. He did so in order to rescue his wife Sītā, whom Rāvaṇa had abducted.
Tiruppāvai 13 *Nācciyār Tirumoḻi* 1.10, 4.7, 14.9 *Tiruppāvai* 13	Kṛṣṇa's defeat of the demon Bakāsura Rāma felling Rāvaṇa's head (also *Tiruppavai* 12)	Kaṁsa dispatched Bakāsura to kill Kṛṣṇa. He took the form of a stork (*baka*) and swallowed Kṛṣṇa. But unable to bear Kṛṣṇa's heat, he began to vomit blood and Kṛṣṇa. Kṛṣṇa then killed it by splitting its beaks apart. During the battle between Rāma and Rāvaṇa, as Rāma cut off Rāvaṇa's head, another sprouted in its place. Rāma eventually felled all of his heads, chopped off his twenty arms, and pierced his heart with his arrow.
Tiruppāvai 15 *Nācciyār Tirumoḻi* 1.10, 4.5, 7.1, 14.9	Kṛṣṇa's defeat of the demon Kuvalayapīḍa	As Kṛṣṇa approached Kaṁsa's wrestling arena, a terrible elephant confronted him (on Kaṁsa's orders). It caught hold of Kṛṣṇa and a fight took place. Kṛṣṇa killed it by flinging it to the ground.
Tiruppāvai 17	Trivikrama (also *Tiruppāvai* 3 and 24)	See note to *Tiruppāvai* 3.
Tiruppāvai 24	Trivikrama (also *Tiruppāvai* 3, 17)	See above to *Tiruppāvai* 3.
Tiruppāvai 24	Rāma's defeat of Rāvaṇa (*Tiruppāvai* 12, 13)	See note to *Tiruppāvai* 13.
Tiruppāvai 24	Kṛṣṇa's defeat of the demon Śakaṭāsura (also *Tiruppāvai* 6)	See note to *Tiruppāvai* 6.

(Continued)

Table 3. *(Continued)*

Tiruppāvai and *Nācciyār Tirumoḻi* Verse Number	Reference to Myth	Myth Narrative
Tiruppāvai 24	Kṛṣṇa's defeat of the demon Vatsāsura	A demon sent by Kaṁsa disguised himself as cow and infiltrated Kṛṣṇa and Balarāma's herd of cows. Both of them spotted the demon. Kṛṣṇa caught the demon-cow by its hind legs and tail and dashed it against two trees, thus killing it.
Tiruppāvai 24 *Nācciyār Tirumoḻi* 12.8, 13.8, 14.2	Lifting of Govardhana mountain	The cowherds worshiped Indra for rain. Kṛṣṇa once suggested that they instead worship the mountain Govardhana instead. This mountain is thought to embody Kṛṣṇa. The cowherds did so. Enraged, Indra sent a devastating storm. Kṛṣṇa lifted the mountain over Gokula like an umbrella, thus protecting the cowherds.
Tiruppāvai 25	Reference to Kṛṣṇa's birth	Kṛṣṇa was born as the eighth child to Vasudeva and Devakī, sister of Kaṁsa, king of Mathurā. Fearing that Kaṁsa would kill this child like all the others, Vasudeva smuggled him out to the village of Gokula. He exchanged the baby boy for the baby girl just born to Yaśodā and Nandagopa.
Tiruppāvai 25	Kṛṣṇa's defeat of Kaṁsa	After Kṛṣṇa's defeat of the wrestlers (see above), Kaṁsa was infuriated. He ordered that everyone should be killed. Kṛṣṇa leapt on him and killed him, thus fulfilling the prophecy.
Tiruppāvai 26 *Nācciyār Tirumoḻi* 2.2 13.2	Mahāpralaya (Kṛṣṇa asleep on a banyan leaf) Also *Tiruppāvai* 4	In the final deluge when the world is submerged in water, Kṛṣṇa is said to float around as an infant on a banyan leaf.
Tiruppāvai 27 Nācciyār Tirumoḻi 1.3, 8.3, 10.7, 12.4, 12.9, 13.9	Govinda* (also *Tiruppāvai* 28 and 29)	A name for Kṛṣṇa; Tender of Cows.
	Reference to lifting of the mountain Govardhana (also *Tiruppāvai* 24)	See note to *Tiruppāvai* 24.
Tiruppāvai 30 Nācciyār Tirumoḻi 9.1, 10.9,	*Kūrma avatāra* (churning the ocean of milk)	This references the episode when the gods and demons churned the ocean of milk to secure the nectar of immortality. Viṣṇu assumed the form of the tortoise and bore the mountain Mandara on his back, to prevent it from sinking.
Tiruppāvai 30	Mādhava* (also *Tiruppāvai* 9)	See note to Tiruppāvai 9.
Tiruppāvai 30	Keśava* (also *Tiruppāvai* 7)	*See note to Tiruppāvai 7.*

Table 4. Myths and Names that Occur in the Nācciyār Tirumoḻi

Nācciyār Tirumoḻi Verse Number	Reference to Myth	Myth Narrative
Nācciyār Tirumoḻi 2.3, 4.10, 14.10	The rescue of the elephant Gajendra	Viṣṇu rescued an elephant that was his great devotee by vanquishing a crocodile that tormented it.
Nācciyār Tirumoḻi 2.1	Śrīdhara	Refers to the inseparability of Viṣṇu and Śrī. He who bears Śrī.
Nācciyār Tirumoḻi 2.6, 2.7, 11.7,	One who spanned the ocean	Refers to the episode in the *Rāmāyaṇa* where Rāma built a bridge across the ocean to Laṅka in order to rescue his wife Sītā.
Nācciyār Tirumoḻi 3.9, 4.6, 4.7	Kaṁsa's net	Refers to the various plans Kṛṣṇa's uncle, Kaṁsa, put into action in order to destroy him. These include sending demons, who took, for instance, the forms of an elephant, bird, and cart.
Nācciyār Tirumoḻi 4.6, 4.7, 7.6, 12.8	Splitting the *maruta* trees	Refers to the instance where Krsna's mother Yaśodā bound him to a mortar. Krsna dragged himself between two trees that then collapsed.
Nācciyār Tirumoḻi 4.7	The defeat of the seven bulls	Refers to Krsna's defeat of seven demons, who had taken the form of seven bulls. In vanquishing them, he won the hand of Nappiṉṉai.
Nācciyār Tirumoḻi 4.7, 11.9	The defeat of Śiśupāla Marriage of Rukmiṇī	Kṛṣṇa defeated Śiśupāla, who sought to marry Rukmiṇī. Rukmiṇī, who was in love with Kṛṣṇa, sent a message to him, and he spirited her away on the day of her wedding.
Nācciyār Tirumoḻi 6.6, 7.5,	Madhusūdhana	A name of Viṣṇu. The name refers to Viṣṇu's defeat of the demon Madhu. Two demons, Madhu and Kaiṭhaba emerged from Viṣṇu's ear and aimed to wreck havoc on the world. Viṣṇu awoke in time to destroy them.
Nācciyār Tirumoḻi 8.5	Tore the body of Hiraṇya with his long nails flecked with blood	Refers to Viṣṇu's descent as Narasiṁha to defeat the demon Hiraṇyakaśipu. He had received a boon from Brahmā that he could be killed by neither man nor beast, neither on heaven nor on earth, neither by day nor by night, or by any known weapon. Viṣṇu took the form of a man-lion, held him up, and disemboweled him with his nails during twilight.

(Continued)

Table 4. *(Continued)*

Nācciyār Tirumoḻi Verse Number	Reference to Myth	Myth Narrative
Nācciyār Tirumoḻi 10.4	Slashed the nose of Śūrpaṇakhā	Refers to the episode in the *Rāmāyaṇa* where Rāma's brother Lakṣmaṇa slashed the nose of the demoness Śūrpaṇakhā, sister of Rāvaṇa. She tried to seduce the two brothers and when that failed, turned on Sītā.
Nācciyār Tirumoḻi 10.7	Danced with the pots	A legend peculiar to the Tamiḻ tradition. Kṛṣṇa is supposed to have performed a dance with pots of the eve of a battle with the demon Bāṇa, whose daughter Uṣā was in love with his grandson. The dance takes place in Kuṭantai, identified with the present-day town of Kumpakōṇam in Tamiḻ Nāṭu.
Nācciyār Tirumoḻi 11.8	Rescued the earth in the form of a shameful pig	Refers to Viṣṇu's descent as a boar, to rescue the goddess earth, Bhū Devī, submerged in the cosmic ocean.
Nācciyār Tirumoḻi 12.5	Danced on the head of the serpent	Kṛṣṇa vanquished the serpent, Kāliya, that was poisoning the water of the Yamunā. He marked his victory by dancing on its crest.
Nācciyār Tirumoḻi 12.6	Kṛṣṇa at Bhaktivilocana/ Bhaktilocana	Kṛṣṇa and his friends approached Bhaktivilocana hungry and tired and requested food from Brahmins who were performing a sacrifice. They refused him, but their wives eventually fed them.
Nācciyār Tirumoḻi 12.7	Defeat of the demon Pralamba at Bāṇḍīram	Balarāma, Kṛṣṇa's brother, defeated Pralamba, who disguised himself as a cowherd and joined the two boys and their friends. When they reached Bāṇḍīram, he revealed his true form, but Balarāma just struck him down with a forceful blow.

Glossary

Adhyayanotsavam: The Festival of Recitation. Twenty days of recitation of the *Nālāyira Divya Prabandham* in Śrīvaiṣṇava temples in South India.

Akam: Lit. interior, private. Refers to a subgenre of Tamiḻ Caṅkam poetry that deals with love.

Alaṅkāra: Ornamentation/adornment of the gods.

Aṁśa: Emanation. Refers also to the concept of the *āḻvār* as emanations of Viṣṇu.

Ammi: Flat grinding stone used in the South for making pastes. It is a central feature in the South Indian wedding ceremony.

Anaṅga: A name of Kāma. Literally, the limbless one. It refers to the myth where he was burned to ash by Śiva.

Antaryāmin: The god who resides in all things and in all sentient beings.

Anubhava Grantha: A text of/for enjoyment; in Śrīvaiṣṇava parlance, it refers to the commentarial text.

Anubhava: Enjoyment, relish. As a Śrīvaiṣṇava concept, refers to the enjoyment of the god.

Anyāpadeśārtha: The literal interpretation of a text.

Anyārha śeṣatva: Lit. servanthood to no other (deity/person). Refers to exclusive devotion to Viṣṇu.

Araiyar: King/reciter. Hereditary Brahmin ritual performer in Śrīvaiṣṇava temples.

Arjuna: One of the five Pāṇḍava brothers of the *Mahābharata*. Son of Indra. He is Kṛṣṇa's interlocutor in the *Bhagavad Gītā*.

Artha: Wealth, prosperity. One of the four goals of life.

Avatāra: Viṣṇu's descent/incarnation into this world in order to protect *dharma*.

Ācārya: Teacher, preceptor.

Ādi Śeṣa: The thousand-headed serpent upon which Viṣṇu reclines on the ocean of milk. In Śrīvaiṣṇava theology, this serpent is regarded as the foremost (*ādi*) of Viṣṇu's servants (*śeṣa*).

Āḻvār: Those who dive deep. It is a title given to twelve Vaiṣṇava poets who lived between the sixth and ninth century in South India.

Āmpal: Water lily, also known as *alli*. *Nymphaea lotus*.

Āśrita Pāratantriya: Lit. dependence to those who have sought refuge. It refers to Viṣṇu's attribute of being dependent on his devotees.

Āyarpāṭi: Tamiḻ. Gokula. The land of the cowherds, and the place that Kṛṣṇa was raised.

Baladeva/Balarāma: Older brother of Kṛṣṇa. He is considered to be an emanation of Viṣṇu's thousand-headed serpent, Ādi Śeṣa.

Bhakti: Devotion.

Bhakti Yoga: The discipline/practice of devotion.

Bharata: One of the four sons of King Daśaratha. He is the younger brother to Rāma.

Bhagavad Gītā: The Song of God. Kṛṣṇa's discourse to Arjuna on the nature of action, sacrifice, and exclusive devotion to him.

Bhāgavata Purāṇa: The Legend of God. It consists of eighteen chapters. Kṛṣṇa's story, the bulk of the book, is contained in books 10 and 11.

Bhū Devī/Bhūmī: The goddess earth, who is considered to be Viṣṇu's secondary consort.

Brahmin: Priest. Refers to the priestly caste in Indian society.

Campakam: Evergreen tree that produces fragrant white/yellow flowers, *Michelia champaca*.

Caṅkam: To come together. Refers to the (mythic) Tamiḻ literary academy. Also refers to the earliest extant Tamiḻ literary corpus, the Caṅkam anthologies (1st-3rd centuries C.E.).

Caṅku: Conch/conch shell. The word refers to a conch shell, Viṣṇu's conch, and to a woman's bangles.

Ceṅkaḻunīr: Red/purple Indian water-lily, *Nymphaea odorata*.

Cerunti: A kind of sedge. Or golden-blossomed pear tree.

Cetana: Sentient beings.

Devakī: Kṛṣṇa's natural mother and sister of Kaṁsa.

Dharma: The right manner of conduct. It includes religious, political, and legal behavior. One of the four goals of life.

Divya Deśa: Divine Place. There are 108 sites sacred to Śrīvaiṣṇavas. These are the sites that were sung by the *āḻvār* poets. Of these 108, 106 are terrestrial. The last two (107 and 108) are the transcendent realms of Viṣṇu.

Draupadī: The heroine of the *Mahābharata* and wife of the five Pāṇḍava brothers.

Dvarakā: The coastal capital city of Kṛṣṇa.

Gajendra: Viṣṇu's elephant-devotee who was tormented by a crocodile and was rescued by Viṣṇu, who killed the crocodile.

Garuḍa: The king of the birds and Viṣṇu's vehicle.

Gokula: Land of the cowherds. Also known as Āyarpāṭi (Tamiḻ).

Gopī: The cowherd maidens of Vṛndāvana (Gokula, Āyarpāṭi).

Guṇa: Quality, virtue, attribute.

Hanumān: Son of the wind and Rāma's trusted monkey friend. Rāma's messenger.

Jñāna Yoga: The practice of cultivating discerning knowledge.

Kainkarya: Loving service to Viṣṇu.

Kalyāṇa Guṇa: Lit. auspicious qualities, virtues, specifically those associated with Viṣṇu.

Kaṁsa: Kṛṣṇa's uncle and king of Mathurā.

Kaṇṇaṉ: Tamiḻ equivalent for Kṛṣṇa.

Karma Yoga: The discipline of cultivating desireless action.

Katampa: Seaside Indian oak, *Wendlandia notoniana*.

Kayal: A carp fish, *Cyprinus fimbriatus*.

Kāma: The fulfillment of desire. One of the four goals of life.

Kāmadeva: The god of desire.

Kāyā: A tree with purple flowers, *Memecylon malabaricum*.

Koṅku: Silk-cotton tree, *Bombax gossypinum*.

Kurukai: Wild poppy, *Argemone mexicana*.

Kuruntai: A kind of broad-leaf jasmine, *Nyctanthes arbor-tristis*.

Kuyil: Indian cuckoo.

Kūṭal: Joining, coming together. An ancient name for Maturai. Also a game of divination played by young girls to divine the fate of their love.

Kuvaḷai: Blue water lily. Equivalent to the Sanskrit *nīlotpakam*.

Lakṣmaṇa: Rāma's younger brother.

Lakṣmī: Viṣṇu's consort and goddess of wealth and auspiciousness.

Līlā Vibhūti: The realm of play. It refers to the terrestrial world.

Mahābhārata: An epic of one hundred thousand verses that tells of the adventures of the five Pāṇḍava brothers, their ancestors, and their relatives.

Maṇipravāḷa: Lit. gems and coral. A specialized form of Tami̲l prose that combines Tami̲l and Sanskrit and was used most elaborately by the Śrīvaiṣṇavas in their commentaries.

Marukai: A fragrant plant with bright red flowers.

Maruta: A tropical tree.

Mathurā: The city of Kṛṣṇa's birth.

Māci: Month of the Tami̲l solar calendar that usually falls between mid-February and mid-March.

Māṇikkavācakar: c. late ninth century C.E. One of the most important poets of the Tami̲l Śaiva *bhakti* movement. Author of the *Tiruvācakam*, of which the *Tiruvempāvai* is a part.

Mārkaḻi: Month of the Tami̲l calendar that usually falls between mid-December and mid-January.

Mārkaḻi Nīrāṭṭa Utsavam: The festival of bathing held in Mārkaḻi (December–January) and celebrated at Śrīvilliputtūr exclusively for Āṇṭāḷ. Commemorates her observance of the *pāvai* vow.

Muttukkuṟi: Divination with pearls. An enactment performed by the Araiyars at Śrīvilliputtūr, Śrīraṅgam, and Āḻvār Tirunakari.

Mokṣa: Liberation from the cycle of birth and death. One of the four goals of life.

Nappiṉṉai/Nīlā: A cowherd girl that Krishna married by conquering seven bulls. She is considered to be the third consort of Viṣṇu.

Nammāḻvār: Lit. our *āḻvār*. The most important of the twelve *āḻvār*. He composed four texts, of which the most is important is the *Tiruvāymoḻi*.

Nandagopa/Nandagopāla: Kṛṣṇa's foster father and the chief of the cowherds of Gokula.

Nālāyira Divya Prabandham: The compilation/anthology of four thousand Tami̲l poems of the *āḻvār* revered by the Śrīvaiṣṇavas as revealed text.

Ñāḻal: Tigerclaw tree, a thorny deciduous tree, *Erythrina variegata*.

Nāthamuni: The tenth-century preceptor of the Śrīvaiṣṇavas who is credited with recovering the entire corpus of Tami̲l poems of the *āḻvār* that came to be known as the *Nālāyira Divya Prabandham*.

Nāyaṉmār: Leaders. The sixty-three saints of the Tami̲l Śaiva *bhakti* tradition.

Nāma Saṅkīrtana: The recitation of the names of god.

Nirhetuka Kṛpa: The causeless grace of god.

Nityasūri: Eternal divine beings, who reside perpetually in the transcendent realm with Viṣṇu.

Nōṉpu: Lit. vow/ritual observance undertaken by married women or young virgin girls. In the case of the *Tiruppāvai* it refers to the Mārkaḻi vow where unmarried girls bathe at dawn every morning, abstain from particular foods and activities, and praise Kṛṣṇa.

Paṅkuṉi: Month in the Tamiḻ solar calendar that falls between mid-March and mid-April.

Para bhakti: Supreme devotion. In Śrīvaiṣṇava theology it refers to the second phase of mystical experience and follows *bhakti*. It is characterized by mental perception of god.

Para Jñāna: Supreme knowledge. In Śrīvaiṣṇava theology it refers to a temporary vision of god.

Paratva: Viṣṇu's transcendence.

Parama Bhakti: The final phase of the theistic mysticism in Śrīvaiṣṇava theology, where the mystic experiences a complete and eternal union with god.

Parāśara Bhaṭṭar: A twelfth-century teacher and disciple of Rāmānuja. He is credited with writing a *taṉiyaṉ* in Sanskrit for the *Tiruppāvai*.

Paṟai: Lit. ritual drum. In the *Tiruppāvai* it symbolizes grace of Viṣṇu and performing loving service to Viṣṇu.

Pāñcajanya: The name of Viṣṇu's conch. It is associated with the demon Pañcācana who took the form of conch. Viṣṇu/Kṛṣṇa killed the demon and appropriated the conch. As the conch was born from the demon Pañcācana, it received the name, Pāñcajanya (born from Pañcācana).

Pāratantriya: The quality of dependence. The devotees' dependence on Viṣṇu. Complete dependence on Viṣṇu is a necessary precursor for surrender to him.

Pāvai: Lit. doll or woman. It also refers to a particular kind of vow or a genre of poetry called the *pāvai pāṭṭu*. In addition, it is a metonym for the vow (*nōṉpu*) undertaken by young girls during the month of Mārkaḻi (December–January).

Pāyiram: An introduction, preface, or prologue.

Periyāḻvār: Lit. the great *āḻvār*. See Viṣṇucittaṉ.

Periyavāccāṉ Piḷḷai: Thirteenth-century commentator on the entire *Nālāyira Divya Prabandham*.

Phala Śruti: Lit. the fruit of listening. It refers to the benedictory verses that concludes a poem, or a section of a longer poem.

Prāpaka: The means to achieve the goal.

Prāpya: The goal to be achieved, Viṣṇu.

Puṟam: Lit. exterior, public. Asubgenre of Tamiḻ Caṅkam poetry that dealt with kings, politics, and war.

Puruṣakāra: The mediator, who aids the devotee in reaching Viṣṇu. There are several mediators and chief among them is Viṣṇu's consort, Śrī.

Puruṣārtha: The aims of life. In Sanskrit literature on *dharma*, there are four aims of life—*dharma* (code of conduct, law, etc.), *artha* (wealth), *kāma* (desire), and mokṣa (liberation from the cycle of birth and death).

Pūtanā: Ademoness sent by Kam.sa to kill Kṛṣṇa.

Rāma: The seventh incarnation of Viṣṇu. The hero of the *Rāmāyaṇa*.

Rāmānuja (1017-1137 C.E.): Arguably the most important preceptor of the Śrīvaiṣṇavas, credited with instituting a number of temple reforms. He also wrote a number of commentaries, including one on the *Bhagavad Gītā*.

Rāmāyaṇa, Vālmīki: The Sanskrit epic that narrates the exploits of the divine prince Rāma.

Rāvaṇa: The anti-hero of the *Rāmāyaṇa*. The king of Laṅka.

Rukmiṇī: One of Kṛṣṇa's primary consorts.

Saṁsāra: The cycle of birth and death.

Saṁśleṣa: Union.

Saulabhya: Viṣṇu's accessibility to his devotees.

Sauśīlya: Graciousness.

Sītā: The heroine of the *Rāmāyaṇa*, Rāma's wife.

Svāpadeśārtha: Inner, esoteric meaning of a text.

Svabhava: Essential attributes, qualities.

Svarūpa: Essential nature.

Svātantriya: Lit. independence. In Śrīvaiṣṇava theology, it refers to Viṣṇu's independence, that is, his ability to act alone and be the sole arbiter of grace.

Śaraṇāgati: Total and exclusive surrender to Viṣṇu.

Śārṅga: The name of Viṣṇu's bow.

Śeṣa: Lit. remainder. Servant/Slave. It is used in reference to the human soul, who is owned by god (*Śeṣi*(n)—owner) Also, the name of Viṣṇu's serpent that serves as his bed. He is considered to be the exemplary servant.

Śrī: Radiance, fortune, splendor, auspiciousness. Another name for Lakṣmī, the primary consort of Viṣṇu. The Tamil̲ equivalent is Tiru.

Śrīvaiṣṇava: The community that worships both Śrī (Lakṣmī) and Viṣṇu and accepts the Tamil̲ songs of the *āl̲vār* as revealed.

Śrīraṅgam/Tiruvaraṅkam: The temple town located near modern Tiruccirāppaḷḷi (Trichy) is the most important of the Śrīvaiṣṇava sites.

Śrīvilliputtūr: The temple town, seventy-five kilometers northeast of Maturai, considered to be the birthplace of Viṣṇucittan̲ (Periyāl̲vār) and his daughter, Āṇṭāḷ.

Śūrpaṇakhā: Sister of Rāvaṇa.

Tan̲iyan̲: Laudatory verses appended to the compositions of the *āl̲vār* and *ācāryas*.

Tai: Month in the Tamil̲ solar calendar that falls between mid-January and mid-February.

Tirumāliruñcōlai/Māliruñcōlai: The grove of Māl. A sacred temple site near the city of Maturai, and one of the 108 *divya deśa* sacred to Śrīvaiṣṇavas.

Tiruvempāvai: A Śaiva poem by Māṇikkavācakar describing the *pāvai* vow.

Tulasī: Indian basil.

Upāya: Way, means, path. In Śrīvaiṣṇava theology it refers to the path to Viṣṇu. Viṣṇu is both the means and the goal.

Upeya: The goal. In Śrīvaiṣṇava theology it refers to Viṣṇu.

Vaikuṇṭha: Viṣṇu's paradise.

Valampuri: Another name for Viṣṇu's conch. A conch which has its spirals oriented to the right/clockwise (*valam*) as opposed to a conch with spirals directed counter-clockwise (*iṭampuri*).

Vāḷ: Cutlass fish.

Vātsalya: Tender, maternal affection. An attribute of Viṣṇu.

Vanamālā: Viṣṇu's garland of unfading flowers.

Veda: Set of four texts (*Ṛg*, *Sāma*, *Yajur*, and *Atharva*). Hindus consider these to be revealed texts.

Vēṅkaṭam: A mountain site sacred to Viṣṇu and one of the 108 *divya deśa* sacred to Śrīvaiṣṇavas.

Vibhīṣaṇa: Rāvaṇa's brother, who defected and surrendered to Rāma.

Viśiṣṭādvaita: Qualified nondualist philosophy systematized by Rāmānuja.

Viṣṇucittaṉ: One of the twelve *āḻvār* poets. He composed the *Tiruppallāṇṭu* and *Periyāḻvār Tirumoḻi*. He is also known as Periyāḻvār. He is referred to in the final verses of Āṇṭāḷ's poems and hagiography suggests that he was her father.

Vṛndāvana: The Forest of Vṛndā (basil plants). The land of Kṛṣṇa's childhood.

Vyājya: Pretext.

Yaśodā: Kṛṣṇa's foster mother, who raised him in Vṛndāvana/Gokula.

Bibliography

PRIMARY SOURCES IN TAMIḺ AND MAṆIPRAVĀḶA ORGANIZED BY TITLE

Āṇṭāḷ aruḷicceyta Tiruppāvai: Sri Uttamūr Tirumalai nallāṉ Cakravarti Vīrarāghavācāryār Iyaṟṟiya Prapandha rakṣai eṉṉum uraiyutaṉ. Madras: Ubhaya Vedanta Grantha Malai, 1986.

Āṇṭāḷ aruḷicceyta Nācciyār Tirumoḻi: Sri Uttamūr Tirumalai nallāṉ Cakravarti Vīrarāghavācāryār Iyaṟṟiya Prapandha rakṣai eṉṉum uraiyutaṉ. 2nd ed. Chennai: Ubhaya Vedanta Grantha Malai, 1997.

Cūṭikkoṭutta Nācciyār aruḷicceyta Tiruppāvai. P. B. Aṇṇaṅkarācāriya Svāmikaḷ Iyaṟṟiya Tiruppāvai Naṟumaṇam eṉṉum viśēṣa uraiyuṭaṉ. Kāñcīpuram: Aṇṇaṅkarācāriya Institute, 1971.

Guruparamparaprabhāvam 6000. Maṇipravāḷa Text. Eds. Srinivasa Appankar Swami et al. Chennai: Ganesh Publications.

Nācciyār Tirumoḻi Vyākhyāṉam. (Periyavāccāṉ Piḷḷai) Ed. Krishnaswami Iyengar. Trichy: Srinivasa Press.

Nālāyira Divya Prabandham. Tamiḻ text. Ed. Aṇṇaṅkarācāriya Kāñcīpuram: Aṇṇaṅkarācāriya Institute, 1972.

Nālāyira Divya Prabandham. Tamiḻ text. Ed. Krishnaswami Iyengar. Trichy: Srinivasa Press.

Śrīvilliputtūr Sthala Purāṇam. Tamiḻ text. Publication Information Unavailable.

Tamiḻ Lexicon. Vol. 1–7. Madras: University of Madras, 1982.

Tiruppāvai Mūvāyirappaṭi Vyākhyāṉam. (Periyavāccāṉ Piḷḷai.) Ed. Aṇṇaṅkarācāriya Kāñcīpuram: Aṇṇaṅkarācāriya Institute, 1970.

Tiruppāvai Vyākhyāṉam. (U.V.K. Srinivasa Iyengar Swami). Ed. Krishnaswami Iyengar. 4th ed. Trichy: Srinivasa Press, 1991.

SECONDARY SOURCES

Ate, Lynn Marie. "Periyāḻvār's Tirumoḻi: A Bālakṛṣṇa Text from the Devotional Period in Tamiḻ Literature." Ph.D. diss., University of Wisconsin-Madison, 1978.

Battar, Vijayabhaskara. *Śrīvilliputtūr Śrī Āṇṭāḷ*. Śrīvilliputtūr: Srinidhi Publications, 1996.

Benton, Catherine. *God of Desire: Tales of Kāmadeva in Sanskrit Story Literature*. Albany: State University of New York Press, 2006.

Bharati, Srirama, trans. *The Sacred Book of Four Thousand*. Chennai: Sri Sadagopan Tirunarayanswami Divya Prabandha Pathasala, 2000.

Branfoot, Crispin. "'Expanding Form': The Architectural Sculpture of the South Indian Temple, ca 1500–1700." *Artibus Asiae*, vol. 62, no. 2, (2002). pp. 189–245.

Bryant, Edwin. *Krishna: The Beautiful Legend of God (Śrīmad Bhāgavatam Book X)*. London: Penguin Books, 2003.

———. "The Date and Provenance of the Bhāgavata Purāṇa and the Vaikuṇṭha Perumāḷ Temple." *Journal of Vaishnava Studies*, vol. 11, no. 1, (2002). pp. 51–80.

Carman, John, and Vasudha Narayanan. *The Tamiḻ Veda: Piḷḷāṉ's Interpretation of the Tiruvāymoḻi*. Chicago: University of Chicago Press, 1989.

Chari, S. M. S. *Philosophy and Theistic Mysticism of the Āḻvārs*. New Delhi: Motilal Banarasidass, 1997.

Cutler, Norman. *Songs of Experience: The Poetics of Tamiḻ Devotion*. Bloomington: Indiana University Press, 1987.

———. *Consider our Vow: Translation of Tiruppāvai and Tiruvempāvai into English*. Madurai: Muttu Patippakam, 1979.

Dehejia, Vidya. *Slaves of the Lord: Path of the Tamiḻ Saints*. New Delhi: Munshiram Manoharlal, 1988.

———. *Āṇṭāḷ and Her Path of Love*. Albany: State University of New York Press, 1990.

Filliozat, Jean, trans. *Un Texte Tamoul de Devotion Vishnouite Le Tiruppāvai d' Āṇṭāḷ*. Pondicherry: Institut Français D'Indologie, 1972.

Fuller, C. J. *The Camphor Flame: Popular Hinduism and Society in India*. Princeton, N.J.: Princeton University Press, 1992.

Goldman, Robert P., et al., trans. and eds. *Rāmāyaṇa of Vālmīki: An Epic of Ancient India*. Vol 1–6. Princeton, N.J.: Princeton University Press, 1984–2009.

Hardy, Friedhelm. *Viraha Bhakti: The Early History of Kṛṣṇa Devotion in South India*. Delhi: Oxford University Press, 1983.

Hart, George L. *The Poems of Ancient Tamiḻ: Their Milieu and Their Sanskrit Counterparts*. Berkeley and Los Angeles: University of California Press, 1988.

———. *Poets of the Tamiḻ Anthologies: Ancient Poems of Love and War*. Princeton, N.J.: Princeton University Press, 1979.

Hawley, John Stratton. *Three Bhakti Voices: Mirabai, Surdas and Kabir in Their Times and Ours*. New Delhi: Oxford University Press, 2005.

———. "The Damage of Separation: Krishna's Loves and Kali's Child. *Journal of the American Academy of Religion*, vol. 72, no. 2, (June 2004). pp. 369–93.

Heifetz, Hank, trans. *Origin of a Young God: Kālidāsa's Kumārasambhava*. Berkeley and Los Angeles: University of California, Press, 1985.

Hopkins, Steven P. *An Ornament for Jewels: Love Poems for the Lord of Gods by Vedāntadeśika.* New York: Oxford University Press, 2007.

———. *Singing the Body of God: The Hymns of Vedāntadeśika in Their South Indian Tradition.* New York: Oxford University Press, 2002.

Hudson, Dennis. "Āṇṭāḷ's Desire." *Vaiṣṇavī: Women and the Worship of Krishna.* Ed. Stephen J. Rosen. New Delhi: Motilal Banarasidass, 1996. pp. 171–211.

———. "Āṇṭāḷ Āḻvār: A Developing Hagiography." *The Journal of Vaishnava Studies,* vol. 1, no. 2, (1993). pp. 27–61.

———. "Piṉṉai: Krishna's *Cowherd* Wife." *The Divine Consort: Rādhā and the Goddesses of India.* Eds. John Stratton Hawley and Donna Marie Wulff. Boston: Beacon Press, 1987. pp. 238–62.

———. "Bathing in Krishna: A Study in Vaiṣṇava Hindu Theology." *The Harvard Theological Review,* vol. 73, no. 3/4. (July–Oct. 1980), pp. 539–66.

Jagannathachariar, C. *The Tiruppāvai of Śrī Āṇṭāḷ: Textual, Literary and Critical Study.* Madras: Arulmigu Parthasarathy Swami Devasthanam, 1982.

Mani, Vettam. *The Puranic Encyclopedia: A Comprehensive Dictionary with Special Reference to the Epic and Puranic Literature.* Delhi: Motilal Banarasidass, 1975.

Miller, Barbara Stoler, trans. *The Bhagavad-Gita: Krishna's Counsel in Time of War.* New York: Bantam Dell, 1986.

Narayanan, Vasudha. "Brimming with Bhakti, Embodiments of Shakti." *Feminism and World Religions.* Eds. Arvind Sharma and Katherine Young. Albany: State University of New York. 1999. pp. 25–77.

———. "The Realm of Play and the Sacred Stage." *Gods at Play: Līlā in South Asia.* Ed. William Sax. New York: Oxford University Press, 1995. pp. 177–204.

———. *The Vernacular Veda: Revelation, Recitation, and Ritual.* Columbia: University of South Carolina Press, 1994.

———. *The Way and the Goal: Expressions of Devotion in Early Śrīvaiṣṇava Commentary.* Washington, D.C.: Institute for Vaishnava Studies, 1987.

Peterson, Indira Viswanath. *Poems to Śiva: The Hymns of the Tamiḻ Saints.* Princeton, N.J.: Princeton University Press, 1989.

Pollock, Sheldon, ed. *Literary Cultures in History: Reconstructions from South Asia.* Berkeley and Los Angeles: University of California Press, 2003.

———. "Rāmāyaṇa and the Political Imagination." *Journal of Asian Studies,* vol. 52, no. 2, (May 1993). pp. 261–97.

Ramanujan, A. K. *Hymns for the Drowning.* New York: Penguin Books, 1993.

———. *Poems of Love and War From the Eight Anthologies and the Ten Long Poems of Classical Tamiḻ.* New York: Columbia University Press, 1985.

———. "On Women Saints." *The Divine Consort: Rādhā and the Goddesses of India.* Eds. John Stratton Hawley and Donna Marie Wulff. Boston: Beacon Press, 1982. pp. 316–26.

———, and Norman Cutler. "From Classicism to Bhakti." *The Collected Essays of A. K. Ramanujan.* New York: Oxford University Press, 1999. pp. 232–59.

Reynolds, Holly Baker. "To Keep the Tāli Strong: Women's Rituals in Tamiḻnaḍ, India." Ph.D. diss., University of Wisconsin-Madison, 1978.

Rosen, Stephen, ed. *Vaiṣṇavī: Women and the Worship of Krishna*. New Delhi: Motilal Banarasidass, 1996.

Rukmani, T. S. *A Critical Study of the Bhāgavata Purāṇa*. Varanasi: Chowkhamba, 1970.

Sarada, S. "Andal Charitram." *Kalakshetra Rukmini Devi: Reminiscences by S. Sarada*. Madras: Kala Mandir Trust, 1985. p.138.

Selby, Martha. *Grow Long Blessed Night: Love Poems from Classical India*. New York: Oxford University Press, 2000. pp. 17–21.

Sharma, Arvind, and Katherine Young, eds. *Feminism and World Religions*. Albany: State University of New York Press, 1999.

Simha, S. N. L. *Tiruppāvai of Godā: Our Lady Saint Āṇḍāḷ's Krishna Poem*. Bombay: Ananthacharya Indological Institute, 1982.

Śrī Āṇṭāḷ: Her Contributions to Literature, Philosophy, Religion and Art. Acompilation of lectures during the All India Seminar on Andal: August 13–15, 1983. Madras: Sri Ramanuja Vedanta Center, 1985.

Sriram, V. *Carnatic Summer: Lives of Twenty Great Exponents*. Chennai: East West Books, 2004. pp. 10–14.

Sundaram, P. S., trans. *Āṇḍāḷ: Tiruppavai and Nachiyar Tirumozhi*. Bombay: Ananthacharya Indological Institute, 1987. Tharu, Susie, and Lalitha K., ed. *Women Writing in India Vol. 1: 600 BC–early 20th century*. New York: The Feminist Press, 1991.

Venkataraman, C. *Araiyar Cēvai*. Madras: Tamiḻ Puttakālayam, 1985.

Venkatachari, K.K.A. *The Maṇipravāḷa Literature of the Śrīvaiṣṇava Ācāryas*. Bombay: Ananthacharya Institute, 1978.

Venkatesan, Archana. "Double the Pleasure: Reading Nammāḻvār's *Tiruviruttam*." *Passages: Relationships between Tamiḻ and Sanskrit*. Eds. M. Kannan and Jennifer Clare. Pondicherry: French Institute of Pondicherry and Tamiḻ Chair, University of California, Berkeley, 2009. pp. 257–69.

———." Who Stole the Garland of Love: Āṇṭāḷ Stories in the Śrīvaiṣṇava Tradition." *Journal of Vaishnava Studies*, Vol 15, no. 2, (Spring 2007). pp. 189–206.

———. "AWoman's Kind of Love: Female Longing in the Tamil Alvar Poetry." *Journal of Hindu Christian Studies*, vol. 20, (2007). pp. 16–24.

———. "Divining the Future of AGoddess: The Araiyar Cēvai as commentary at the Śrīvilliputtūr Āṇṭāḷ Temple." *Nidan: The International Journal of Hinduism*, vol. 17, (2005). pp. 19–51

———. "Āṇṭāḷ and Her Magic Mirror: Her Life as Poet in the Guises of the Goddess." Ph.D. diss., University of California, Berkeley, 2004.

Venkatesananda, Swami. *The Concise Srimad Bhagavatam*. Albany: State University of New York Press, 1989.

Waghorne, Joanna, Norman Cutler, and Vasudha Narayanan, eds. *Gods of Flesh/Gods of Stone: The Embodiment of Divinity in India*. Chambersburg, Penn.: Anima Publications. 1985.

Younger, Paul. "Singing the Tamiḻ Hymn Book in the Tradition of Rāmānuja: The Adyayanōtsava Festival in Śrīraṅkam " *History of Religions*, vol. 21. no. 3, (1982). pp. 272–93.

———. "Ten Days of Wandering and Romance with LordRaṅkanātaṉ: The Paṅkuni Festival in Śrīraṅkam Temple, South India." *Modern Asian Studies*, vol. 16, no. 4, (Oct. 1982). pp. 623–56.

Zvelebil, Kamil. *History of Tamil̲ Literature*. Leiden: E. J. Brill, 1975.

———. *The Smile of Murugan: On Tamil̲ Literature of South India*. Leiden: E. J. Brill, 1973.

ELECTRONIC SOURCES

Bhakti List Archives. Online. Available: http://www.Ramanuja.org/sv/bhakti/about.html. August 8, 2009

Sathakopan, Oppilliappan Varadchari. Sri Andal's Nacciyar Tirumozhi. Online. Available: http://www.sundarasimham.org/e-booksS2.htm. August 8, 2009.

Sathakopan, Oppilliappan Varadchari. Sri Andal's. Tiruppāvai. Online. Available: http://www.sundarasimham.org/e-booksS3.htm. August 8, 2009.

Ratnam, Anita. Naachiyar: Mystic Search for the Divine. Online. Available: http://www.arangham.com/repertor/nachiyar/nachiyar.html. August 8, 2009.

Raman, Jayanthi. Krishna Bhakti, 2006. Online. Available: http://www.jayanthiraman.com/Productions/productions.htm. August 8, 2009.

Index

abhiṣeka (ritual ablutions), 33, 34
ācārya (teacher), 195
ācārya paramparā (lineage of teachers), 94
acetana (insentient beings), 201
adamātmaṉ, 89
Adhyayanotsavam (Festival of Recitation), 6, 33, 35
Ādiśeṣa, 114
Ahalyā, 227
ahaṁkāra (self-importance), 124
ajnāna (ignorance), 191, 204
akam (interior), 112, 194
akavacīr, 44*n*19
Akrūra, 99, 232
Aḻakar Kōyil, 199
alaṅkāra (ornamentation), 33, 34, 47*n*52, 119
alkul, 105
Āḻvār Tirunakari, 35, 200
Amar Chitra Katha, 38
ammi, 205
āmpal flowers, 40, 109
aṁśa (emanation), 114
āṉaiccāttaṉ, 98
Anaṅga, 193
Andal Kalyanam, 37
Aṅgada, 228
Aniruddha, 114, 233–34
Annangaracharíar, 82, 83
Annangaracharíar Press, 42
Āṇṭāḷ, 17–18, 43*n*3, 81, 133, 224–25 (see also *Nācciyār Tirumoḻi*; *Tiruppāvai*)
  Annual Bathing Festival of, 34
  commentary of works of, 31–33
  enactment of, at Śrīvilliputtūr Āṇṭāḷ temple, 34–35
  historical, and place among *āḻvār*, 5–7
  story of, 4–5
  and women poet-saints of India, 7–16
Āṇṭāḷ and Her Path of Love, 38–39
Āṇṭāṉ, Tirukaṇṇamaṅkai, 225
Antarī, 205
antarīkṣa (the heavens), 122
antaryāmin (in-dweller of sentient beings), 98, 122
antāti, 143
anubhava, 31, 33, 49*n*76
anubhava grantha, 31, 33, 49*n*76

anyāpadeśārtha (literal meaning), 82
anyārha śeṣatva, 124
Araiyar Cēvai (service of the Araiyars), 35–36
Araiyars, 133, 199
Ārāyirappaṭi, 82
Arjuna, 216, 230
Aṟputatiruvantāti, 8
artha pañcaka (five truths), 119, 132
Arundale, Rukmini, 37
āśritapakṣapādam (impartial protection), 123
āśrita paratantra (devotion to devotees), 93
atamaṉ, 89
Attuḻāy, 117
avatāra, 16, 89, 98, 114, 116, 122, 131
Aveṉcīr, 44*n*19
Āyarpāṭi, 12, 17, 18, 87, 113, 116, 123, 129, 143, 199, 201, 218 (see also *Vṛndāvana*)
Ayodhyā, 191

Bakāsura, 107, 199, 231
Baladeva. *See* Balarāma
Balarāma, 111, 114, 218, 232, 233
Bāṇa, 233–34
Bāṇḍīram, 218
Benton, Catherine, 191, 192
Bhagavad Gītā, 83, 85, 92, 136, 137, 216, 230
bhagavat-anubhavam (enjoyment of god), 103
Bhāgavata Purāṇa, 17, 18, 45*n*26, 46*n*33, 83, 123, 133, 193, 196, 199, 230–34
bhāgavatas (those who worship Viṣṇu), 102
bhaktas (devotees), 102
Bhaktilocana, 218
bhakti mārga (exclusive devotion), 137
bhakti songs, 6
bhakti yoga (the discipline of devotion), 209, 230
Bharata, 217, 227, 228, 229
Bharatanātyam, 37
Bhaṭṭar, Parāśara, 135, 143, 224
Bhīṣma, 215
bhoga (worldly experience), 198
Bhū Devī, 6, 8, 15, 16, 38, 190, 191, 205, 215, 225
brahmamuhūrta, 86
Brahmins, 35, 38, 85, 88, 99, 142, 204, 225
Bryant, Edwin, 45*n*26, 230

Caṅkam poems, 121, 194, 202, 218
  and anthologies, 7
  of war, 18–19
Caṅkam Tamiḻ, 144
caṅku (conch), 28–30, 47*n*44
Cāṇūra, 233
carama śloka, 230
ceṅkaḻunīr, 109
cetana (sentient beings), 138, 201
Cilappatikāram, 32, 33, 219
ciṟṟil. *See* sandcastles, song of
Citralekhā, 233
clothes, song for, 154–56, 196–97
collective union, 121
collective voice, 26–27
communal worship, importance of, 96–110, 133
conch bangles, song for, 215–16
cūṭikkoṭuttavaḷ, 4
Cutler, Norman, 8, 17, 18, 19, 49*n*75, 143

Damanakotsava (Festival of the Damanaka Flower), 191
Dāmodaraṉ. *See* Viṣṇu
dark rain clouds, song to, 208–10
Dāsa, Tiruvaḻuti Valanādu, 135
Daśaratha, 227, 228
Dehejia, Vidya, 14, 19, 38, 108
desire, song of, 219
deva, 32
Devakī, 197, 231
devaloka (the world of the gods), 122
dharma, of women, 38
divination, song of, 157–58, 198–200
divya deśa, 6
Divyasūricaritram, 37

Kṛṣṇa, 9, 12, 15, 16, 18, 19–22, 24, 26–27, 33, 35, 37, 40, 81, 82, 83, 85, 86, 90, 92, 96, 98, 99–102, 103, 105, 107, 110–16, 118–22, 124–26, 128–31, 134, 135, 136–40, 194–96, 204, 211, 216, 217, 218, 219, 220–21, 224, 229, 230–34
  vow and quest for, 88
kṛṣṇānubhavam (the enjoyment of Kṛṣṇa), 86, 103, 121
kṛṣṇasaṁśleṣa (union with Kṛṣṇa), 86, 195, 196–97, 198
Kumbhakarṇa, 104
Kurukṣetra, 230
kuruntai tree, 196
Kuṟuntokai, 32
Kuśa, 229
kūṭal, 198, 199
kuvaḷai, 89
Kuvalayāpīḍa, 199, 232
Kuyil, song to, 159–62, 201–3

Lakṣmaṇa, 96, 114, 193, 227, 228
Lakṣmī, 115, 199, 225
lament, song of, 213–14
laukika (worldly), 89
Lava, 229
līlā vibhūti (material world of play), 119
liturgical recitation, 33
Lokācārya, Piḷḷai, 132
love-sickness, 199

Māci, 192, 193
Mādhavaṉ. *See* Kṛṣṇa
madhyamaṉ, 89
Mahābhārata, 92, 123, 135, 215, 229–30
Mahādevīyakka, 8
Māliruncōlai, 13
Māmāyaṉ. *See* Kṛṣṇa
Māmi, 102
maṇḍala (magical diagrams), 192, 193
maṇḍali, 38
maṅgalāṣāsanam, 128
Mani, Vettam, 230
Māṇikkavācakar, 19, 46*n*27, 111
Maṇipravāḷa, 31, 47*n*48, 82, 83, 189
Maṇipuri dance, 37
maṇṭapa, 34
Mārīca, 228
Mārkaḻi (December–January), 12, 17–18, 33, 51, 85–87, 108
  bathing in, 34–35, 133
Mārkaḻi Nīrāṭṭa Utsavam (Festival of Ceremonial Bathing in Mārkaḻi). *See* Mārkaḻi
maruta trees, 199
Mātali, 203
mātavi, 117
Mathurā, 93, 130, 217, 218, 219, 231, 232
Maturai, 198, 219
Māyaṉ, 93
Māyāvatī, 233
meditative sleep. See *yoga nidrā* (meditative sleep)
Meghadūta, 208, 209
metonomy, 30
metonymy, 30, 194
Mīrā, 9, 37, 38
Mithilā, 227
mokṣa, 38, 132, 137
Mount Kailāśa, 7
muni (sages), 96
muṟacu, 18–19
mūrti (embodiment), 98
Muṣṭika, 233
Muttā, 7
muttukkuṟi (divination with pearls), 35–36, 199–200
Mūvāyirappaṭi, 82

Naachiyar: Mystic Search for the Divine, 37
Nācciyār Tirumoḻi, 8, 10, 11, 12–13, 14–15, 32, 37, 38, 39, 41–42, 47*n*43, 82, 90, 101, 111, 127, 140, 142, 143, 144 (*see also* Āṇṭāḷ)
  and *Araiyar Cēvai* at Śrīvilliputtūr, 35–36

paratva (transcendence), 102, 132
Paripāṭal 11, 17, 46*n*30
parrot, significance of, 202, 202–3
pāvai nōṉpu, 12, 17, 84, 88, 133, 192
pāyiram (preface), 84, 85–93
pēraravam (great sound), 97
Periyāḻvār. *See* Viṣṇucittaṉ
Periyāḻvār Tirumoḻi, 5, 6, 11, 37
Periya Nampi, 117
periyāy (supreme), 122
Pēyāḻvār, 81
phala śruti verses (benedictory verses), 5, 47*n*43, 101, 142, 143, 144–45, 193, 205, 214, 216
piccai (alms), 88
Piḷḷai, Periyavāccāṉ, 31–33, 41, 49*n*76, 81, 82, 83, 85, 88, 89, 90, 98, 99, 106, 116, 118, 121, 132, 135, 189, 190, 191, 192, 193, 195, 196, 197, 198, 199, 201, 202, 204, 205, 206, 208, 209, 210, 211, 213, 214, 215, 216, 217, 219, 220, 227
Pradyumna, 193, 233
Pralamba, 218, 232
prāpaka, 86
prāpya, 86
pūjas, 33
puram (exterior), 112, 124, 194
Puṟanāṉūru, 44–45*n*20
Purāṇic Encyclopedia, 230
Purṣusottamaṉ, 89
puruṣakāra (intermediary figure), 17, 111, 114, 115, 116, 118, 119, 121, 206, 215
puruṣārtha kaiṅkarya (the goal of life as loving service to god), 140
puruṣārthas (the goals of life), 84, 119
puruṣārtha svarūpa (the nature of the goal), 132
Pūtanā, 96, 231
Putuvai. *See* Śrīvilliputtūr
pūvai, 127

questions and answers, song of, 220–21

rākṣasa, 107, 108
Rāma, 106, 107, 118, 122, 128, 132, 134, 191, 193, 195, 196, 205, 209, 213, 217, 227, 228, 229
Raman, Jayanthi, 37
Rāmānuja, 32, 47*n*52, 116–17, 190, 212, 224
Ramanujan, A. K., 8, 18
Rāmāyaṇa, 83, 92, 102, 105, 107, 114, 118, 122, 126, 132, 135, 190, 192, 197, 208, 209, 213, 217, 227
Rāmāyaṇa, Vālmīki, 31, 33, 49*n*76, 227–29
Raṅganātha, 5
Raṅgarāmānuja, 82
Ratī, 17, 233
Ratnam, Anita, 37
Rāvaṇa, 92, 106, 107, 123, 130, 213, 228, 229
Rukmavatī, 233
Rukmi, 233
Rukmiṇī, 115, 215, 233

sacred places, song of, 217–18
sādhana (practices), 138
Śakaṭa, 97
Sāma, 192, 193
Śambara, 233
sambhoga (union), 120
saṁsāra (cycles of birth and death), 124, 125, 195
sandcastles, song of, 194–95
sannyāsis (renunciants), 88
śārṅga, 91
śaraṇāgati (surrender), 137, 139
Sarayū river, 192, 229
sarveśvaraṉ (god of gods), 120
Sathakopan, Sri Varadachari Oppiliappan, 83
Śatrughna, 227
sattva guṇa (virtue of luminosity), 192
saulabhya (accessibility), 131, 135, 138
sauśīlya (graciousness), 135

Śayana tirukkōlam (The Depiction of the Attitude of Repose), 33, 119
self-delusion, 124
self-mutilation, 14
self-portraits, verbal, 143
sensuality, 14
sexual union, 46, 86, 111, 116, 121, 122, 137, 197
Singing the Body of God, 39
Śiśupāla, 123, 196, 199, 234
Sītā, 32, 92, 102, 106, 107, 115, 118, 119, 135, 190, 196, 205, 208, 211, 215, 220, 227, 228, 229
Śiva, 7, 8, 212, 233, 234
Songs of Experience, 49*n*75, 143
Śrī, 120
Śrī Devī, 6, 13, 15, 205
Srinivasa Press, 42
Śrīraṅgam, 4, 35, 200, 216, 224
śrītvam (the character of Śrī), 120
Śrīvilliputtūr, 3–4, 12, 33, 34, 101, 119, 133, 142–43, 200, 212, 225
śṛṅgāra (desire/love), 209
strītvam (womanly nature), 124
Sugrīva, 228
Sumitrā, 227
Sundararāja Perumāḷ, 212
Śūrpaṇakhā, 118, 132, 135, 228
svabhāva, 135
svāpadeśārtha (esoteric meaning), 82, 91
sva svarūpa (the nature of one's self), 132
svātantriya (quality of independence), 113, 124, 213, 215, 217
Swami, Srinivasa Aiyyankar, 83

Tai, 147–50, 191–93
tai nīrāṭal, 17–18
tāli (sacred thread in marriage), 204
Tamiḻ *bhakti* poems, 41
Tamiḻ poetic meters, 44*n*19
Tamiḻ syntax, 39
taṉiyaṉs (laudatory poem), 9, 145
  Nācciyār Tirumoḻi, 224–25
  Tiruppāvai, 223–24
taṉṉumai, 19
Tāṭakā, 227
Therīgāthā, 7
Tiruiraṭṭaimaṇimālai, 8
Tirukkōṭṭiyūr, 224
Tirumāliruncōlai groves, song in, 211–12
Tirumaṅkaiyāḻvār, 35, 48*n*57
Tiruneṭuntāṇṭakam, 35, 48*n*57
Tiruppallāṇṭu, 11, 128, 132, 133
Tiruppāvai, 9, 11–12, 14, 25, 32, 36, 38, 39, 40, 41–42, 81, 191, 192, 194 (*see also* Āṇṭāḷ)
  Āḻi Maḻai Kaṇṇā, 54, 90
  Amparamē Taṇṇīre, 67, 114–15
  and Āḻvār concordance, 94t
  Aṅkaṇmā Nālattu, 72, 124–25
  Aṟṟivvulakam, 74, 128–29
  baths in, 17–18
  Ciṟṟañciṟukālē, 79, 136–41
  demarcation between devotee and consort in, 15–16
  drums in, 18, 19
  ēl ōr empāvāy (refrain) in, 19–20
  Ellē Iḷaṅkiḷiyē, 65, 110
  Ēṟṟa Kalaṅkaḷ, 71, 122–23
  as imagined reality, 16
  Kaṉaittiḷaṅ Kaṟṟerumai, 62, 106
  Kaṟavaikaḷ Piṉ Ceṉṟu, 78, 136–39
  Kaṟṟukkaṟavai, 61, 105
  Kīcu Kīcu, 57, 98
  Kīḻvāṉam Veḷeṉṟu, 58, 99–100
  Kūṭārai Vellum, 77, 134–35
  Kuttu Viḷakkeriya, 69, 118–19
  Mālē Maṇivaṇṇā, 76, 132–33
  Māri Maḻai Mulañcil, 73, 126–27
  Mārkaḻi Tiṅkaḷ, 51, 85–87
  Māyaṉai Maṉṉu, 55, 91–93
  Muppattu Mūvar, 70, 120–21
  myths in, 236t–38t
  Nāyakaṉai Niṉṟa, 66, 113
  Nōṟṟuccuvarkam, 60, 103–4
  Ōṅki Ulakaḷanta, 53, 89

Tiruppāvai (*continued*)
  Orutti Makaṉāy Piṟantu, 75, 130–31
  Puḷḷiṉvāy Kīṇṭāṉai, 63, 107–8
  Puḷḷum Cilampiṉa Kāṉ, 56, 96–97
  ritual lives of, 33–34
  structure of, 20–23
  taṉiyaṉ, 223–24
  Tūmaṇi Māṭattu, 59, 101–2
  Uṅkaḷ Puḻaikkaṭai, 64, 109
  Untu Mata Kaḷiṟṟaṉ, 68, 116–17
  Vaiyattu Vāḻvīrkāḷ, 52, 88
  Vaṅkakkaṭal, 80, 142–45
  vows in, 17
Tiruppāvai Jīyar. *See* Rāmānuja
Tiruvālaṅkāṭṭu Mūtta Tiruppatikams, 8
Tiruvāymoḻi, 6, 82, 134, 143, 204, 211, 221
Tiruvempāvai, 19, 46*n*27, 48*n*53, 108, 111
Tiruviruttam, 32
Tiruvyāmoḻi, 46*n*41
tulasī plant, 4, 40, 104
tūtu/sandeśa (messenger) poems, 201–2
tuyileṭai (waking-up), 94

upamāna (known object), 90
upameya, 90
upāya, 86
upāya svarūpa (the nature of the means), 132
upeya, 86
ūṟṟam uṭaiyāy (unknowable), 122
Uṣā, 233, 234
Uttamaṉ. *See* Viṣṇu
Uyyakoṇtār, 143
Uyyakoṇṭār, 223

Vaikuṇṭha, 88, 122, 140
Vaikuṇṭhaṉ. *See* Kṛṣṇa
Valampuri, 91, 207
Vālin, 228
Vāmana, 89
vaṅka-k katal, 145
vārppaṭam (bronze casting procedure), 214
Vasiṣṭha, 128
Vasudeva, 197, 231
Vaṭapatraśāyi (lord who reclines on a banyan leaf), 133
vātsalya (maternal love), 106, 123, 124, 132z
Vedānta Deśika, 6, 39
Vedas, 122
Veeraraghavachariar, Uttamur, 82, 83, 189, 191
Vēṅkaṭam, 127, 201, 208, 209, 210, 211, 224
Venkatesananda, Swami, 230
Vibhīṣaṇa, 92, 107, 122, 213, 229
violence, 13–14
virodhi svarūpa (the nature of an antagonist), 132
viśiṣṭādvaita philosophy (qualified nondualism), 86, 190
Viṣṇu, 4, 6, 13, 16, 18, 19, 23, 28–30, 32, 34, 39, 41, 83, 85, 86, 88–90, 103, 106, 114, 115, 118, 120, 122–23, 128, 132, 133, 135, 136, 141, 142, 144, 190, 191–2, 193, 195, 198, 199, 201, 204–6, 211, 212, 214–21, 227, 229, 231
Viṣṇucittaṉ, 4, 5, 11, 37, 128, 133, 141, 142, 205, 213, 214, 215, 217, 220
Viṣṇu-Nārāyaṇa, 83, 86–87, 98 (*see also* Viṣṇu)
Viṣṇu Purāṇa, 230
Viśvaksena, 206
Viśvāmitra, 128, 227
Vṛndāvana, 24, 26–27 (*see also* Āyarpāṭi)
vyājya (pretext), 139

white conch, song to, 206–7
wordly sleep, 106

Yamunā, 92, 217, 231, 232
Yaśodā, 12, 18, 86, 92, 111, 114, 126, 129, 199, 218, 231
Yogamāyā (divine illusion), 231
yoga nidrā (meditative sleep), 88, 106
yogi (ascetics), 96
Yudhiṣṭhira, 229